DIVINE FAITH
&
MIRACLES

Divine Faith
&
Miracles

by

Dr. Douglas J. Wingate

Life Christian University Press
P.O. Box 272360, Tampa, FL 33688
813-909-9720
Visit our website at www.lcus.edu

ISBN: 978-0-9837091-0-7

Printed in the United States of America

TABLE OF CONTENTS

CHAPTER ONE

ON A COLLISION COURSE WITH GOD

"THE PRESIDENT OF THE UNITED STATES, John F. Kennedy, is dead."

Stunned and in disbelief, I stared at the intercom speaker on the wall of my eighth grade classroom. As Walter Cronkite delivered the awful news, his voice did not have even a hint of his usual reassuring tone. As a thirteen-year-old boy, I idolized the President. I had seen and heard him in person just five days earlier when he visited Tampa, my hometown in Florida. How could he be dead? Who could have done such a thing? The teacher was visibly shaken and not much help as I fought to hold back the tears that filled my eyes, desperately trying to be brave. But I was devastated.

No other single event would impact my life and destiny as much as the events of that November day in 1963.

Over the next two months, my dreams to gain an appointment to the Air Force Academy, go on to law school, and then enter political life lost all of their appeal. If the President of the United States could be assassinated in the twentieth century, how could a little boy hope to make a difference, no matter how lofty his goals? What new purpose in life could inspire me? The solution to my dilemma would drastically change the course of my life.

Three months later, I sat spellbound watching *The Ed Sullivan Show* on Sunday night, February 9, 1964. The Beatles from England were on – and every tuned-in living room in America felt the impact of this musical phenomenon. It was no different in my home, as I began to envision a new career path opening up for me. I was already a drummer in the school marching band. It was one of the tools I had intended to use to get an appointment to the Air Force Academy. Certainly they would need drummers in the Drum and Bugle Corps. But now I saw the possibility of getting rich and famous through entertainment. I thought to myself, *I'll grow up to be a musician like The Beatles. Nobody assassinates musicians.* (As it turned out, even that wasn't true.)

By the time I was fifteen, I was playing in local nightclubs. Then other doors started to open. One month after graduating from high school, my band was the opening act for a concert with the legendary Jimi Hendrix. We began to play concerts with all of the biggest rock stars of the day. We were even the stage band for a Rock & Roll Revival tour where I played drums for Chuck Berry and The Coasters. I was living my dream – and life was exciting! But with that life came the abuse of alcohol and drugs to the point that by the time I reached my twenty-third birthday, I was no longer in control of my life.

I started realizing, with the help of a friend, that I needed an alternative to getting high on drugs and alcohol. My friend was on a spiritual search for answers to problems in her life. We both got into Hinduism and Yoga. Then one day while I was on a road trip with the band, I called and she informed me that she had "gotten saved" while attending a church service that my mother invited her to.

Soon after that she decided to return to Boston to take care of her grandfather. Before she left, she said something to me that cut straight to my heart. She said, "You are so hung up on your Rock Star ego trip, that if Jesus is the only way to heaven, you are going to hell for eternity, just because you think that it is not hip to be a Christian."

I had attended church as a young boy, but they never talked about "getting saved" at my church. I still had my Sunday-school Bible somewhere in storage at my parent's house, so I dug it out and started to read the Bible and check out these claims that Jesus was the Son of God and Savior of the world.

After reading Matthew, Mark, Luke, and most of John, I came to John 16:33, where Jesus said, **"In the world you will have tribulation; but be of good cheer, I have overcome the world."** Right after reading that, Jesus called my name and spoke to me, personally. It was so real inside me, it seemed I heard an audible voice. Jesus said, "Doug, I'm alive, and I'm the Lord."

I immediately knew what to do. I slid out of my bed, got on my knees, and asked Jesus to come into my heart and life. After reading that much of the Scripture, I was convinced His claims and His promises were all true. I'd heard Jesus speak directly to me. I wanted Jesus to be the Lord of my life.

That November night I found more than faith for salvation and assurance of a place in heaven after this life. I discovered a journey of faith that would produce almost indescribable miracles throughout all of this incredible experience called life.

I hope to impart to you, in this book, the secrets of faith I have learned that have allowed me to be transformed from that drug-addicted, alcoholic rock drummer to where I am today as the Founder and President of Life Christian University. LCU is a ministry university established in 1995, with over 100 campuses throughout the world. As I write this, in the spring of 2010, over 14,000 students have attended LCU and are serving in ministry. Some of the most notable names in ministry today, men and women of God who have authored books that we use in our courses, have earned degrees from LCU by their scholarly writing.

I have had the honor of preaching and teaching the Word of God all over the world, from Moscow, Russia, to Mumbai, India. My experience is only one of many countless thousands of stories of how faithful and miraculous God and His Word are. He proves – time and again – the words of the Apostle Paul from 1 Corinthians 1:26-27:

> **For you see your calling, brethren, that not many wise according to the flesh, not many mighty, not many noble, are called. But God has chosen the foolish things of the world to put to shame the wise, and God has chosen the weak things of the world to put to shame the things which are mighty.**

If God is able to do these things in my life, considering where I started, my question is, "What can God do in your life?" Let me encourage you and challenge you to read this book thoroughly. God has an awesome divine destiny for you. In order to achieve all that God wants you to do, you will have to be transformed by the renewing of your mind. You will have to grow in faith a little more each day. But the miracle-working God that we serve is more than able to lead you every glorious step of the way.

May God richly bless you with ever-increasing faith.

CHAPTER TWO

WHO CAN RECEIVE A MIRACLE?

I AM ALWAYS AMAZED by the controversy among Christians about faith, specifically the "faith message" or "word of faith." The reality is that all faith works the same way, even faith for salvation. The primary elements of faith are believing and confessing what the Bible says God has done for mankind. Romans 10:9-10, the classic scripture for receiving salvation, stresses these two points very distinctly.

ARE ALL GOD'S PROMISES AVAILABLE TODAY?

The controversy seems to surround the question of how many of God's promises are still available to us today. For God to make all of His covenant promises available to believers today would require the miraculous power of God to be in manifestation for every area of life. Herein lies the problem.

Many Christians don't believe that God still does miracles today, even though the salvation that they possess is, undeniably, the greatest miracle that God has ever produced. For God to turn a sin-riddled spirit, wholly devoid of anything remotely righteous or holy, into a righteous habitation, suitable for His Holy Spirit to dwell in, is the most fantastic, mind-blowing miracle in the universe!

Other Christians believe that God still does miracles today, but He does them randomly and mysteriously for reasons unknown to man. They don't believe it is possible to have one's faith become a factor in receiving one of these random and mysterious miracles.

Still others believe that even though God has indeed made miracle promises that are available to Christians today, His sovereignty means that He does not have to fulfill anything that He has promised, other than the promise of salvation. I am always perplexed as to why they are sure that He has to keep His promise to save those who receive Jesus as Savior but does not have to keep His promises to those who receive Jesus as Healer, Provider, or Prince of Peace in their home.

Then there are those who believe that God does not lie (Numbers 23:19), Jesus doesn't change (Hebrews 13:8), and God magnifies His Word even above His name (Psalm 138:2). These Christians believe everything God has promised is still available to them through faith.

This raises the question: Does believing that all the promises are still available give Christians in need a false hope? Not when the hope that is offered them is firmly rooted in Scripture and is one of the covenant promises of God's Word that Jesus and the Apostles of the early Church ministered to people.

BLINDED TO THE BLESSINGS OF LIFE

It is interesting that many of the same Christians who do not believe that all the promises of God are still available today are the ones who have believed a lie of the devil concerning how God empowers His Church. Satan has deceived many Christians into believing that the work of the Holy Spirit that began on the day of Pentecost and continues throughout the Book of Acts in the early Church is not available for the Church today. Most Charismatic Christians call this experience the Baptism of the Holy Spirit, based on the promise of Jesus in Acts 1:5, **"But you shall be baptized with the Holy Spirit not many days from now."** Satan has even caused some Christians to fear this Holy-Spirit-empowering experience because he has deceived them into believing that he, himself, is the author of such an experience. A very clever deception, don't you think? To lay claim to something that Jesus promised and only the Holy Spirit of God can give, and to make Christians cower in fear that they will somehow become demon-possessed instead of Holy-Spirit-empowered.

The first and, maybe, the most important aspect of this empowering experience is the uncanny ability to spiritually discern the true meaning of a scripture as you meditate on it (1 Corinthians 2:14). Without this ability a Christian will be spiritually blinded to probably 90% of the blessings of life that are promised in God's Word.

EXPERIENCING THE MIRACULOUS

This brings us to some questions about the title of this book, *Divine Faith & Miracles.* Is there a difference between experiencing a supernatural result from having exercised your faith in God's Word and experiencing a miracle?

A miracle is a supernatural intervention by God into the ordinary course of events in the life of a person. The simple truth is that miracles are produced two ways. The first is by exercising faith, either alone or in combination with the faith of another. When a person or persons successfully exercise faith in one of God's promises, they receive a miracle.

The second way a miracle is produced is by one of the gifts of the Spirit being in operation, such as the working of miracles, gifts of healings, or special faith. In this case the miracle is produced irrespective of the recipient's faith, although they occur most often in an atmosphere of faith, where the miraculous Word of God is being preached with power. A thorough discussion on these issues will come later in the book. But for now, the good news (Gospel) is that faith in God and His Word actually works, producing a flow of miraculous events in the life of an honest and diligently sincere believer.

EVER-INCREASING FAITH

Ever-increasing faith is the idea that God can cause your faith to grow as you respond to Him. As you take the steps to do what this book will teach you, God will increase your faith every single day of your life. It never has to stop growing. You can keep growing in faith – in fact, you'll be required to keep growing in faith all the days of your life in order to accomplish what God has ultimately called you to do. Most Christians don't even have an idea what God has ultimately called them to do, because it's so huge, that if He showed it to them right now, it might frighten them.

Maybe He's given you a glimpse of the vision He has for your life, and even that glimpse has startled you a bit. You've said, "Who? Me?" The devil has lied to every single person who has ever heard the call of God. He tells them, "Not you! Everybody knows about you. You can't be the one called to do that!"

Satan's negative message comes in many ways, through a variety of people and circumstances. But, the reality is, God has called you, and the potential is there for your faith to be constantly increasing so you can accomplish what He's set before you to do. If all God wanted to do was to make sure that we got saved so we could go to heaven, He would just have taken us to heaven immediately after we got saved. That way, we could just skip the "growing-up" part. But no, we're the ones who are called to preach the gospel - the angels don't do that job. We're the ones who must be transformed to the point where, by both our lives and our words, we are really ministering to everyone who needs the Word of God - and that's everybody on the planet!

CHAPTER THREE

FAITH – A MIRACULOUS GIFT FROM GOD

THE MOST IMPORTANT THING that can be said about faith is that it is a miraculous gift from God. Ephesians 2:8 says, **"For by grace you have been saved through faith, and that not of yourselves; it is the gift of God, not of works, lest anyone should boast."** This verse tells us that even the faith to be saved does not originate with us but is a gift from God, given at the time you hear God's Word.

This miraculous gift, however, does not come without a response to the Word of God from each individual person. This decision and the corresponding gift of faith from God begins when we respond to the Bible's claim that Jesus is the Son of God and that there is no other way to go to heaven at the end of this life, except by receiving Jesus as our own Savior and Lord. Faith enough to receive Jesus as Lord is imparted to the human spirit and perceived by the human mind before one confesses Jesus as Lord, which is the reasonable response to this exceptionally good news.

The classic scripture that describes this process is

found in Romans 10:9-10:

> **That if you confess with your mouth the Lord
> Jesus and believe in your heart that God has
> raised Him from the dead, you will be saved.
> For with the heart one believes unto righteous-
> ness, and with the mouth confession is made
> unto salvation.**

When we examine these two verses, we see that the
order of "believing in your heart" and "confessing with
your mouth" are changed from verse to verse. In verse 9
the most important aspect of obtaining salvation is listed
first, that is to "confess with your mouth the Lord Jesus."
The reason that this is so vital is that believing in your
heart that God raised Jesus from the dead is not sufficient
in and of itself to gain salvation without the decision to
receive Jesus as your own personal Lord. Satan himself
believes that God raised Jesus from the dead, but he can
never gain redemption. Countless hundreds of thousands
of people throughout the world attend churches that
embrace the resurrection of Jesus as fact, but never
receive Jesus as their own personal Lord because the
importance of "confessing with your mouth the Lord
Jesus" is not emphasized and no invitation is given to do
so. So these unfortunate church-attending people go
through life thinking that they are going to heaven when
they die, having never been born again by confessing
Jesus as their own personal Lord.

Most Christians accomplish this vital step by praying
a prayer that includes this confession along with repentance of sin and asking for Jesus to come into their hearts.
That is certainly my preference when leading someone to
the Lord, but according to these verses, a prayer isn't even

required. It is fair to assume that when someone desires to confess Jesus as Lord that they are repentant for their sins and are inviting Jesus to come into their hearts, but it is preferable to be sure by covering those issues with instruction and prayer.

Then we see in verse 10 the chronological order by which the process evolves: **"For with the heart one believes unto righteousness, and with the mouth confession is made unto salvation."** The first thing that happens when a person hears the gospel with an open heart, is that the Word of God is able to accomplish a miraculous transformation of the human spirit by the "washing of water by the Word," the same process God used to cleanse the Church in Ephesians 5:26. Once the human spirit is cleansed or made righteous by the Word, it becomes a suitable habitation for the Holy Spirit. This does not mean, though, that the Holy Spirit comes in automatically without the confessing of Jesus as Lord. Both steps are absolutely essential. Once the confession or decision by prayer is made, the Holy Spirit does come in instantly, bringing eternal life, and the new birth into God's family is complete.

WINNING UNSAVED "BELIEVERS"

I once shared this teaching with the students at a friend's Bible school. I told them that I prefer witnessing to and praying with easy cases, not with doubters who want to argue religion. The first thing I ask someone I want to witness to is, "Do you believe in your heart that God raised Jesus from the dead?" If they answer, "Yes," then I ask the second question, "Have you asked Jesus into your heart to be your personal Savior?" If they say, "No," then I explain this necessary step for salvation from

Romans 10. Then I ask them if they would like to pray to receive Jesus right now and be assured of eternal life.

I stressed to the Bible school students that winning souls who already believe in the resurrection of Jesus is somewhat like shooting fish in a barrel. One girl came to me the next week and shared this testimony. She had been shopping in a bookstore and, as she was leaving, she was a bit frightened by a man who looked like he might be in a motorcycle gang. He had parked his bike just outside the door, so she hurried past him to her car. When she began to open the car door, the Lord prompted her to go back and ask him the questions that we had covered in class.

She was obedient and went back and said, "Sir, do you mind if I ask you a question?" He agreed and she asked if he believed in his heart that God raised Jesus from the dead. He told her that he attended Sunday school as a boy and has always believed since that time. She then asked if he had ever received Jesus as his own personal Savior, and then proceeded to explain Romans 10:9-10 to him.

When she asked if he would like to receive Jesus right now, to her amazement, he said, "Yes." In a matter of five minutes she led this rough-looking biker to the Lord. Glory to God!

The good news is that all faith in God works the same way that faith for salvation works. It all becomes a matter of believing in your heart and confessing with your mouth.

FAITH ALWAYS PRODUCES A MIRACLE

The Bible itself is impossible to believe without receiving miracle faith from God. In order to believe the Bible you must first examine the claims of the central figure of the Bible, Jesus Himself. If you examine the life and ministry of Jesus with an open heart and personal honesty within yourself, God will impart to you the faith to be born again. Then the Holy Spirit will take up residence in your spirit, and you can begin the journey of ever-increasing faith. Until someone is born again, the entire Bible appears to be one big fairy tale. The stories about God creating the human race from Adam and Eve, or the story of Noah and the flood, or Moses and the Red Sea, all are beyond belief without the Holy Spirit convincing you through an internal miracle of God.

The Bible, then, is a book for the family of God only. The Holy Spirit's presence in our lives makes us a spiritual family, often with stronger family bonds than we have with those who are blood relatives. The good news is that anyone who is currently outside of this family can be birthed into this family by believing on Jesus as their own personal Lord and Savior. If you have already experienced the miracle of the new birth and are part of the family of God, I want to introduce you to the reality that you can constantly grow in faith for greater victory in life, every single day. Your faith for every area of life can grow and produce miraculous results.

If you have not made Jesus King of your life, then you are not reading this by accident. God is at this moment speaking to your heart!

Will you receive Jesus Christ right now?

Here is how you can receive Christ:
1. Admit your need (I am a sinner.)
2. Be willing to turn from your sins (repent).
3. Believe that Jesus Christ died for you on the cross and rose from the grave.
4. Through prayer, invite Jesus Christ to come in and control your life through the Holy Spirit. (Receive Him as Lord and Savior).

CHAPTER FOUR

WHY DO WE NEED DIVINE FAITH?

WHY DO WE NEED DIVINE FAITH? Scripture gives us many reasons to develop strong faith in God. We will list twenty-five of the top reasons in this chapter – but my prayer is that every day you will discover more and more reasons of your own!

REASON #1: WE CAN'T PLEASE GOD WITHOUT FAITH

The first reason we need faith is because we can't please God without it. Hebrews 11:6 says, **"But without faith it is impossible to please Him, for he who comes to God must believe that He is, and that He is a rewarder of those who diligently seek Him."**

God does exist. He isn't an idea that man thought up – even though most false religions are ideas that man thought up with Satan's inspiration. False religions were inspired by Satan to keep men in the turmoil of trying to earn their way to God. Half of the world is trying to get God off their case through religious works. The rest want to believe that He doesn't even exist. For years, scientists have been coming up with theories to explain the creation without God.

Even before becoming a Christian, I had no problem with believing that God existed. If you just look at the handiwork of God's creation, you have to say, "There's got to be a God of order who created this universe. It just couldn't have happened randomly, no matter what the theorists say."

Darwin's Theory of Evolution, that life just spontaneously issued forth out of the primordial ooze and evolved in complexity from there, is only a theory – and an extremely flawed one. For one thing, I can prove by the laws of the universe that we're in a state of de-evolution, not evolution. Think about the star of every solar system. What are stars made up of? Gases. What happens when you burn gas? It burns up. In the universe as it is right now, every star will ultimately burn up. Every planet that revolves around a star in a solar system has a decaying orbit. It's being drawn into that star and eventually will collide with it. That means everything is terminal. That means it's in a state of de-evolution rather than evolution. It wasn't designed that way by God, but man's sin caused all of creation to go out of tilt. The Bible tells us that all of creation is groaning for the revealing of the sons of God (Romans 8:19-22).

One day, God will make a new heaven and a new earth, and everything will change back to His original plan. But, until then, it's in a state of de-evolution.

In recent years, scientists have come up with the "Big Bang Theory." Now, I agree with the "Big Bang Theory" in one sense, because God spoke and "Bang!" it happened. The whole universe came into existence. That was a big bang, there was no question about it. But I don't believe in the big bang the way the secularists have described it, that the universe just happened without plan or forethought on the part of a Supreme Being. Believing that takes more faith than believing that God exists and that He is the Creator of all things.

REASON #2: JESUS TOLD US TO HAVE FAITH

Another primary reason why we need to have faith is simply because Jesus said, **"Have faith in God"** (Mark 11:22). If Jesus said it, that ought to settle it with us. The literal translation of what Jesus said to His disciples was, "Have God's faith."

This is an important point. Although we may talk about developing or strengthening our faith, the reality is, we don't possess faith on our own. It's a gift of God. From the very start of our life as a Christian until the time we leave the planet, the faith we have is always a gift from God.

When we first really heard the Gospel, the claims of what the Lord Jesus said about Himself and about His life, we thought, "My goodness, could this be true? What if Jesus really is who He said He was, the Son of God? He said, 'No man comes to the Father, but by Me.' What if to reach mankind, He took on a human form and lived among men? What if He paid the price for man's sin, then died in my place so I could have eternal life? What if the same Holy Spirit who was in Adam and Eve could suddenly come to live in me and transform me? I'd be able to come into God's presence and live forever with the life of God on the inside of me."

As our heart begins to hear and receive the truth of God's Word, God imparts faith to us. This faith enables us to say, "I know that if I pray and ask Jesus to come into my heart, He's going to come in and I'm going to be born again." We're now convinced of that. But we weren't convinced of that just a few minutes earlier.

Maybe you were saved at a church service, or maybe someone presented the Gospel to you one-on-one. However it was that you got saved, just a few minutes earlier, you didn't have the faith to be saved. You didn't have the faith to pray for salvation. Then, suddenly, a revelation came to you about who Jesus really was and you stepped right out of the kingdom of darkness and its stranglehold, and stepped right into eternal life. Praise God!

That's what happens in us when we begin to have God's faith. God's faith is unlimited and moves in the realm of the miraculous. Jesus said God's faith was available to us. In fact, He instructed us: "Have God's faith." This takes the limits off: our faith can keep growing until it touches the miraculous working of God.

REASON #3: WE NEED FAITH BECAUSE
WE ARE SAVED THROUGH FAITH

We've already seen how the gift of faith is given to us and that's what saves us. Ephesians 2:8-9 gives us this additional insight into the human heart: **"For by grace you have been saved through faith, and that not of yourselves; it is the gift of God, not of works, lest anyone should boast."**

You see, if we could earn the favor of God through our works, then we'd have bragging rights before God. We'd be able to stand before Him and say, "Look what I've done! I've earned my brownie points, so to speak. I've earned my merit badges. I've earned the right to be able to stand in Your presence."

But the Bible says no man can glory in God's presence

(1 Corinthians 1:29). Only Christ can glory.

All we need to be concerned with is the fact that Jesus already did it all. As I live out my Christian life, I don't need to be concerned about trying to get any recognition myself. I'm going to be recognized from the Lord for being faithful and obedient. That's the key, that's the secret.

Everywhere I minister, I tell people, "I can't find a downside to serving the Lord." There isn't one. As you go through this life serving God, He will constantly increase the anointing on your life. As you understand more of Him and His ways, you'll be so blessed. In the process of ministering, you'll get the opportunity to see and experience miracles like you've only dreamed of. You'll also have many personal encounters with the Lord. Eventually you'll just say, "I feel like I'm on a magic carpet ride of miracles in life."

God is an awesome God who will astound you every single day. God will cause you to walk in divine health, divine prosperity, and divine peace in your home – and you'll realize you didn't earn any of it! He just does that for you as a gift! As you go, you'll be used by Him to transform people's lives, and see people saved, healed, and delivered, knowing it doesn't have anything to do with you. Jesus deserves all the credit and glory. All God is asking you to do is show up and be faithful and obedient.

Jesus said believers would lay hands on the sick and they would recover (Mark 16:18). I know I couldn't heal a gnat's wing – so it's a good thing that God says, "Just put your hands on them." That's all that we need to do – our part is simple. But as we do it in faith, going wherever God sends us, preaching and proclaiming the words that God gives us, we will see miracles happen. On three occasions, I've seen hospitalized people healed by God and released from the hospital, and eventually declared completely healed by the doctors. One of these had terminal cancer.

Obey God and you, too, will see miracles. At the end of this incredible, miraculous life, you're going to step into God's presence. You'll know everything you experienced wasn't about you, that Jesus deserves all the glory, and that you don't deserve a single bit of any reward. Then you'll hear Jesus say, **"Well done, good and faithful servant.... Enter into the joy of your Lord"** (Matthew 25:21).

Then He will reward you as though you had done it all yourself! Where's the downside to that kind of a life of obedience?

Not only will God reward you in heaven, He'll make sure you get so many rewards on this side too, that you'll be embarrassed. I've been so blessed that I was afraid to tell anybody about it - you know how some people become so envious when you talk about being blessed! One day, God reproved me. He said, "Don't ever apologize for being blessed of the Lord."

We want to preach the good news everywhere, especially in those places that need it the most. And the good news that we preach is that God is a God of faith and wants to reward all who will diligently seek Him. Why should we apologize when it works for us?

REASON #4: WE ARE MADE RIGHTEOUS BY FAITH

Foundational to all faith is the understanding of our righteousness.

Romans 1:16-17 says:

For I am not ashamed of the gospel of Christ, for it is the power of God to salvation for everyone who believes, for the Jew first and also for the Greek. For in it the righteousness of God is

revealed from faith to faith; as it is written, "The just shall live by faith."

Notice that the righteousness of God is revealed from faith to faith. Your understanding of your right-standing with God is going to increase continuously from faith to faith.

You didn't get just a little bit of righteousness, just enough to be acceptable to God. No, in the realm of the Spirit, God transformed you from being an evil sinner and an enemy of God, to being the very righteousness of God in Christ. Romans 3:21-22 says:

But now the righteousness of God apart from the law is revealed, being witnessed by the Law and the Prophets, even the righteousness of God, through faith in Jesus Christ, to all and on all who believe.

We have been made totally acceptable to God, as acceptable as Jesus Himself. That's what was imparted unto us – the very righteousness of Christ Himself, was imparted unto every single believer.

Romans 9:30 says, **"What shall we say then? That Gentiles, who did not pursue righteousness, have attained to righteousness, even the righteousness of faith."** In other words, our righteousness is based on our faith in the work Jesus Christ did and His imparting of righteousness to us.

God doesn't look at the natural you with all the shortcomings and frailties that you are so conscious of. He looks at you with the fullness of your potential, because He looks at you through Christ. Ultimately, in the realm of the Spirit, He's already re-created you to look just like Jesus. Righteousness has already been imparted to you. Yet, most Christians walk around so aware of both their sin nature and their own personal sin that they are not expecting anything much from God. They feel too unworthy to approach God for help.

That's why an understanding of righteousness is absolutely essential for you to be able to exercise faith. You must know that you have just as much right to go into the throne room of God as the Lord Jesus Himself. Now, that concept alone seems completely arrogant to a lot of Christians. They think that exercising faith is presumptuous, that it's commanding God or ordering Him around. No, nothing could be further from the truth.

The reality is, God wants to do so much more in your life than you can imagine. He wants you to come to Him and ask Him to fulfill His promises. He wants to bless you more than you can ever conceive. He wants to do more for you than any Christian has ever asked Him to do. Those covenant promises are all, **"Yes, and in Him Amen"** (2 Corinthians 1:20) – that means, "Yes, yes, yes," every time.

But most people don't receive the blessing of all the covenant promises. Since they've been talked out of believing that the promises are for the body of Christ today, they don't spend the time exercising and developing their faith in these areas. They think that confession only applies to confessing sin, not confessing what God has done for them in Christ. They think they are being humble.

The fact is, true humility is to agree with God and to say whatever God says about yourself. You need to settle it in your mind that what He says about you is reality. The seen, natural realm that you and I know and live in every single day was created by the realm of the Spirit. When God says something from the realm of the Spirit, it supercedes everything in this natural realm – and it will change everything in this realm.

God sees you in a completely different light – and He wants you to see yourself the way He now sees you. In other words, if God says you're the head and not the tail, hallelujah, that's what you are (Deuteronomy 28:13a). If He says you're above and not beneath, that's where you're located (Deuteronomy 28:13b). If He says you're seated in heavenly places with Christ Jesus (Ephesians 2:6), that's not only the positional truth that God sees, that's the truth He wants you to see. He wants you to be able to take that positional truth and make it a reality in your life.

CRAWL UP IN YOUR DADDY'S LAP

I have a little girl, who is my princess. I know the love I have for my daughter and the relationship I have with her. Little girls are just so special. I remember when she was small. Every time she reached up to me and said, "Daddy, hold me," what do you think I did? She could get anything she wanted from her daddy. I would often hold up her little hand, point to her little finger, and tell people, "That's the little finger that I'm wrapped around."

The love that the Father in heaven has for each one of us, individually, is so much greater than any earthly father among us could possess. Knowing how much I love my daughter helps me realize God's love for me. I can picture walking right into His presence and, just like my little girl does, reaching my hands up to Him so He can lift me into his lap.

REASON #5: WE HAVE PURIFIED HEARTS BY FAITH

In Acts 15:6, we read about the apostles and elders coming together to discuss what should be done about the growing number of Gentiles who believed in Jesus.

Peter described what occurred when the Holy Spirit sent him to minister to the Gentiles (recorded in Acts 10).

"So God, who knows the heart, acknowledged them by giving them the Holy Spirit, just as He did to us, and made no distinction between us and them, purifying their hearts by faith" (Acts 15:8-9).

The phrase, "purifying their hearts by faith" refers to the washing and cleansing of the human spirit, one of the two parts of the heart (the other being the soul). Our spirits must be made righteous and holy before the Holy Spirit will take up residence there. Exercising faith in God's Word and the revelation that Jesus is the only Savior and Lord is what cleanses the spirit. Upon praying to receive Jesus, also known as confessing Him as Lord, the human spirit is cleansed and the Holy Spirit comes in to reside in this purified spirit.

REASON #6: WE ARE JUSTIFIED BY FAITH

Romans 3:28 says, **"Therefore we conclude that a man is justified by faith apart from the deeds of the law."** To be justified means to be considered "just" before God. One person put it this way: "It's just-as-if-I'd never sinned." We've been justified. All the claims of justice have been met by the Lord Jesus. He made this incredible, miraculous exchange. He took our sin upon Himself and imparted His righteousness to us. What a radical concept – but it's the truth!

It's so hard for people in the world to believe that God would do this, and make right standing with Him a free gift. They think, "No, surely, I've got to earn my way to God. I've got to keep all the rules, and if I don't, I must do some sort of penance."

This tradition of "works" came from the Judaic roots of Christianity, from the Law of Moses, the worship in the Tabernacle, and the sacrifices for sin. Jesus was the great fulfillment of everything required in the Law of Moses and every part of the Tabernacle worship. He was the High Priest, He was every article of the Tabernacle, He was the sin offering. Everything the priests did, year after year, was a rehearsal of the redemptive work of God that Christ was going to do. God put the precedents all in place, because He didn't want His people to miss the Christ - the Messiah. Unfortunately, many of the Jewish people had their eyes on the rehearsal, on the pattern, rather than on the real, when Jesus came.

Even many Christian denominations have put many burdens of legalism within the framework of their theology and practice. They perpetuate the idea that, somehow, we've got to earn our acceptability, our way to God. The reality is that even the best people, who seem so moral and upright, have a sin nature built into them. Without Christ, they are in such a totally sinful condition that they are completely unacceptable to God and severed off from Him.

The gap between our lives and the holiness of God was so huge, there was nothing we could do to earn the favor and acceptance of God. It was beyond our abilities. But praise God, it was all done for us by the Lord Jesus Christ and became a free gift to us when we received Jesus as Lord and Savior. This was all accomplished by faith - we were justified without the deeds of the law.

Galatians 2:16 says,

Knowing that a man is not justified by the works of the law but by faith in Jesus Christ, even we have believed in Christ Jesus, that we might be justified by faith in Christ and not by the works

of the law; for by the works of the law no flesh shall be justified.

It was the faith of Jesus Christ that produced this work for us. Praise God, you can't earn it - it's a free gift to be received.

REASON #7: WITH JUSTIFICATION COMES PEACE

Romans 5:1 adds to this concept saying, **"Therefore, having been justified by faith, we have peace with God through our Lord Jesus Christ."** I don't know about you, but when I got born again, I felt like a thousand-pound weight rolled off my back. I got rid of so many confused ideas about the universe and my life in it. All of that burden rolled away, and everything suddenly became simple and true. I was justified freely by faith, and now I had peace with God, a peace that surpasses all understanding (Philippians 4:7).

What a marvelous purchase Jesus made when He paid for our peace! He delivers this peace to us as a gift from the God of Peace. Only through Jesus can we discover that God is not mad at us. He loves us and treasures us as His offspring, the children of the Father. He desires to shower our lives with blessings, not hardship. All He asks in return is that we make Jesus Lord of every area of our lives by faith. And when we do this, we find a constant flow of spiritual peace and rest coming to us from the Father's presence.

REASON #8: WE HAVE ACCESS
TO GOD'S GRACE BY FAITH

Faith gives you the access into God's grace. Romans 5:2 says, **"through whom also we have access by faith into**

this grace in which we stand, and rejoice in hope of the glory of God."

Grace is God's free gift to us of all the good things He has in His kingdom – but they can only be accessed by faith in the Lord Jesus, the mediator between man and God. This verse tells us we stand in grace, rejoicing in hope of the glory of God. Biblical hope is nothing like "a-wishing and a-hoping." Biblical hope is a confident expectation of good. By faith, we can stand in that "confident expectation."

Through faith in Jesus, we have free access to all of God's grace. God's grace is many-faceted. It includes financial provision, healing, and wholeness. It includes God's undeserved and unmerited favor. It includes His divine influence on your inner man. It includes an inner strength that will empower you to do what you could not do before.

Hebrews 4:16 says, **"Let us therefore come boldly to the throne of grace, that we may obtain mercy and find grace to help in time of need."** By faith, we can approach God's throne of grace and and obtain everything He has promised us as a free gift. Faith pulls in that grace.

REASON #9: WE ARE BAPTIZED IN THE HOLY SPIRIT BY FAITH

Jesus told His disciples to wait in Jerusalem for the "promise of the Father" (Luke 24:49, Acts 1:4). The disciples obeyed and were baptized with the Holy Spirit, with the evidence of speaking in other tongues, a supernatural gift which changed the Church forever.

After the Holy Spirit was given to the disciples on the day of Pentecost, Peter immediately offered both the gift of salvation and the gift of the Holy Spirit to three thousand Jews. **"Then Peter said to them, 'Repent, and let every one of you be baptized in the name of Jesus Christ for the remission of sins; and you shall receive the gift of the Holy Spirit'"** (Acts 2:38).

In Galatians 3:14, Paul tells us that we, too, **"might receive the promise of the Spirit through faith."** We need the Holy Spirit in every area of our lives: spirit, soul, and body. Our souls need to be constantly filled with the Spirit of God.

REASON #10: WE ARE HEALED BY FAITH

There are several examples in the Bible where Jesus told someone that it was their own faith that made their healing possible. Here are three of those stories:

But Jesus turned around, and when He saw her He said, "Be of good cheer, daughter; your faith has made you well." And the woman was made well from that hour (Matthew 9:22).

Then Jesus said to him, "Go your way; your faith has made you well." And immediately he received his sight and followed Jesus on the road (Mark 10:52).

And He said to him, "Arise, go your way. Your faith has made you well" (Luke 17:19).

You, too, can build yourself up in faith to receive healing from the Lord. Things may come against your body, but you can turn them back by faith in the covenant promises of God. You can learn to walk in divine health and fulfill your course.

REASON #11: WE ARE PROSPERED BY FAITH

God wants to bless you financially, so you can fulfill the ministry He has given you. He also wants you to be well-supplied so you can give to every good work. In 3 John 1:2, John writes, **"Beloved, I pray that you may prosper in all things and be in health, just as your soul prospers."**

Soul prosperity is the process of faith, of becoming mature in Christ. As you immerse yourself in the covenant promises of God they come alive to you, and you realize that God has already provided everything you need.

REASON #12: WE ARE SANCTIFIED BY FAITH

The faith that is in us has a sanctifying force. After we are saved, we learn that our lives need to change. This is a process that occurs as our thought processes are transformed, sanctified, and set apart for the Lord's purposes.

In Acts 26:18, the Apostle Paul recounts how Jesus spoke to him saying that he would be a minister and a witness to the Gentiles, sent to:

> **"...open their eyes, in order to turn them from darkness to light, and from the power of Satan to God, that they may receive forgiveness of sins and an inheritance among those who are sanctified by faith in Me."**

This is the process: our eyes are opened, we turn from darkness to light, and our sins are forgiven. By faith we then begin to walk in the blessings of our inheritance in the kingdom of God as we renew our minds to the Word of God (Romans 12:2). Like Paul, we can become useful to the Lord.

REASON #13: OUR RIGHTEOUSNESS IS REVEALED FROM FAITH TO FAITH

We have seen that the beginning of divine faith is to believe that God is and that He will reward us as we diligently seek Him. After that, there are multiple levels of faith that we can keep growing to and going to. Romans 1:17 says, **"For in it the righteousness of God is revealed from faith to faith; as it is written, 'The just shall live by faith.'"**

Understanding our right-standing with God is a process, because righteousness is revealed from faith to faith. We are so accustomed to walking by our emotions. We might not *feel* righteous every single day, but we need to learn to walk by faith, and not by sight or feeling.

In fact, our faith will never work until we understand our righteousness. We must see ourselves as God sees us, what Jesus has made us to be. The more we learn to walk in faith, the more God is able to reveal to us over and over again, how we have access to His throne because of His imparted righteousness. Jesus said we can ask anything that we want (John 14:13, 14; 15:7; 16:23).

The truth is, we can never dream as big as what God has already planned!

REASON #14: WE LIVE BY FAITH

We have seen how the revelation of the righteousness of God within us comes to us progressively from faith to faith. This revelation keeps growing in us until we not only sense it from time to time, but we are actually living in an atmosphere of faith – we abide there. Galatians 3:11 says, **"But that no one is justified by the law in the sight of God is evident, for "the just shall live by faith."**

Hebrews 10:38 says the same thing: **"Now the just shall live by faith; But if anyone draws back, My soul has no pleasure in him."** We realize that God cannot have pleasure in people who recoil from Him, who draw back from believing Him and fellowshipping with Him. It's not that you lose your salvation, it's that to please God, you must continue growing in faith. We were created to live by faith.

REASON #15: WE STAND BY FAITH

We stand by faith. Not all battles are won in a day. There are times when answers come suddenly, and times we must stand by faith, waiting to see the things God has promised us come to pass.

Watch, stand fast in the faith, be brave, be strong (1 Corinthians 16:13).

That your faith should not stand in the wisdom of men, but in the power of God (1 Corinthians 2:5 KJV).

Therefore take up the whole armor of God, that you may be able to withstand in the evil day, and having done all, to stand (Ephesians 6:13).

In addition, Paul writes that as ministers, we build others up so they can stand against all the wiles of the devil.

Not that we have dominion over your faith, but are fellow workers for your joy; for by faith you stand (2 Corinthians 1:24).

REASON #16: WE WALK BY FAITH

In 2 Corinthians 5:7 we read, **"For we walk by faith, not by sight."** What we see with our eyes might be a fact, but it is not necessarily the truth. Your body may experience symptoms that say you are sick, but the higher truth of God's Word says, **"by His stripes you were healed"** (1 Peter 2:24). We aren't moved from our stand of faith by hearing a bad report because we know that the Truth can change the facts.

REASON #17: WE ARE THE CHILDREN OF GOD
BY FAITH

If you have put your faith in Christ Jesus, you are a child of God. Galatians 3:26 says, **"For you are all sons of God through faith in Christ Jesus."**

John 1:12 says, **"But as many as received Him, to them He gave the right to become children of God, to those who believe in His name."**

REASON #18: CHRIST DWELLS IN OUR HEARTS
BY FAITH

Ephesians 3:17 says, **"that Christ may dwell in your hearts through faith."** Jesus is always there. He has promised that He will never leave you (Hebrews 13:5b). This indwelling is different from the indwelling of the Holy Spirit who lives in our spirit because we are born again.

This refers to the conscious exercise of our faith to let Christ (the Anointed One, along with His anointing for our lives) dwell in us. In other words, there is a tangible presence of Christ that we are able to obtain and maintain as we walk by faith.

REASON #19: WE RECEIVE FOR OTHERS BY FAITH

Only two times in the Bible did Jesus say someone had "great faith." Both of these individuals came to Jesus to receive healing for another. Here are their stories:

> **Then Jesus answered and said to her, "O woman, great is your faith! Let it be to you as you desire."And her daughter was healed from that very hour (Matthew 15:28).**

> **The centurion answered and said, "Lord, I am not worthy that You should come under my roof. But only speak a word, and my servant will be healed. For I also am a man under authority, having soldiers under me. And I say to this one, 'Go,' and he goes; and to another, 'Come,' and he comes; and to my servant, 'Do this,' and he does it."**

> **When Jesus heard it, He marveled, and said to those who followed, "Assuredly, I say to you, I have not found such great faith, not even in Israel!"**

> **Then Jesus said to the centurion, "Go your way; and as you have believed, so let it be done for you." And his servant was healed that same hour (Matthew 8:8-10,13).**

This Roman soldier understood how the kingdom of heaven works. He knew that Jesus operated under authority, and that what He commanded happened.

There is a story of a man who came before a great king and made such an extraordinary request that all who heard it gasped. In the uncomfortable silence that followed, many were sure the king was deciding how to punish any fool who would ask for so much.

Finally the king spoke: "Your request is granted."

Later, the king's most trusted aide took him aside and asked, "Oh, King, I must know! Why would you grant such an extraordinary request? Surely you know it will consume one-third of the total wealth of your kingdom."

The king replied, "Yes, I know it will greatly diminish my wealth. However, the size of his request honored me."

In the same way, Jesus was honored by the centurion's great faith that He would be able to do this. In fact, I feel we can insult the Lord by our lack of faith in Him. He knows the full price He paid for our redemption. When someone turns down one of the benefits that He purchased at so great a price, it breaks His heart. Yet many believers walk away from so much that He died to give them. He's happy they will be in heaven, but He'd rather that they would receive blessings from Him all the days of their lives on earth as well.

REASON #20: WE INHERIT THE PROMISES BY FAITH

Hebrews 6:12 tells us, **"do not become sluggish, but imitate those who through faith and patience inherit the promises."** It takes faith and patience. You can't give up on faith. You cannot take faith vacations! You must stay consistently in faith.

Any book you read on success will always include the principle of perseverance. The kingdom of God works the same way because we are opposed by the principalities of the kingdom of darkness. True faith includes the idea of relentless, persistent pursuit of the promises of God.

REASON #21: ANYTHING NOT DONE IN FAITH IS SIN

In Romans 14:23 Paul gives us another good reason to develop our faith. He writes, **"But he who doubts is condemned if he eats, because he does not eat from faith; for whatever is not from faith is sin."** Here Paul is dealing with people eating meat that had been sacrificed to idols, then sold in the market. People who were weaker in faith thought, "Oh, my goodness, I'd be cursed if I ate something that was sacrificed to an idol." But if you were a person of stronger faith, you'd realize "It's just meat. I'm not going to pick up any demonic influence by eating meat that an idol-worshiper sacrificed to their so-called god. I'm not going to let that bother me."

But if a fellow believer would be offended if you ate meat that had been sacrificed to an idol, Paul advises our thoughts should be, "I'm not going to eat this meat. I'm not going to cause my brother, who Christ died for, to stumble because I want meat instead of just vegetables." This is not a good time to exercise the liberty that comes to us through faith.

In this passage, Paul is saying that anything not done in faith is sin. That is, if you know what to do and you don't do it, then it would be a sin. God calls us to a progressively higher level in our walk with Him. Jesus said that the way to life is narrow, and it seems like the way gets narrower and narrower, the further you go down the road. The longer you've been saved, it seems the more the Lord requires of you. I've been saved for thirty-six years and in the ministry for thirty-five years as I write this book. I sometimes feel that the way for me is as narrow as a tightrope. I want to do everything "just so," because I don't want any of the opposition of the devil to get through, and I want to be pleasing unto the Lord.

REASON #22: BY FAITH WE OVERCOME THE WORLD

In 1 John 5:4 we read, "**For whatever is born of God overcomes the world.**" "Whatever" is a thing. John goes on to say, "**And this is the victory that has overcome the world – our faith.**" If faith is the "whatever" that overcomes the world, that means our faith is also the "whatever" that's born of God. If faith is born, then it must be alive.

Some may say, "I didn't know faith was alive." It is. Paul tells us in 1 Corinthians 13:13, "**And now abide faith, hope, love, these three.**"

Abide means "to live." Another way of saying this would be, "Now these three things live." Faith is a living, vital force, just like love and hope. Anything that emanates out of God Himself is alive, because God is alive. He is life itself and the source of all life.

Paul continues in verse 14, "**but the greatest of these is love.**" Why is love the greatest of the three? Because that's the essence of God Himself. If you were to summarize what God consists of – it's love. That is His very nature. And the thing He wants emanating to us from His presence more than anything else is His love.

Faith, hope, and love are all forces of life. Every time we receive a higher level of any one of them, we are receiving more of the life of God. As you grow in faith, hope, and love, you are adding more of God's life to yourself. All those things come by meditating on God and His covenant promises, looking at His character and His nature, and letting that be imparted to you. We need living, vital faith, because it is by our faith that we overcome this world.

REASON #23: BY FAITH IN GOD'S PROMISES, WE BECOME PARTAKERS OF THE DIVINE NATURE

Second Peter 1:2 says, **"Grace and peace be multiplied to you in the knowledge of God and of Jesus our Lord."** How do we get grace and peace multiplied to us? In the knowledge of God. Those who love knowledge and love knowing God better are going to have grace and peace multiplied to them continually.

Verse 3 tells us, **"As His divine power has given to us all things that pertain to life and godliness, through the knowledge of Him who called us by glory and virtue."**

God has already done everything for us in the realm of the Spirit. He has given us all things that pertain to life and godliness. As we gain knowledge of Him, all these things that add life and godliness to us are going to increase in our lives.

Verse 4 says, **"by which have been given to us exceedingly great and precious promises, that through these you may be partakers of the divine nature, having escaped the corruption that is in the world through lust."** There are so many more incredible, great, precious promises in the Word of God than people have ever realized were in there. By knowing and receiving these great promises, we become "a partaker of the divine nature." The more we exercise faith and receive the great promises of God, the more we partake of His nature and become like Him. If there's one reason I want to have more faith, it's this: to be like God, to be Christ-like. I want to have the nature of God that He intended for human beings to have. He says that we can do that by receiving these great and precious promises into our lives.

REASON #24: BY FAITH WE CALL THINGS INTO BEING

We have this great privilege to "partake" of God's nature and to do some of the very same things He does. By faith we speak as God does, that is, calling things into being. Romans 4:17 says, **"(as it is written, 'I have made you a father of many nations') in the presence of Him whom he believed – God, who gives life to the dead and calls those things which do not exist as though they did."**

A lot of people don't understand exactly what it means to "call those things which do not exist as though they did." An example of this can be seen in the way God made the physical universe. God wanted to create a family to love, to have fellowship with. He had to create a physical universe to place a physical man in. When He spoke and created the universe, He called things which did not exist into being.

Jesus operated in this principle when He was on the earth. In the midst of the storm, He said, **"Peace, be still!"** – and the wind ceased and there was a great calm (Mark 4:39). To a leper, He said, **"Be cleansed"** – and immediately his leprosy was cleansed (Matthew 8:3). He said to a fig tree, **"'Let no fruit grow on you ever again.' Immediately the fig tree withered away"** (Matthew 21:19).

When we first started the university, I also pastored a church. Since divine healing and health is a great passion of mine, we had healing school every Wednesday night. After a year of teaching on healing every week, when I'd ask if anybody needed prayer for healing, nobody responded anymore, because everybody was walking in divine health.

One day God told me, "I want you to teach on prosperity every Sunday morning until I tell you to stop." Now, as a pastor, I was already concerned that when visitors heard a sermon about prosperity, they would think we were all about money. But God said, "If you preach as much on prosperity as you do on healing, your people will get great results in that area as well."

That put things in a different light. Now my response was, "Here am I Lord, send me. I will preach that every Sunday morning until You say to quit." I had to tell our visitors, "Look, don't think this is the only message we ever deal with. We have a whole university; we deal with every theological topic there is. However, the Lord told me specifically to teach on this."

It was incredible how much I learned during that period of time! And as we began unfolding these truths, people in the congregation started getting financial miracles. Some amazing things began to happen.

One lady, who was a realtor, suddenly started writing huge, five-, six-, seven-thousand dollar tithe checks. I thought, "What's happening? If these are tithe checks, that tells me some serious money is coming in!" Her husband, who was also a realtor, had invested in real-estate. He died years earlier, and she had inherited the business. She was selling a little here and there, but she had owned some properties for years that just would not move.

She told me the things she was learning somehow sparked her faith, and suddenly, every property that she couldn't sell was selling and everything that she wanted to lease, was leasing. God was blessing her.

My father-in-law, a salesman in the recreational vehicle industry, also suddenly started writing huge checks. I asked him, "What's going on?"

He said, "This is fun! I've got the favor of God just

dripping from me. I've got sales coming in from every-where - it's really unlimited. I'm so busy it's making my head spin."

Many in the congregation started getting new jobs, new positions. That's because the application of the Word of God in any area will bring God's results in that area.

We've been told too long that poverty was a sign of humility, that a Christian should be poor and humble, as though the two terms were synonymous. But "poor" is actually synonymous with "ignorant." And ignorance can be cured with knowledge - specifically knowledge of God's Word.

We want to obtain knowledge and grow in faith in all different areas, but especially in areas where we lack. When someone discovers new ways to apply their faith, it's often a shock to them. They say, "Wow, I didn't even know I could believe God in this area!"

Now, in our lives, we obviously are not going to speak any universes into existence or call forth new planets. What is it that we call into existence that isn't already in existence? For example, in the area of finances, there's already enough money in the world to take care of you. But, if it's not in your account, it's one of those "things which do not exist." It does not exist in your account, and it needs to be there! It's not a matter of form or religious incantation; it's not just saying, "Money, be here," or "Money, come." Not that it's bad to do those things, but it's also a matter of obeying God's promptings and doing things in faith that you know are going to produce the income and the substance.

The Lord showed me this about our ministry. He said, "Don't you know that I know every single deutsche mark, I know every single peso, I know every single dollar, and every single yen?" He listed all these different currencies, then He said, "I know where all that money is in banks all over the world, and I've got your name written on money in all these different places. My plan is to draw money out of those banks and into your bank account, so you will be able to fulfill what I've called you to do. It's going to take money to do what I've called you to do. But I've already marked it all and it's coming in."

That's good news! The Gospel is good news – and along with our salvation come so many other things that are part of that good news, too! God's going to take care of us, and He's got ways for us to grow in faith to be able to receive everything Jesus died to give us.

REASON #25: WE NEED FAITH TO FINISH OUR COURSE

We have been looking at the question, "Why do we need faith?" We've seen that we need faith to be saved, to begin a walk with God. We need faith to continue that walk victoriously and to overcome all the problems of life. One final reason we need faith is to finish our course. Did you know you could even die in faith? What a comforting thought! A believer can leave this planet without fear, being "fully persuaded."

Hebrews 11:13, speaking to the Old Testament people of faith says, **"These all died in faith, not having received the promises, but having seen them afar off were assured of them, embraced them and confessed that they were strangers and pilgrims on the earth."** Now, if you remember, Old Testament saints did not receive salvation even though they served God. When they died they went to a holding place called "Paradise" or "Abraham's Bosom." They couldn't go directly into the presence of God until after

Jesus paid the price for man's sin. I like to say they were "saved on credit" – on credit of what Jesus was going to do in the future, the sacrifice that would make all believers the righteousness of God. Meanwhile, they were in Paradise, awaiting the day Messiah was going to come to earth.

Remember when Jesus was transfigured on the mountain in front of Peter, James, and John? They saw Moses and Elijah talking with Jesus. They had come from Abraham's Bosom to discuss God's plan with Jesus. I'm sure they were encouraging Him: "You're about ready, Messiah! You're just about to go to the cross and pay the price for all man's sin. We know what's coming after that! You're going to come get us and take us to heaven!" They were excited about the plan of God. Jesus was excited about it. I'm excited about the plan of God. We ought to all be excited about the plan of God!

The Old Testament saints were the "captivity" that Ephesians speaks of when it says, **"He (Jesus) led captivity captive"** (Ephesians 4:8). He delivered all of them and took them to heaven into the presence of God. His work on the cross "remitted" – completely removed – their sin. Their sin was separated from them completely, and now they were perfectly acceptable to God. They were perfectly righteous and could stand directly in the very presence of God. They died in faith believing that the Messiah would come and take them from Abraham's Bosom to heaven, where they'd get to see God face-to-face and live with Him for all eternity.

We, too, need to die in faith. The reality is, nobody on planet Earth gets out of here alive! All of us are going to go through the door of death. And even though we're born again, death is still the unknown, because we haven't experienced it.

But we don't need to be afraid of dying. I have no fear of death, whatsoever. Once, I was on a picnic with my son and one of his little friends. The little boy asked me, "What do you fear the most?" As I thought about it, I realized I've been in the Word and near the Lord so long that I don't have any fear. I replied, "Come to think of it, I'm not afraid of anything." As soon as I said that, I realized there was something I feared. I added, "Actually, I do fear one thing. I fear not fulfilling what God has called me to do." I fear not being pleasing unto God – that would be a tragedy in my life. I told the little boys, "So, I live every single day of my life to hear those words, 'Well done, good and faithful servant. Enter into the joy of your Lord.'"

Every day counts – every minute of every day counts. We've got to live uprightly before the Lord, pursuing Him completely all the time. I'm not totally legalistic about this: I do float around my swimming pool and enjoy fellowship with my family and other friends. We sometimes go out to dinner and just "hang" a little bit. But the rest of the time, I'm on the go and I'm fulfilled. I don't always sleep many hours at night. I don't know any other way to live. I understand what the prophet Jeremiah meant when he said, **"But His word was in my heart like a burning fire shut up in my bones"** (Jeremiah 20:9). I feel full of the fire of God and the power of God.

We die in faith, knowing that it's going to be "promotion day," it's going to be a graduation day. We haven't experienced this, so in that sense there's a fear of the unknown: you don't know what it's like to have your body shut down, but you know that your spirit and soul will immediately be accompanied by angels into the presence of God.

People ask, "Aren't you afraid to get on an airplane and fly around the world? What about plane crashes?

What about terrorists?"

I've spent so much time meditating on Psalm 91 that I'm fully persuaded I'm not going out by terrorists. I'm not going out by a plane crash, or anything else. Psalm 91 says the angels will bear me up. That means that if I'm in an airplane and the engines go out, God's going to bear that whole airplane up on angels' wings and it's still going to land.

Then one day, the Lord assured me He would not need angels to hold my plane in the sky. He said, "I know your schedule and where I am sending you far better than you do. And I know every airplane that you are going to fly in. I make sure that the equipment is maintained perfectly and you'll always fly on reliable aircraft."

I'm not going down in an airplane, or in a car crash or anything else. I'm going to go the full distance. I'm going to complete my course and fulfill my divine destiny. In Psalm 91:15-16, God promises, **"He shall call upon Me, and I will answer him; I will be with him in trouble; I will deliver him and honor him. With long life I will satisfy him, And show him My salvation."** Long life doesn't include early death.

We don't need to leave this planet until we are satisfied with long life. I take this as God's guarantee that I won't be dying early and leaving while I still have responsibilities to my family. I know some people may think that is arrogant or crazy, but I am convinced that's the will of God for all of us. It's the plan of God, and we walk it out by faith. And the more I live it, the more I realize the truth of it every single day. Living without fear of death is a great joy.

Of course, there is also the possibility that we may still be alive when Jesus comes back. If so, we'll be the

Church that's raptured. We'll be transformed in the twin-kling of an eye and given a glorified body instantly. What a wonderful experience! I can't think of anything more radical! If you're a fan of science fiction movies, you've seen the special effect that makes it look like you've jumped into hyper-space and are exceeding the speed of light. All the planets and stars just suddenly fly right by your face. Could you imagine having that experience? Flying right through the heavens into the third heaven of God – no space ship or space suit, just a glorified body. Phew! I'd like that experience!

25 REASONS WHY WE NEED DIVINE FAITH

#1: We can't please God without faith.

#2: Jesus told us to have faith.

#3: We need faith because we are saved through faith.

#4: We are made righteous by faith.

#5: We have purified hearts by faith.

#6: We are justified by faith.

#7: With justification comes peace.

#8: We have access to God's grace by faith.

#9: We are baptized in the Holy Spirit by faith.

#10: We are healed by faith.

#11: We are prospered by faith.

#12: We are sanctified by faith.

#13: Our righteousness is revealed from faith to faith.

#14: We live by faith.

#15: We stand by faith.

#16: We walk by faith.

#17: We are the children of God by faith.

#18: Christ dwells in our hearts by faith.

#19: We receive for others by faith.

#20: We inherit the promises by faith.

#21: Anything not done in faith is sin.

#22: By faith we overcome the world.

#23: By faith in God's promises, we become partakers of the divine nature.

#24: By faith we call things into being.

#25: We need faith to finish our course.

CHAPTER FIVE

A DEFINITION OF FAITH

WHEN WE DEFINE "FAITH" according to the Bible and understand what it's talking about, it'll give us a better perspective - God's perspective. Hebrews 11:1 gives us a biblical description of faith. It says, **"Now faith is the substance of things hoped for, the evidence of things not seen."** Let's do a word study on this verse and see what God has to say about faith.

The Greek word for faith in Hebrews 11:1 is the word *pistis*. It is the most common New Testament word for faith. It comes from the Greek root word *peitho* which means "to convince by argument." Isn't that interesting? Isn't that what it often takes for us to be convinced of something? Somebody makes a valid, reasonable argument and we are persuaded and convinced.

The word itself, *pistis,* means "a firm persuasion or conviction based upon hearing." We're still talking about hearing a convincing argument, but it's now about much more than just hearing with our natural ears. It's now the hearing of understanding. We receive biblical faith when we are firmly persuaded to the point of total conviction concerning something we have heard.

The Greek word translated "substance" in Hebrews 11:1 is *hupostasis*, which means "setting under" or a "firm foundation" - a solid, bedrock foundation. What does the Bible say about Jesus? He's "the Rock." What did Jesus say about the two men who built their houses, one on a rock and one on the sand? The man who heard the Word of God and did it was the one who built his house on the solid foundation of God's Word, on a solid rock. Faith is this solid foundation, this firm foundation. This word is also translated "confidence." We have persuasion with total confidence because we are on bedrock.

The word translated "hope" in this verse is the Greek word *elpis*, which means "an anticipation, usually, with pleasure or a favorable and confident expectation having to do with the unseen and the future." In other words, hope is the belief that something good is waiting for you in the future.

NATURAL HOPE VS. SUPERNATURAL HOPE

Even unsaved people have a natural form of hope - you have to have hope just to stay alive. We have seen that faith, hope, and love are living, vital forces. God has built hope in every single human being. Part of our nature, given by God, is to hope in a better tomorrow, in a good future. Negative situations can impact a person's natural hope over and over and over again until their hope is eradicated. When they run out of hope, they see no reason to stay on this planet. When you hear about people attempting suicide, it's because they became absolutely hopeless.

As a Christian, you can have a supernatural supply of

hope. Romans 5:5 says, **"Now hope does not disappoint, because the love of God has been poured out in our hearts by the Holy Spirit who was given to us."** This gives us a clear picture of how, as Christians, we can always continue to hope, because the love of God is poured into our hearts by the Holy Spirit who's been given unto us. As soon as the Spirit of God takes up residence in your spirit, you have a new hope that you never had before. You have hope that emanates out of the realm of the Spirit, so it far transcends any natural, human hope that you had before. All of a sudden you have a hope of eternity, of forever living with God in heaven.

Not only that, as you begin to study God's Word, you start to see God's promises concerning every area of need in your life.

WORKING DEFINITIONS OF FAITH

A number of different translators have brought out some additional shades of meaning in their translation of this verse.

Weymouth wrote: **"Now faith is a confident assurance of that for which we hope."**

Moffat wrote: **"Now faith means we are confident of what we hope for."**

Berkley wrote: **"Faith forms a solid ground for what is hoped for."**

Adding all these thoughts together, a conclusive translation of Hebrews 11:1 would be: "Now our firm persuasion and conviction is the solid foundation for those things that we expect with great anticipation."

BELIEVE IN THE BEST, NOT THE WORST!

Here is another working definition of faith: "Faith is believing in your heart that something you can't see with your eyes is going to come to pass." It's interesting that fear has the same definition: "Fear is believing in your heart that something you can't see with your eyes is going to come to pass." One is being persuaded to accept the truth from God's Word and the other is being persuaded to accept a lie from Satan. Satan is quick to plant his negative thoughts in your mind to cause you to expect bad things. You begin to ask yourself, "What if this happens?" Your mind begins to wander, playing out scene after scene. We are actually taught to do this – they call it critical thinking: "Imagine every negative thing that could possibly happen, everything that could go wrong." If you spent all your time doing that, you'd get so depressed, you wouldn't even get out of bed in the morning!

I understand planning and preparing, but when you do things with God, you don't have to plan on the worst. You can avoid it. You need to learn how to bypass those things. As Brother Kenneth E. Hagin said concerning walking in divine health for many years, "Now, that doesn't mean that I haven't had all these marvelous opportunities to be sick. I just decided to pass them up." He learned how to turn the symptoms back.

We don't have to believe for the worst. We can constantly be walking in faith and turning the negative things around.

Faith is believing that God loves you enough to fulfill His promises to you. Have faith in God's love, in His nature, in His character. We dishonor God's love for humankind when we think He doesn't care about these things.

GOD MEANT WHAT HE SAID

Faith is believing that God meant what He said when He said it. So many preachers all over the world spend all their time trying to explain to the people who follow them why God didn't mean what He said when He said it.

A classic case is when somebody had the most righteous and holy grandmother on the planet. Granny was taught "Sickness is the plan of God. God sends it your way to teach you things," and "You're humble if you're sick and poor." Granny died, even though everybody else was praying for her to be healed. The preacher concludes, "My grandma was the most righteous, holy person I've ever known. If it was God's will to heal anybody, He would've healed her. So, it must not be God's will to heal everybody. He must have some divine purpose in sickness and disease." Because they haven't experienced divine healing, they come up with all these different "human" ideas and reasoning to explain why God didn't really mean it when He said, "By His stripes we are healed."

In doing Greek word studies of Bible verses, I've read after Greek scholars who were not Spirit-filled. To rightly divide the Word of Truth, you have to understand the spiritual meaning behind every bit of Scripture. Very seldom does anyone who's not baptized in the Holy Spirit get much revelation outside of the realm of salvation. But once a person is baptized in the Spirit, then God is able to quicken to them covenant promises in all these different areas of life.

I've read translations that some very accurate Greek scholars have written. As I see the precision of the words the Holy Spirit chose and what the definitions of those words are, God begins to show me things, and I'll start dancing around my office, shouting, "Whoo, hoo! Glory to

God! Man, this guy's got a handle on it."

Then I read the margin, where they have added their own explanation, basically, "This is what God said, but this is not what He meant."

I ask, "What? Why would you bother to learn the original languages well enough to be able to teach exactly what the words in the Scripture are and then deny what they're saying?" They have missed it – they are trapped in their non-spiritual interpretation of the Word of God. We need to have the Spirit of God available to reveal to us what the Bible means and how God's kingdom works.

CHAPTER SIX

HOW FAITH COMES AND WHERE IT BEGINS

FAITH COMES BY HEARING AND HEARING. Romans 10:17 says, **"So then faith comes by hearing, and hearing by the word of God."** This is talking about spiritually hearing the will of God. Some have said, "The reason the word 'hearing' is in there twice is because faith comes by hearing and hearing, and hearing and hearing, and hearing and hearing." I agree. No matter how many times you need to hear the Word concerning a specific promise to get in faith, that's how many times you have to hear it to get in faith!

Several years after Brother Hagin started the Healing School at Rhema Bible Training Center, he turned it over to Keith Moore. Brother Moore would give out "prescriptions" from the Word of God. He'd say, "This is Healing School, so we are going to pass out prescriptions for your healing. You are going to have to go home and take this medicine. I prescribe that you take all of this, once an hour, every waking hour of the day."

Then he'd say, "Imagine if you went to a doctor for a

prescription and the directions said, 'Take this medication two times a day for three weeks straight.' You couldn't expect to go home and take it twice the first day and say, 'Well, I did it, and it didn't work. The next day I was still sick, and a week later I was still sick.'"

The doctor might well ask, "How many of the pills did you take?"

"Well, I took two."

"What did the prescription say?"

"It said, 'Take two a day for three weeks.'"

The doctor would then reply, "No wonder! If you had taken the medicine as directed it would have worked!"

Sometimes Brother Moore would instruct them: "Say this scripture one thousand times."

They would say, "What! I don't have the time to say it a thousand times."

He'd say, "What do you mean? You told me the doctors told you that you are terminal, that you are going to die. You don't have the time not to say it."

"But that would be a lot of work. It's too hard."

"Yeah, well, dying is worse! No matter how many times you've got to say this scripture, hearing and hearing it coming out of your own mouth, to be in faith and produce the results – isn't that worth it?"

Brother Hagin told about a woman who came up in his prayer line. Before he laid hands on her, he asked, "Now, if the Lord tells you something to do in order to be healed, will you do it?"

She said, "Well, yeah, if it's easy."

What's the option? Staying sick! Even if it's a little bit of work, you better do what God says to do.

GOD'S WORD IS SPIRITUALLY DISCERNED

Hearing comes by the Word of God because it reveals the will of God. Brother Hagin taught "Faith begins where the will of God is known." Some people do not know that God wants to heal them when they are sick just as much as He wanted to save them before they got saved. He wants to prosper them; He wants to give them peace in their home and in their marriages. All these blessings come to us by faith as we understand God's will.

Many people read the words of the Bible but they can't really understand them. They know the words, but cannot discern what the will of God is even from those very words. That's because the things of the Spirit of God are spiritually discerned (1 Corinthians 2:14). Now, that's bad news for those who aren't Spirit-filled.

But it's good news in that Satan doesn't have a clue what the Word of God means either. People ask, "How do you know that? Isn't Satan all-knowing?" No, he's a fallen angel with very limited knowledge and very limited power. He's got the ability to force the demons to do his bidding, but he's limited. He doesn't know what you think. And he doesn't know what you say in a conversation between you and God, because the Bible says you are able to speak mysteries with God (1 Corinthians 14:2).

In this passage, Paul was referring specifically to speaking in tongues, but I believe it applies to any spiritual conversation we have with God. In another place, Paul tells us if we speak with the tongues of men and of angels but don't have love, it's useless noise (1 Corinthians 13:1 paraphrased). Paul then proceeds with his famous discourse on the God kind of love, but he has also identified something important here – speaking in tongues can either be in the language of men or of angels. It would be logical to think that the fallen angels could understand what we say to God in angelic tongues. But that's why God has required that these conversations be spiritually discerned. The demons can understand the language and the words, but they're just like some of the Greek scholars who don't have any spiritual understanding of the meaning of the Scriptures they are translating. They can't interpret what you're saying – it's a mystery, a secret, between you and God.

There are other reasons Satan and the demons just don't get it. First of all, the kingdom of darkness doesn't operate by any of the principles of God. God's kingdom operates by love, and Satan's kingdom is totally devoid of love. God's kingdom operates by unity and agreement, and Satan's kingdom is totally devoid of unity or agreement. It operates strictly by competition for power and oppression. Since the demons don't understand love, unity, or agreement, they are clueless as to how the Word of God works, how faith works, and about the mysteries you speak to God – whether you pray in tongues or with your understanding.

In fact, Satan's schemes don't even factor into the equation concerning you and what God has called you to do. Once you understand how insignificant he is and how little his schemes really matter, it's going to make a world of difference in your life.

THE BEGINNING OF FAITH

The very beginning of faith is this: " **Every good gift and every perfect gift is from above, and comes down from the Father of lights, with whom there is no variation or shadow of turning**" (James 1:17). Everything good in life comes from God. Everything bad in life comes from the devil. Jesus said, **"The thief does not come except to** steal, and to kill, and to destroy. I have come that they may have life, and that they may have it more abundantly" (John 10:10).

You need to have these things settled in your mind:

- Sickness is not sent by God to teach you some lesson.
- Poverty is not a blessing of heaven to make you humble.
- Every bad thing in life comes from the devil.
- Every good thing in life comes from the Lord.

Once you understand these things, you are going to be light years ahead of ninety percent of the Body of Christ who are still confused on many of these issues. Once you know that only good comes from God, you are freed from the fear that He may do something harmful to you. Then you are to able to draw near enough to Him to access all the good things He wants to give you.

HOW TO BE UNSTOPPABLE

The reality is that Satan cannot keep you from getting answers to your prayer. He cannot prevent the blessings of God from coming into your life. He cannot stop you from receiving the anointing you need to be able to fulfill what God has called you to do. He cannot even remotely begin to stop you from fulfilling what God has called you to do.

Now, he does stop some people because he trips them up with sin and causes them to fall. He works through flaws in their Christian character where they haven't totally decided to make Jesus Lord as well as Savior. Jesus is saying to you, "Hi, I'm Jesus. I'm Lord, and you're not." Once you've decided you're not Lord and He is, and you make Him Lord of every area of your life, you're safe! You're on good ground. You're suddenly going to be "in the will of God."

Now, that doesn't mean that Satan can't try to disrupt your life or attack you in some way. I heard one minister say something that will be a great encouragement to you: "There are only two times that Satan will attack your life. Number one is when you're out of the will of God, and number two is when you're in the will of God." Isn't that so comforting! Satan is going to try to attack your life, but when you're in the will of God and you're in faith, you can turn his attacks back. When you're not in the will of God, you're pretty helpless and you get overrun. And so it's a matter of walking by faith, moment-by-moment obeying the voice of the Lord and doing what He tells you to do. Then Satan can't stop you from fulfilling your destiny.

RIGHTLY DIVIDING THE WORD OF TRUTH

To understand divine faith, we need to know how to "rightly divide the Word of Truth." In 2 Timothy 2:15, Paul wrote, **"Be diligent to present yourself approved to God, a worker who does not need to be ashamed, rightly dividing the word of truth."** What does it mean to rightly divide the Word of Truth?

One of the first things is to be able to rightly divide between the Old Testament and the New Testament. We need to understand that the Old Testament Law was done away with. We don't have to go through all the different forms of trying to observe the Law to be able to receive the grace of God. Jesus did all that for us. So, we understand that now everything's received by faith, not by works.

Next we need to understand that many of the things people suffered in Old Testament times were a result of the curse of the Law – which we've been delivered from. Both the blessing and the curse of the Law are found in

Deuteronomy 28.

I remember the first time I read the covenant promises of blessing in the first fourteen verses. I said, "Wow! That's good news!" Then I read verse 15:

If you do not obey the voice of the Lord your God, to observe carefully all His commandments and His statutes which I command you today, that all these curses will come upon you and overtake you.

As I read that long list of curses, I thought, "Whoa, man! That's terrible!" Later I found out that we've been redeemed from the curse of the Law because Jesus became a curse for us. I discovered you could read Deuteronomy 28 and say, "Not only am I promised these blessings, I'm delivered from these curses! I don't have to experience any of these things." I don't know what the "botch of Egypt" is exactly, but I'm glad that it's not God's plan for my life!

EVERY SCRIPTURE HAS MEANING

Another way to rightly divide the Word of Truth is to look for the spiritual import behind every passage of Scripture the Holy Spirit highlights for us. The Bible says:

All Scripture is given by inspiration of God, and is profitable for doctrine, for reproof, for correction, for instruction in righteousness, that the man of God may be complete, thoroughly equipped for every good work (2 Timothy 3:16-17).

When we get the spiritual understanding of what the Holy Spirit means behind a particular verse, it always increases our faith.

And since faith in all areas of life comes the same way, faith can be related from one area to another area. For example, maybe you've had a breakthrough in your faith for finances. You finally understood what God was trying to show you. Where you once had such a struggle, you now have a peaceful confidence that your needs will be supplied – with enough left over that you can be a generous giver. Suddenly, you are attacked with symptoms of sickness in your body. You can transfer what you learned about trusting God in the realm of finances to the realm of healing. The victories you've won in one area can be leveraged into victory in another area.

If you constantly spend your time in the Word, allowing the Holy Spirit to reveal to you the meanings of different passages of Scripture, you will see an overall increase in all areas of your faith.

It's been said that when Albert Einstein was asked, "What is the most interesting phenomena in the universe?" he replied, "Compound interest." Exponential growth over a period of time is truly amazing. This sort of exponential growth can happen to your faith.

You've seen the graphs that show how savings accounts increase over time because of compound interest. Imagine a graph showing the growth of your faith. Your learning curve is no longer at the bottom of the chart, because you have been steadily building on a solid foundation. As you continue to invest your time in studying God's Word and discovering what God is saying to you out of each scripture the Holy Spirit shows you, the graph of your faith will continue to climb higher and higher until it is going almost straight up. The principle of compound interest will be working to give you a supernatural return of ever-increasing faith!

CHAPTER SEVEN

LET THE BIBLE
INTERPRET ITSELF

PERHAPS YOU HAVE HEARD the theological term "hermeneutics." It's a Greek word for the study of the interpretation of Scripture. The first law of hermeneutics – or the first rule for interpreting Scripture – is this: "Let the Bible interpret itself in the light of God's revealed character and God's revealed will."

GOD'S REVEALED CHARACTER

This throws a lot of people off from the very beginning because they don't know what God's revealed character is. They look at the Old Testament and say, "It looks to me like God is a terrible, awful judge. If you do the wrong thing, He'll send an angel to slay 187,000 of you all in one night." They see God as an austere judge. They don't understand that the Old Testament was written under the Dispensation of Judgment and the Law. As New Testament believers, we're under a different dispensation, the Dispensation of Grace. We have a new covenant and a new revelation of God's character.

What does God look like for those who believe on Jesus Christ as Savior and Lord? It's simple: Look at Jesus, because when you look at Jesus, you are seeing God. Whatever Jesus looks like, whatever character traits He displays, that is exactly God's true nature. He exhibits the same loving character that Jesus displayed while He was ministering on earth.

The Bible tells us that Jesus is the exact image of God in the earth and the revealer of His will and character. Colossians 1:15 says Jesus **"is the image of the invisible God, the firstborn over all creation."** In John 8:29, Jesus told the Jews, **"And He who sent Me is with Me. The Father has not left Me alone, for I always do those things that please Him."** Isn't that good to know? Everything Jesus did was always pleasing to the Father. All the healings, all the miracles, the feedings of the multitudes, all the times He blessed people – all these pleased the Father, because it is the Father's nature to bring blessings.

A third scripture makes this point even more emphatically. John 14:8 records that Philip said to Jesus, **"Lord, show us the Father, and it is sufficient for us."** In other words, "We'll be satisfied if You show us the Father."

Jesus told him:

"Have I been with you so long, and yet you have not known Me, Philip? He who has seen Me has seen the Father; so how can you say, 'Show us the Father'?

"Do you not believe that I am in the Father, and the Father in Me? The words that I speak to you I do not speak on My own authority; but the Father who dwells in Me does the works.

"Believe Me that I am in the Father and the Father in Me, or else believe Me for the sake of the works themselves" (John 14:9-11).

Jesus plainly came out and told Philip, "Hey, if you have seen Me and the things that I do, you've seen God the Father. You've seen exactly the way He is. He's not any different from what I'm revealing to you."

DOES GOD "CAUSE" SICKNESS AND PROBLEMS?

Although in our King James Bible and in many other translations, there are places where it says plainly that God caused certain things to happen, that isn't really the meaning in the original Hebrew. In the English language, the relationship between the agent producing an effect and the effect itself can be clearly expressed. Some Hebrew scholars have said that in the Hebrew language there is no such causative tense. God set a system of blessing in motion, yes, but He did not cause the curse. People bring judgment on themselves if they walk out from the umbrella of God's protection. Their lives are reaping the harvest of all the negative seed that they've sown. A lot of the judgment blamed on God was actually the death and destruction that Satan brings to people's lives when they don't do things God's way. God allows these things to happen because He has given mankind a free will and has bound Himself to His Word and limited Himself to respond to the prayer of faith and its corresponding actions.

When we walk according to the Word of God in knowledge and in faith, we stay under a protective covering of the Lord. This does not mean that we don't have some opposition to our faith. But as we continue to grow in faith, we can overcome all opposition.

HOW MANY PEOPLE DID JESUS MAKE SICK?

We have seen that to understand the character and will of the Father, all we have to do is look at Jesus. When we look at Jesus and His life, we see the true picture of what God is really like.

What a contrast to the view of God as the cause of sickness and disease that some people have read into the Old Testament.

How many people did Jesus turn away when they asked, "Lord, please heal me" or "Please heal my daughter"? How many times did Jesus say, "No, healing is not for you. It's not God's will"? He never once said that.

There were times when people came to Jesus who did not have faith to be healed, and even then, He didn't turn them away. Mark 9:22-24 tells the story of the father of a demon-possessed boy who wasn't too sure if Jesus would help. He begged Him, "If you can do anything, have compassion on us, and help us."

Jesus told him, "If you can believe, all things are possible to him who believes."

The father of the child cried out with tears, "Lord, I believe; help my unbelief." He was just being honest: "I've got some belief, but I've got some unbelief. Will You help me with the part where I'm having a hard time believing?"

Jesus immediately healed the man's son. In effect He was saying, "Sure. I'll be glad to. It's My nature to help you get over your unbelief and to get in faith. Here is a miracle to show the power of God."

Jesus wants to help all of us get over our unbelief and into the place of faith. Most of the time we don't realize how much we've been affected by negative thoughts and negative teaching. We've been bombarded with negativity, and there are still little traces of it here and there that we haven't completely eradicated from our believing and our expectation of God. But the more we get the picture of Jesus and His will and the revelation that this is also the will of God the Father in Heaven, the more we're going to receive from God through divine faith.

INTERPRET THE WORDS OF THE BIBLE IN CONTEXT

The second rule concerning the interpretation of Scripture is that specific words that could be translated in different ways must be interpreted by the context in which they are written. For example, take the word "love." In the Greek, there are four words for love, so you can get very specific in describing what type of love it is. But in English, we have only one word to use to communicate this concept. Therefore, we must study the context to see what level of love we're talking about. We say, "I love pizza," "I love music," "I love people," and "I love my wife." We love all those things differently and on different levels, because there are different types of loves. (Guys, you're in trouble if you love pizza the same way you love your wife!)

An even better example is found in the two Greek words *logos* and *rhema*. In the New Testament, *logos* is translated "word" and it refers to the whole counsel of God's Word. *Logos* is the complete expression of God's thoughts and will – the ideal, heavenly version in the eternal realm. Over the centuries, God spoke this Word to His prophets, who wrote it down. Then God made sure, sometimes by miraculous means, that His Word survived. The Scriptures were canonized and retained for us to be able to see the things He wanted us to know in the twenty-first century. There are covenant promises concerning every issue of life. Everything we have to deal with in this life is covered somewhere in the Bible, the written Word of God.

Rhema is also translated "word," but it means "a specific word or utterance, as that understood to be for you as an individual." Out of the whole counsel of God found in the Bible, God will highlight one specific promise or give specific directions.

The day you were born again, a *rhema* word came to you. You believed it for yourself and the power of this Word impacted your life. Billions of people could take advantage of the words concerning Jesus Christ being Lord and Savior. One day, you took God at His individual word, and realized, "Oh, my goodness. This is for me! Forget the other six billion people on the planet. This is for me! I'm receiving Jesus as my Lord and Savior today."

On that day, you were born again. The Holy Spirit moved into your spirit, and you were translated from the kingdom of darkness into the kingdom of God's dear Son. You became a member of the family of God and part of the army of God. All this happened in an instant, upon your confession of Jesus as Lord. You received the full impact of that *rhema* word that you believed.

Other covenant promises become alive in us the same way. Maybe a minister laid hands on you and you received your healing through one of the gifts of the Spirit in operation. Because you've experienced it, you know miraculous healing is available and that it's possible. But so far, you haven't been able to exercise your own faith and get the same result.

Then one day, you hear Jesus say, "That promise is for you, too!"

Suddenly you see it. "I can pray the prayer of faith and receive it right now!" Maybe you've had some of those experiences.

Receiving healing by exercising your own faith is the highest level of healing because then you're not dependent on anybody else. You don't have to wait until the healing evangelist comes to town. You don't have to wait until somebody at your church is obedient to flow in the Holy Ghost. Your healing is now between you and God – and you will be able to receive every time.

A VERY SPECIFIC WORD

Let's look at some accounts in the Bible where individuals received a very specific word from God, a *rhema* word. In Luke, chapter 5, Jesus was teaching by Lake Gennesaret. Peter and his partners were also on the shore of the lake. They had been fishing all night long. When Jesus showed up, they were cleaning their nets. That's a bad sign. When you catch something, you are mending your nets, when you're cleaning your nets, that's an indication you didn't catch anything. They were cleaning the seaweed out of them so they would be ready for the next fishing trip.

The multitude listening to Jesus kept growing larger, and Jesus decided it would be a good idea to get into a boat and teach from there. Peter made a decision that changed the course of his life: he let Jesus into his boat. I suggest that to everybody, "Let Jesus in your boat." That's the way you start.

As Jesus spoke, Peter was moved by His teachings. He realized, "I'm listening to supernatural words. This is a different kind of man." When Jesus finished teaching, He told Peter, "Now launch out into the deep and let down your nets for a catch."

Peter's first thought was that Jesus' plan was not a good idea. "Jesus, I know You are a good teacher, I know

You're anointed because I've never heard words like this. But I am a professional fisherman, so I know a lot more about when and where to catch fish than You do." Peter at first argued with Jesus, saying, "Master, we've toiled all night long. We threw the nets over this side of the boat and that side of the boat, but we never caught anything!"

Then it dawned on Peter, "Wait a minute! This man is speaking miracle words." Jesus had asked him to do something easy enough to do, simply let your nets down for a catch. You notice Jesus didn't say, "Let your nets down and let's just see what happens. Maybe you will catch something and maybe you won't." He didn't say that. He said, "Let your nets down. You are going to get a catch when you do."

Peter reconsidered and said, "I know we've let down the nets all night long, but nevertheless, at Your Word I'll do it again." He recognized there was power in those words. He immediately let down the nets and caught so many fish that the nets started breaking. Peter called for his partners to come and help. Soon both boats were so full of fish that they were about to sink! Both Peter and his partners realized, "This man speaks things and miracles happen. He must be the Son of God. He's the Messiah we were looking for!"

Peter cried out, "Oh, Lord, I'm a sinful man, depart from me!" I always wondered about that. Jesus was in a boat - so where was He going to go? Peter didn't know Jesus could walk on water yet, so, how could Jesus depart?

Instead of departing, Jesus invited them to join Him, saying, **"Follow Me"** (Matthew 4:19). Jesus added, "Fear not. From now on you're going to catch men instead of fish" (Luke 5:10 paraphrased). Peter, Andrew, James, and John immediately left everything and followed Jesus. The miraculous catch of fish convinced them to obey the Lord's *rhema* word: "That's it, that was His Word. He said follow Him, so that's what we are going to do."

When Jesus speaks a *rhema* word to us, our response should also be "Nevertheless, at Your word." When He has spoken into your heart, you say, "That's it! That solves it for me, I'm not doing anything else but what He says." That's faith.

Peter heard another *rhema* word in Matthew 26:34, but this time, he did not receive it. Jesus tried to warn Peter that he would deny Him three times before morning. Peter and all the disciples boldly declared this would not happen, but of course, it did. Then in Matthew 26:75 we read, **"And Peter remembered the word of Jesus who had said to him, 'Before the rooster crows, you will deny Me three times.' So he went out and wept bitterly."** Peter heard a *rhema* word from the Lord, but he did not believe it. After it came to pass, he wept when he remembered that word.

NOTHING IS IMPOSSIBLE

Another example of someone receiving a *rhema* word is found in Luke 1:30-37. This is just so powerful! The angel Gabriel came to tell Mary that she's going to be the mother of Jesus, the Messiah. He told her:

> **"Do not be afraid, Mary, for you have found favor with God. And behold, you will conceive in your womb and bring forth a Son, and shall call His name Jesus. He will be great, and will be called the Son of the Highest; and the Lord God will give Him the throne of His father David. And He will reign over the house of Jacob forever, and of His kingdom there will be no end" (Luke 1:30-33).**

Those were heavy words. Mary did not doubt the angel's words, but she wondered how God was going to do this amazing thing. She asked the angel, **"How can this be, since I do not know a man?"** She was betrothed to be married to Joseph. In the Hebrew tradition, when a couple was betrothed, they were legally under a marriage contract, but they had not yet consummated the marriage by coming together sexually. They would do that only after a huge feast was given to celebrate their marriage. Mary and Joseph were still awaiting their wedding feast. Mary was asking the angel, "How is God going to produce this? I haven't slept with my husband yet."

We find the angel's reply in verses 35-37:

"The Holy Spirit will come upon you, and the power of the Highest will overshadow you; therefore, also, that Holy One who is to be born will be called the Son of God. Now indeed, Elizabeth your relative has also conceived a son in her old age; and this is now the sixth month for her who was called barren. For with God nothing will be impossible."

One day, I was doing a word study in a Greek word study concordance, following all the places where the Greek word *rhema* was used. I was reading along through Matthew and Mark and *rhema* would be translated "word," or "saying." Then all of a sudden, in Luke 1:37, I saw the word "nothing." *"Rhema"* was in the negative form so it was actually "no *rhema*" or "no word," and the translators chose to use the word "nothing." What the angel actually said to Mary was, "With God no word that He speaks shall be impossible."

This accurate translation clarifies a couple of things

72

for us. Some people have read, "With God nothing is impossible," and their mind says, "Oh man, I could ask for all kinds of stuff." No, you need to get a specific *rhema* word from the Lord.

I know people who have tried to believe God for all kinds of goofy things. "I believe, God, that I'm going to inherit the Taj Mahal." Did God tell you that? For one thing, if it's owned by somebody else, and you think you're going to inherit it, then that is covetousness – and you need to repent. Or "I believe God's going to cause a Corvette to show up in my front yard tomorrow with my name on the registration, and I'll find the keys in my mailbox." Well, did God say that was going to happen? You're stretching it – and setting yourself up for a really great disappointment.

People could save themselves a whole lot of trouble by not dreaming things up that are not necessarily the promise of God. Believe me, if you just stick with the things that God really has promised you, you're going to be plenty busy believing God and having the true blessings of the Lord active in your life. The angel said, "Nothing that God speaks – if He can get His *rhema* word across to you and get you to believe it – is impossible."

Mary knew this angel represented God Himself. When he said, "This is going to happen to you," she believed him.

She said, **"Let it be to me according to your word."** In other words, "According to the *rhema* that you've delivered, the *rhema* of God to me, let it happen to me." She was totally submitted to God's Word.

In 1977, I took a pilgrimage to Israel. I had some Christian friends staying on a kibbutz in Jerusalem for a year. Two other friends and I decided to visit them.

Instead of taking the official tour buses, we decided to rent a car and drive around. I don't know if that was the wisest thing to do, but we did see things other people don't get to see. We drove to Nazareth and started walking around through all the little markets. Suddenly, I realized I was separated from my two friends. I thought, "Oh, great! I'm lost in a foreign country, and I don't speak the language. I wonder if I'll ever get back to America!" I wandered around for two hours, looking for my friends. Finally, I saw a huge church in the center of town. Curious, I walked inside, where I saw a Franciscan priest standing next to some sort of stone structure.

I said, "I'm lost. What is this place?"

He answered, "Oh, this is the Church of the Annunciation."

Of course! I thought. *This is Nazareth!*

"You mean, where Gabriel announced to Mary that she was going to become the mother of the Son of God?"

He said, "Yes," and started to explain that many believe that the stone "grotto" (or cave) was the actual house where Mary lived at the time of the angelic visit.

As I thought about this, it occurred to me that if that were true, then this place was much, much more. I told the priest, "Then this would also be the place where the Holy Spirit actually did what the angel said He was going to do. He came upon Mary and conceived the Son of God right here!"

Suddenly, tears started streaming down the priest's face. I'm sure he had been asked all kinds of questions about this place, but I could tell that nobody had asked him something that had tapped into the depth of the reality of what had actually happened here. We both realized that we were at the place where God touched the earth and sent His only begotten Son. I started to weep too. We were both standing there, fellowshipping in the Spirit without saying a word, just knowing the reality of where we were standing.

I found my buddies – they showed up a little later at this same church. I see now that God had a divine appointment set up for me to receive this *rhema,* this revelation, this new understanding of things. And that's the way a *rhema* of God's Word comes. You come into this awareness, "God's done something for the world; and He's done something special for you." That builds your faith to receive what He's done.

Once I understood that this verse actually meant, "No word God said as a covenant promise shall be impossible to them who believe," it made a big difference to me. I stopped believing for squirrely things. God was saying, "Look, just wait until you have My *rhema.* Meditate in My Word, the Bible, until you have My *rhema* on something. And then, guess what! Nothing is going to be able to stop this thing from coming to you!" It's been a great delight to watch God answer so many prayers of faith over the years.

On that same trip to Jerusalem, my friends and I went to what they call the Garden Tomb. This is another place that is really important to me: the place where God touched the earth and raised the Son of God from the dead. They have a door over the Garden Tomb that says, "He's not here; He's risen." I told my friends, "I want to hang out in here for a little while." I went into the tomb, closed the door behind me, and locked it. The presence of God was so strong, I wanted to stay there. But soon my friends started knocking on the door – they couldn't believe I had shut and locked the door to the Garden Tomb!

EVERY WORD IS ESTABLISHED

The third rule for interpreting Scripture is that the whole Bible must be compatible with itself as the whole counsel of God. Matthew 18:16 says, **"But if he will not hear, take with you one or two more, that 'by the mouth of two or three witnesses every word may be established.'"** Now, this was part of an Old Testament Law found in Deuteronomy 19:15 which says:

> **One witness shall not rise against a man concerning any iniquity or any sin that he commits; by the mouth of two or three witnesses the matter shall be established.**

The specific application of this concept was when one person accused another of doing something. In such a case, it would be one person's word against another's. If they're both saying something different, they neutralize one another's testimony. But the Bible says that if one person says one thing, and two eye-witnesses say something different, then the weight of testimony is on the side of the two witnesses. You can find this principle put into the laws of the land in courts all around the world. Where did they get it? From the Bible. It was God's principle for man to use in natural, earthly governments.

We use this same principle concerning the Word of God. If we find a word or a doctrine in the Bible used just once, then we can't build a major doctrine around it. There's not enough evidence. But we will find the fundamental doctrines and the fundamental covenant promises repeated over and over again in many places. We'll get many witnesses that say, "This is what God says, and this is what God does. Therefore we can believe God for these things." When we find multiple witnesses in Scripture, we've got a solid foundation for an absolute doctrine of the Church.

My testimony agrees with the witness of Scripture. Today I can say, "I am confident that the covenant for healing and for provision is part and parcel of the covenant for salvation. They are just as much a part of the work of the Cross as salvation itself." Yet some people don't believe this and have received only salvation as the work of the Cross. But I walk in the covenant promises for all parts of life all the time. You can't convince me it doesn't work: I'm far too blessed. Some people say, "Ah, you're just dreaming." Well, don't wake me up! I tell you, I enjoy this dream; it's a good life. It took me a long time to get here, I'm not going back to sickness and poverty!

CHAPTER EIGHT

FIVE INFALLIBLE STEPS OF FAITH

WOULD YOU LIKE TO BE ABLE TO GUARANTEE that your faith is always going to work? I'm going to give you five infallible steps of faith that will work every single time. I was a student at Rhema Bible Training Center when the Lord revealed this to me. He gave me a way that makes it easy to remember all five steps. The first two words rhyme with each other, the last two words rhyme with each other and the prayer of faith is right in the middle. It's like the peanut butter between the two pieces of bread. It's the glue that holds everything together. The five steps are meditation and illumination, then the prayer of faith, then confession and possession.

THE FIRST STEP IS MEDITATION

Meditation is reading, hearing, pondering, and speaking the Word of God in order to gain faith. Now, you'll hear the term "confession" used a lot, but I prefer the term "meditation." Some people refer to meditation as the "confession unto faith." They say, "You've got to confess the Word, and confess the Word, and confess the Word." That's true, but before you're in faith, it's actually meditation. Literally speaking, you are meditating on the Word in order to be "in faith." So, if you're not yet in faith, you are hoping for what has been promised you.

I remember the very first time I heard Brother Hagin say he'd been walking in divine health for more than fifty years. Suddenly, I felt like my spirit started doing Olympic gymnastics on the inside! I said to myself, "That has got to be what the Word of God really promises and now this man is living it out as living proof. I know it's available for me!"

Now, I wasn't "in faith" yet, but I knew that if he could do it, then it's available to everybody because God is not a respecter of persons. I was excited. I said to myself, "Man, I'm going to get a hold of this, and one day, I'm going to be able to say 'I've been walking in divine health for fifty years.'" I knew I needed to spend time meditating on the Word of God. As I write this book, I am able to say I have been walking in divine health for twenty-nine years, and I know that one day I will be able to say, "It's been fifty years."

As soon as the Bible was written, God started instructing His people to meditate on His Word. One of the Hebrew words for "meditation" is *hagah,* which means "to murmur," or literally "to peep or mutter." It refers to speaking under your breath, kind of talking to yourself. I remember thinking that people who talked to themselves were a little insane. [Of course, that's really not the case. It's only if you answer yourself that you're actually insane!]

But it appears that, according to the Bible, one way to put yourself in contact with the reality of God's kingdom is to speak God's Word to yourself. Speak it to yourself, literally mutter it. This is closely related to the idea of a cow chewing its cud over and over and over again. So, we peep, mutter, and speak the Word to ourselves over and over again.

There's another Hebrew word for meditation, *siyach,* which also means to ponder. This refers to the mental activity that takes place when you are pondering something, going over it again and again.

The Greek word for "meditation" is *meletao,* and it means literally to revolve something over and over again in the mind.

Joshua 1:8 is a key verse concerning meditation of the Scriptures. It says, **"This Book of the Law shall not depart from your mouth, but you shall meditate in it day and night."** In other words, God told Joshua to keep this word in his mouth, speaking it to himself day and night.

The verse continues, **"...that you may observe to do according to all that is written in it. For then you will make your way prosperous, and then you will have good success."** It was important for Joshua to observe everything that God had spoken to Moses. Moses was the author of the Pentateuch, the first five books of the Bible, and Joshua was his protégé. Joshua had served with Moses for 40 years, but all of a sudden, Joshua is in charge. Four times in this chapter, God told Joshua, **"Fear not... be strong...be of good courage."** In this verse, God told Joshua how to be "in faith." He says, "This book of the Law has got to stay in your mouth - keep saying it - and then you will be able to do everything that's written in it."

Now, what happens when you obey God's Word, when you walk uprightly and morally, and do what God says to do? A powerful anointing will come upon your life, because God will increase the anointing on a person who will walk in integrity and character. As you observe to do all that is written in His Word, you'll make your way prosperous and you'll have good success in all the affairs of life.

Joshua needed to be successful because he was going

to lead all the children of Israel down the path he took. Wherever he was going to go, they were going to go too. He needed to know how to get "in faith," so God told him exactly what he needed to do.

What was it Joshua meditated on? Remember he didn't have any New Testament scriptures. He only had the first five books of the Bible, the books Moses had written. And yet, it was enough to produce miraculous faith in him and to show him his purpose in life. I'm convinced that as he meditated on the book of the Law, he saw the picture of God's plan of redemption. He received the illumination. In these scriptures, God unfolds the pattern for tabernacle worship, the whole process for the people to rehearse the redemptive work of the Christ, the Messiah that was going to come. As he meditated on these scriptures, Joshua got a chance to see this is all about the Messiah.

"We are the people who are going into the land of promise. Out of us is going to come the salvation of the world. God is going to bring forth the Savior, the Messiah, through us. These are our marching orders, our reason to live. We are God's chosen people. That is the fire that burns in us and that's why we're going to go in and take the land."

Joshua was driven with this passion because he saw a vision of the Christ by meditating on the Word of God. He saw the redemptive plan of God. I'm totally convinced of it. He was obedient to do everything God showed him to do. He won a great victory at Jericho, which was a picture of the tithe. Just like the "first fruit," it was holy unto the Lord. That's why God said, "Don't take any spoils from it." But Achan had disobeyed God's commandment by taking part of the spoil and hiding it in his tent.

When the army lost their next battle against the King of Ai, Joshua was shocked. He went to God and said, "Oh,

in order to be His living witnesses, reaching out to others. But if Satan can take us out in our health or our finances, if we are completely defeated, we cannot be a living witness to anyone!

THE SECOND STEP IS ILLUMINATION

Once we have done enough meditation on the Word of God, we are ready for the next step: illumination. Illumination is when faith comes alive in our hearts. Faith springs up to a whole new level when we get the illumination on a covenant promise. The Greek word for "illumination" is *photizo*. The English word "photography" comes from this Greek word. *Photizo* means "to shine a light on," literally, "to shed rays of light." It also means "to give understanding to." When someone gets a good idea they might say, "Suddenly, the lights turned on."

Illumination is more than just a dawning on our minds, in a natural sense. Illumination is when God is able to bring across spiritual truth from His kingdom in such a way that suddenly our minds are in agreement with our spirits. The scripture we are reading was recorded thousands of years ago, and maybe we've even read it before. But God suddenly shines His light on this Word, and now we understand what it means in a new way.

This is why it is so important to spend time in the Word. God will keep causing lights to shine on every single page as He reveals His covenant promises to us. Suddenly we realize that we possess it now in the realm of the Spirit, because it was something God did for us two thousand years ago, with the work of the Cross of the Lord Jesus Christ. Once we see what's been done for us, we can begin to take the steps to lay hold of it and make it part of our lives.

REVELATION VS. ILLUMINATION

Although some use the words "revelation" and "illumination" synonymously, there is a difference between the two. "Revelation" happens when God's Word is revealed for the first time. It was hidden, it was a mystery. Then God reveals it to someone as a revelation.

God gave revelation to His prophets by the Holy Spirit and by the angels. "Angel" means "messenger" in both Hebrew and Greek. If you study the Bible, you will see that angels actually delivered many messages to the patriarchs and the prophets. The prophets wrote down the revelations that God gave them – and that's how we have God's written Word, the Bible.

"Illumination" is different from "revelation." Illumination is what happens the first time God's Word is made real to you. The Scripture was there, other believers may have understood it, but suddenly God shines the light on it for you, and you see it for yourself. Now it's yours! You have been illuminated.

Revelation may still come to the believer today if God needs to inform that believer of something that cannot be conveyed through the illumination of the Scriptures. Believers today also receive revelation to guide them in decisions concerning life or ministry. For example, God may tell you to move to a certain city. That specific guidance isn't in the Bible, so it would come by revelation.

Many "word-of-faith" Christians use the term "revelation knowledge" when they are referring to illumination. This sounds real heavy, as in "I've got the heavy revies from the Word of God." "Revelation knowledge" seems weightier than illumination. In comparison, illumination may even sound a little wimpy.

A case can easily be made that illumination is receiving knowledge of God's revelation. Illumination is the spiritual hearing from God's Word that reveals God's will. When you have the illumination, you have faith. You believe in your heart. Romans 10:9,10 says:

That if you confess with your mouth the Lord Jesus and believe in your heart that God has raised Him from the dead, you will be saved. For with the heart one believes unto righteousness, and with the mouth confession is made unto salvation.

Believing with the heart and confessing with the mouth is essential. That's how we got saved, and that's the way all faith works.

Illumination is an on-going process. There are countless people who have received salvation based on an illumination of Romans 10:9-10. Then they put their Bible on the shelf and there it sits gathering dust. It's chock full of all kinds of other covenant promises, but these precious promises never come true in their lives because they never open God's Word and let God shine the light on it. Once you are baptized in the Holy Spirit, He can really cause you to believe everything that's in the Book! After that, all the world's available to you by faith in God.

Illumination is a miraculous, supernatural event. Once you have the illumination, faith is there. You realize, "This promise is just as much for me as it was for Jesus or for anybody else. If anybody else has received it, I can too. It's just as much mine as it is theirs!" Once that realization comes to you, you are in faith. God gives illumination as we prepare ourselves for it by reading God's Word and speaking it to ourselves.

REVEALING THE HIDDEN THINGS

The Word of God clarifies the difference between right and wrong and points out things that might be hidden. Through knowing the Scripture and having spiritual illumination we are able to discern the difference between good and evil (Hebrews 5:14).

We see this in the life of the Apostle Paul. Remember the story in Acts 16 about the slave girl who followed Paul and Silas around? Every place they went, she was there, telling the people, "These men are sent from God," and "Everything they say is from the Lord. Listen to them." She was saying the right things, but she was demon-possessed.

She followed Paul and Silas for three days. Paul knew the whole time that something wasn't right. Then all of a sudden, he had the unction of the Spirit of God to cast the demon out of her. Instantly she was delivered, and she couldn't tell fortunes anymore. Her owners were so angry at Paul that they started a riot in that town. But the girl was set free from demonic possession. Paul had studied the Word of God and had his senses exercised to discern between good and evil. God illuminated him and gave him that understanding.

STEP THREE IS THE PRAYER OF FAITH

We have been looking at the five infallible steps of faith, which when exercised concerning God's covenant promises, will produce supernatural intervention from God into the natural course of events of our lives – every single time.

In the first step, we meditate on God's covenant promises, the specific scriptures that deal with the problems of life we are facing. We take those verses and we speak them to ourselves over and over again, until God illuminates the Word to us. This is the second step. When God illuminates the Word to us, it's as if Jesus just spoke and said, "This is for you. This is for you to receive now, in this moment, in this very hour." We become totally convinced that this covenant promise is for us.

Suddenly we know we are "in faith." Does that mean that instantly, every single one of our desires will come to pass? No, not at all. There's a very important step at the very center of the five infallible steps of faith, and that is prayer.

Prayer is involved in every aspect of your relationship with the Lord. Prayer is simply a communication between you and your Father in Heaven. Jesus made us acceptable to God and gave us access to the throne of God's grace. We can go to the Father with great confidence and ask Him for the things Jesus purchased for us.

The "Prayer of Faith" releases your power to receive. We have to come to an understanding that we are simply receiving what Jesus has already done for us. We are not trying to obtain healing, or financial blessings, or peace in our home. That was accomplished by Jesus two-thousand years ago. Once we get the illumination that it is available for us now, it is simply a matter of personally receiving the gift.

It works just like salvation. Salvation was purchased for you two thousand years ago, but you didn't take advantage of it until you received illumination that Jesus was who He said He was - "the Son of God." You became aware that you needed to do something about Him - you needed to receive Him as your own personal Lord. Every other covenant promise of God works exactly the same way. You believe it, and you receive it. It's all a matter of believing and receiving God's covenant promises.

The classic passage of Scripture concerning the prayer of faith is found in Mark 11:23,24:

"For assuredly, I say to you, whoever says to this mountain, 'Be removed and be cast into the sea,' and does not doubt in his heart, but believes that those things he says will be done, he will have whatever he says."

Notice that this is the same pattern we have been studying: first we have to put the Word of God in our mouth. Brother Hagin always pointed out that in this scripture, "saying" is mentioned three times more than "believing."

I've heard Brother Hagin quote Mark 11:23-24 thousands of times. Then he'd say, "You've got to put the Word of God into your mouth." Some people argue, "I don't want to say something like, 'By His stripes I was healed,' because I don't yet believe it." Here's some good advice: say the words as a memory verse that you're working on. One day the illumination will come, and then you'll suddenly believe it!

WHEN YOU PRAY, BELIEVE!

Jesus continued His teaching in verse 24, **"Therefore I say to you, whatever things you ask when you pray, believe that you receive them, and you will have them."** Jesus was giving us the key to the prayer of faith: you must believe that you receive at the time that you pray. That's when the ability to receive this covenant promise is released.

Here's an illustration that will help you stay steady while you are waiting to receiving a promise. Picture yourself asking the Father in Jesus' name for something, and then seeing Him release it out of His hand to you in the realm of the Spirit, at the very time that you prayed the prayer of faith. Now, whether or not the answers impacts you immediately, you still believe that you received it when you prayed.

In other words, if you were praying for healing in your body, and you said, "Father, I see that Jesus died not only for my sins, but also for my healing. By His stripes, I was healed two thousand years ago. He paid the price. Therefore, I believe that I receive right now, in my body, healing for this pain. I thank You for it now Father, in Jesus' name. Amen."

Of course, you'd like the pain to go immediately. But what if it's not immediately removed? Do you say your faith is not working? No! Jesus is saying here that you've got to believe that you received the answer to your prayer at the time you prayed, whether you see it manifest immediately or not.

In a way, it's all about time. This earth operates on the principle of seed time and harvest – which takes time. Even in our natural lives we can see this. Before scientists discovered viruses and bacteria, people did not connect being around a sick person with getting sick themselves – because it did not happen right away. If someone sneezed on them, it wasn't until a day or two later that they started experiencing symptoms. They didn't see the connection – but the "seeds" were planted at the time of the sneeze and they grew. In a similar way, the "seeds" of healing are planted when you pray the prayer of faith. Don't make the mistake of missing the connection because it doesn't happen immediately!

INSTANT RESULTS ARE POSSIBLE!

As you continue to practice the five infallible steps of faith, your faith will constantly increase, and more and more things will be delivered to you immediately after you pray. You'll start seeing some instant results to your prayers.

While I was a student at Rhema, I was incredibly blessed to be able to attend "Healing School" with Brother Hagin every day after class for a year and a half. Every afternoon, I would sit in the front row and receive from this prophet of God. There was a real move of the Spirit of God in Healing School. I learned more about the move of the Holy Spirit in those healing services than in any other place I've ever been.

It was during this time that it became a concrete reality to me that faith works – sometimes almost instantly. Brother Hagin usually ministered the same things in Healing School that he'd been teaching us in class, and at this point we were studying "Christ the Healer." I knew my faith was working! Every day, I was sitting under the Word taught with a powerful anointing, and I was reading and studying at night. I was convinced that I would be able to say like Brother Hagin, "I'll never see another sick day."

Then a flu epidemic swept through Rhema Bible Training Center, the faith school! Many of the students were out sick. I thought, "Oh, man, I'm not going to let that attach itself to me." Lester Sumrall was coming to Rhema the following week to speak to the students and hold a seminar. I was determined not to miss a single bit of Brother Sumrall's ministry. At lunch I went to a restaurant and sat near the front door. A cold front had come through, and I got a blast of cold air every time the door opened. I felt myself get really chilled. I went on to

Healing School and felt okay, but by the time I got home, I started feeling sick. By eight o'clock that night, I had every symptom of the flu that a person can have. I was miserable - dying would have felt better!

I couldn't believe I was sick! I thought, "Well, I'm in faith. I know these covenant promises are for me. I now understand Mark 11:23-24. I'll just pray the prayer of faith." I prayed, "Father, I believe I receive my healing, right now, in Jesus' name."

I stood there expecting my body to suddenly feel better, but it didn't. Instead, I kept getting sicker and sicker. I thought, "I'll just double up on the Word." I took out the book, *Christ the Healer*, and starting reading it. But I was so sick the words were blurry. My eyes couldn't focus at all. This misery continued on through the night.

About three o'clock in the morning, I remembered the story of when John G. Lake was ministering in Africa when there was a terrible outbreak of bubonic plague. He had been ministering to the people, praying for them and serving them. In fact, he'd even been helping to carry the dead out.

Finally a mercy ship arrived with medical missionaries and vaccines for the plague. They urged him to take the vaccine.

He said, "No, I won't need that."

They asked, "Why not? What are you taking?"

He replied, "I'm taking the Law of the Spirit of Life in Christ Jesus. It has set me free from the Law of Sin and Death."

"What is that?" they asked.

He told them, "It's in the Bible. Romans chapter 8."

"We'd like to know more about this," they said, "But

we're really concerned for you. You've been handling people who have died from the plague - and there are germs all over them."

When these people died from bubonic plague, a terrible foam came out of their mouth and their nose. This foam was teeming with living bubonic plague germs.

Lake suggested, "Let's run an experiment so that you'll know I don't need your medicine. Take some foam from a plague victim. Examine it under your microscope and make sure that the disease germs are alive. Then put it in the palm of my hand. When it comes in contact with my body, those disease germs will die because I walk according to the Law of the Spirit of Life in Christ Jesus." Romans 8 had been illuminated to Lake - he knew he was free from the Law of Sin and Death, and that disease couldn't touch him.

The missionaries did as Lake suggested. When they took the foam out of his hand and put it under the microscope, all the germs were dead. He illustrated to them how the power of God was able to keep his body immune from outside invasion of demonic germs.

Suddenly, the light of this truth from Romans 8 was on the inside of me. Before this time, I knew I was in faith, and I knew I was locked in a spiritual battle, but it had not dawned on me to take authority over the devil. Jesus said, "Speak to the mountain." In this case, sickness in my body was the mountain. Satan was the source of this thing, and I needed to rise up in authority over him.

I was filled with righteous indignation, angry that Satan had dared to attack my body: it was the temple of the Spirit of God, and Satan had no authority there.

Finally, at about four o'clock in the morning, I stood

up in the middle of my bed and yelled out at the top of my lungs, "Satan, get your hands off my body. It's the temple of the Holy Ghost, and I walk according to the Law of the Spirit of Life in Christ Jesus." I knew this sickness had to go - now!

After I did that, the Spirit of God came on me. I was able to lie down and go to sleep, which I had not been able to do earlier that night.

Three hours later, at seven o'clock, I woke up completely and totally healed. I was so excited! I thought, "This works! Faith in God works!" I remember going to class that morning, grabbing various friends by the sleeve, and saying, "Hey, guess what? You know what Brother Hagin's preaching? It really does work!"

They all looked at me like I was crazy and said, "Yeah, we know, brother, we know."

I had an excitement and enthusiasm that I couldn't shake because I had seen an instant manifestation. How many of you have had the flu and it lingered on for seven days or so? The flu can be nasty and horrible. So, to me, three hours was an instant manifestation. And because I wasn't in a service, and nobody laid hands on me, I knew this was my own faith at work. This was Jesus saying to me, "Son, your faith hath made you whole."

I thought to myself, "Glory to God. I've got this faith thing working now. From this point in time, I'll be able to tell everybody that I'm walking in divine health and that I don't have any problem with the devil anymore. When he attacks, I'll just turn him back."

Do you know, I had a chance to prove this about two weeks later! It wasn't flu this time, it was food poisoning! My roommate and I were both single guys. Sometimes we put stuff in the refrigerator and forgot how long it had been there. I found a bottle of orange juice. I wasn't sure it was good, but I didn't think it was that old. I took a big swig of it, which was really foolish because it was rotten. I hadn't prayed beforehand, but I figured it was a little too late to pray at that point. I thought, "It'll be all right."

But it wasn't. When I got back from Healing School, I started feeling really sick. I picked up *Christ the Healer* again and started reading through it. Food poisoning is horrible – it feels exactly like the flu. I had all the same symptoms – it was like a repeat of exactly the same kind of sickness.

I must be a slow learner, because it was four o'clock in the morning again when it finally dawned on me – I needed to take authority over the devil! I stood up in the middle of my bed, and yelled, "Satan, get your hands off my body. It's the temple of the Holy Ghost." The power of God came on me again; I lay down in my bed, and fell asleep. I woke up at exactly seven o'clock sharp, completely healed.

This happened in November of 1980 – that was my last sick day. I can testify that I've been walking in divine health since then. Now, I've had some opposition. Like Brother Hagin always said, "I've passed up some marvelous opportunities to be sick." Divine health does not mean perfect health. It just means that when your body comes under the attack of the devil with symptoms of sickness, you are able to resist by faith and turn the sickness back.

Over the past twenty-nine years, I have only missed 5 1/2 days of work, when it was better to stay home until my healing was completely manifested and the symptoms gone. Before my healing in November 1980, I used to miss five to ten days of work per year due to sickness. I'll take 5 1/2 days in twenty-nine years over that, anytime.

In the accounts above, I prayed the prayer of faith and I believed healing was mine according to Mark 11:24. I then had to couple my prayer with Mark 11:23 which has to do with spiritual authority and "speaking to the mountain."

Faith works the same way in the financial area that it does for salvation and healing. Over the years, my wife and I have experienced an incredible transformation in our lives in the area of finances and have seen some amazing financial miracles as well. There was a situation that came up where we had had to believe God for $50,000 over our normal operating expenses – and we saw it come in from an unexpected source within two days!

But I've found that in the case of deep financial problems or chronic illnesses, things don't always change instantly. It would be nice if you prayed the prayer of faith and somebody walked up with a sack of money or a big check a couple of hours later! It would be nice if you could pray the prayer of faith and drop seventy-five pounds in a day. In some situations, it's important to remember that it took you a number of years to get to where you are and it might take you a number of years to get yourself completely out of it. Trust God to illuminate the Word to you and show you creative ideas, to reveal "the way of escape" that He has promised you (1 Corinthians 10:13).

FAITH IS NEITHER FOOLISH NOR PRESUMPTUOUS

Some people get upset when we proclaim the word of faith message, because they think we're preaching that you're never, ever, going to have another problem in life or any opposition: physically, financially, or socially. We know that's not true. Jesus said, **"In the world you will have tribulation."** But then He added, **"But be of good cheer, I have overcome the world"** (John 16:33). We have opposition, but we have simply taken the five infallible steps of faith and have overcome it!

Other people accuse word of faith people of not praying anymore. They say we are always taking authority over the devil and, worse, that we're demanding things of God, as if He's our servant, and we are ordering Him around. Nothing could be further from the truth. We have been given a position we do not deserve, because of what Jesus did. We've been given covenant blessings to enjoy.

We are like Mephibosheth, the grandson of Saul. When David became king, he sent his men to bring Mephibosheth from the place where he was hiding. Mephibosheth thought, "That's it! King David is going to kill me."

But he soon found out that David had a covenant relationship with Jonathan, Mephibosheth's father. David said, "No, no. I came after you, so that I could restore everything from your grandfather's kingdom to you." He said, "Come, Mephibosheth. From now on, you're going to dine at the King's table."

And that's what the Lord Jesus has invited us to do – to come in and dine at the King's table. I'm glad to be an adopted son of somebody who says, "Come in and dine at the King's table." We are God's children, because He has redeemed us and placed us in Christ Jesus. It's an honor and a joy to be His children and His friends.

And because we are His children, we know we have the privilege to receive things from Him. It's not arrogance. It's not a matter of demanding anything of God. Rather, it's a matter of knowing that He's already given us these things in Christ Jesus. He wants us to put a faith-demand on His covenant promises and to be able to receive them.

STEP FOUR IS CONFESSION

"Confession" is speaking the Word after you have received illumination and have believed and prayed the prayer of faith. It is also referred to as "the confession of faith." Confession is where the battle is either won or lost. It is absolutely essential: You must keep saying the same Word of God that got you in position to pray the prayer of faith – even if the promise hasn't yet been manifested.

Satan is going to try to beat you out of receiving what you've already prayed to receive. He's going to try to get you to say, "Well, I guess my prayer didn't work." He'll try to get you to say, "Well, I guess God's promises really aren't true anymore." Or, "They told me God's not in the miracle business anymore. I guess they were right." When Satan and his demons come to taunt you after you've prayed the prayer of faith, you must continue to resist him with the same Word that got you "in faith."

God knows that we will have to stand our ground against Satan, in order to be steadfast and receive the manifestation of the promise. He has given us clear instructions for this phase. In Hebrews 4:14-16, God tells us to "hold fast our confession of faith":

Seeing then that we have a great High Priest who has passed through the heavens, Jesus the Son of God, let us hold fast our confession.

For we do not have a High Priest who cannot sympathize with our weaknesses, but was in all points tempted as we are, yet without sin.

Let us therefore come boldly to the throne of grace, that we may obtain mercy and find grace to help in time of need.

The word "confession" in this passage is the Greek word *homologia* which is from the same root word as *homologeo.* Both are compound words combining *homou*, which means "the same" and *logos* which means "something said." To "confess" means "to say the same thing." When we confess our sin, we are agreeing with God and His Word, saying the same thing about our sin that He does. If He says it's wrong, we should too. When we confess our faith, we are also agreeing with God and His Word, saying the same thing about our situation that He does. If He says, "By His stripes you were healed," we should too!

A DEEPER UNDERSTANDING

Hebrews 4:14-16 tells us we've got to hold fast our confession of faith and come boldly into the throne of God's grace and obtain His mercy when we need it.

God tells us the same thing in Hebrews 10:19-23. We are to have a true heart with full assurance of faith and hold fast to our confession of hope (which is always attached to faith) without wavering:

> **Therefore, brethren, having boldness to enter the Holiest by the blood of Jesus, by a new and living way which He consecrated for us, through the veil, that is, His flesh, and having a High Priest over the house of God, let us draw near with a true heart in full assurance of faith, having our hearts sprinkled from an evil conscience and our bodies washed with pure water.**

> **Let us hold fast the confession of our hope without wavering, for He who promised is faithful.**

God admonishes us to hold fast the confession which we made after we meditated, received illumination, believed the promise, prayed in faith, and received. Hebrews 12:2 says this:

Looking unto Jesus, the author and finisher of our faith, who for the joy that was set before Him endured the cross, despising the shame, and has sat down at the right hand of the throne of God.

Jesus, of course, is the author and finisher of our faith. He got us started on this journey, He's the one who gave us the covenant promises, and He's the one who is going to deliver the covenant promise to us.

HOLDING FAST TO OUR CONFESSION

We all have little skirmishes with the devil when we begin to walk in divine health. As a new "faith" person, you've been studying the Word, and you decide to believe God. Before long, Satan attacks your body with a sickness, but you know Jesus is your Healer, and "by His stripes you were healed" 2000 years ago.

You pray the prayer of faith and you go to work the next day. As soon as you walk in the door, you get hit with a message from the devil. Somebody says, "Man, do you feel as bad as you look, 'cause you look awful! You really better go to bed; you look like you're near death's door."

Maybe you've been witnessing to them, telling them about the promises of God concerning healing. "Oh," they say, "you're doing the faith thing, huh?"

You can get a lot of opposition from the devil even through well-meaning Christian people – through your best friend or your family. They just don't understand that you're in a battle over territory that's been purchased for you by the Lord Jesus, and that you're simply enforcing the victory. He's calling us to rise up in faith. Jesus has already taken the mountain. Now He's positioned us there and says, "Occupy until I come back."

Sometimes it's better to receive your healing resting and resisting at home. It does not show a lack of faith. As I have said, I've missed five and one-half days of work in the last twenty-nine years, when it was easier to stay at home to receive the manifestation of my healing than it was to go to work. I knew I'd be too distracted to fight the good fight of faith at the office. As Brother Hagin often said, "There are things in the natural you can do to help the spiritual."

LIFE IS A TRAINING GROUND

God wants to train you up and develop you in every area of faith. In fact, life itself is a training ground to develop your faith. The times where I learned to believe God and exercise my faith while I was a student were training for my future so I could effectively minister to other people. If you haven't received something from the Lord, how are you going to give it to somebody else? If you aren't walking in some of the covenant promises of God's Word, how can you tell anybody else that they're absolutely true?

About three or four months after I graduated from Rhema, I found myself pastoring a church. I didn't really plan on pastoring, it just kind of happened that way. But, believe me, it takes a lot more faith when God says, "Okay, now I want you to start a church."

My first response was, "Are You sure You have the right person, Lord? I just graduated!" Whatever the Lord speaks to you to do is going to seem like a huge responsibility.

He's going to tell you to do it by faith. You will probably ask, "Lord, do I have enough faith for that?"

Then He will take you back and remind you, "Look at all you've done so far." He will show you your faith victories. All of a sudden you will realize you can rehearse like David did, "Well, let's see, I killed a lion with my bare hands, and a bear with my bare hands. This is a giant. Okay. But he's an uncircumcised Philistine who is defying the armies of the living God." David's righteous indignation rose up and faith came that he could do anything that God had called him to do. He knew he was anointed to take that giant out.

In reality, that's what ministry is. Jesus set the captives free and now we go out and deliver the message. We end up being partners with the Lord, anointed to go forth, take the giant out of other people's lives, and set them free.

As you develop your faith in all areas of life, you become more and more experienced in exercising your faith. You start with something relatively small – yet a faith challenge to someone who is just beginning. You overcome that challenge, but before long there will be a new faith challenge on a higher level. You overcome that and just keep going up, higher and higher, taking ever-increasing steps of faith.

A question comes up from time to time that I want to clarify here: "Can someone else's negative words undo my faith?" It is always easier to maintain faith in an atmosphere of faith, and negativity has a definite downward pull. At times when you are "in the battle" it's best not to surround yourself with negative people, but to seek out like-minded, faith-filled believers. That's why God tells us not to forsake the assembling of ourselves together (Hebrews 10:25).

But, we do not need to be "confession police," worried that someone else's negative words can undo our confession of faith. Such words cannot stop us from receiving from God. Once a person has gone through these first four steps – meditation, illumination, the prayer of faith, and confession – a strong faith has been built within them. That kind of faith will always work.

THE FIFTH STEP IS POSSESSION

Now, finally, we can deal with "possession," the fifth infallible step of faith. We have discussed meditation and illumination, then the middle step – the prayer of faith, then confession, and now possession. "Possession" is the manifestation of the covenant promise, when what you have been believing God for arrives. When it comes into your hands, you no longer have to exercise faith, you no longer have to confess the Word that got you "in faith," you don't even have to stand your ground against the devil anymore.

Here's an illustration in the financial arena. You pray in faith and believe God for a car. You don't know how God is going to answer your prayer, because you don't have any money. But you heard Him say, "Believe Me for a car." You leave the choice up to Him. You're not saying, "Lord, I'm going to believe you for a brand new Corvette. Let's have it sitting in the garage tomorrow morning." That's foolishness. If you don't have any money, He won't tell you to go out and buy anything you want.

You stand in faith, and keep confessing God's promises concerning your car. Soon afterwards, you get a phone call from a relative of yours who "just happened" to think of you. They have a really nice car that they wanted to donate to charity, and they wanted to know if it would be a blessing to you.

You quickly decide, "Yes, that's got to be the answer from heaven." All of sudden, a really nice car has been given to you.

Possession of the promise is when the car arrives, and it's parked in your driveway. What faith do you need to exercise now? You own it - you have the title and the keys. You could go out there, hop in it, start it up and head for church to worship God.

You say, "Hallelujah, it's arrived. I'm blessed!"

Believe me, this is not outside of what God does! Kenneth Copeland was the first person I heard about who gave cars away. He said he was "sowing cars." God prompted him to "sow" what he owned, believing that after he prayed and obeyed, God was going to bring him something else. Later on he started talking about "sowing houses."

I'm not there yet, but I did get into the habit of sowing cars. I sowed a Toyota and got a Town Car. Not a bad deal. Then later on, I sowed a Pontiac and got a Cadillac. I sowed the Town Car and was waiting for my next car. After a while I said, "Lord, I'm still driving my Cadillac. It's been a great blessing, but isn't it about time for me to be driving my next one?"

The Lord spoke to me and said, "Look at your bank account." I said, "It's true, Lord, you've blessed us. We're prosperous." I've always told everyone, "The Lord always gives the best gifts to those who leave the choice up to Him." I was waiting for Him to pick when He said, "Why don't you just go out and buy whatever you want?"

I said, "Okay, Lord, I can receive that!" So, I went out and bought a brand new vehicle. Then I sowed the Cadillac, because I like to always be "one up" on God. (That's a joke!) But I do keep sowing to His kingdom, because I know there will always be a return coming to me.

If you have been standing on a covenant promise concerning healing, "possession" is when all the symptoms lift and you possess relief. You say, "I feel great! God has come through and produced a healing for me." He's brought the manifestation of His covenant promise and it's a wonderful place to be.

UNTIL YOU GET RESULTS

People ask, "How long am I going to have to hear the Word and hear the Word?" The answer is: "Until you get the results you're looking for."

Picture an old-fashioned balance scale. You have a problem in your life, and it has tipped the scale of your life completely down on one side. You start adding faith to the other side: you are meditating on covenant promises and you are speaking them to yourself. You can't see into the realm of the Spirit, but you are tipping the scales in the other direction. At first there is no apparent change – your body still feels the same. The balance is still heavier on the "problem side."

But if you have ever watched someone using a fine-tuned balance scale, you've noticed that once the two sides are nearly equal, adding just a couple more grains can suddenly tip the scale completely the other way. It's the same with receiving our answers by faith. We don't quit, because we know our faith is working, even if we don't see a change. We know at some point in time we will have just enough on the "faith side" to tip the scales on the devil. Suddenly, whatever opposition or problem he's putting in your life just has to go.

So stay in a faith environment. Attend church services that inspire your faith. In services where the Spirit of God is able to move freely, the faith you have been steadily building can suddenly be increased in a dramatic way. Your personal faith can connect with a gift of the Holy Spirit in operation through a minister, and you can suddenly get an instant manifestation – whether you need healing in your body or some other miraculous turn-around.

I was conducting a service where I had a word from the Lord that a couple's finances were changing even as they sat in the church service, and that they were going to find out when they got home.

Another time, I called a couple out and told them, "The Lord just spoke to me and said within two weeks, your financial situation is going to turn around completely. Six months from now, all the burden that's on you is going to be gone, because God is doing something here."

About six months later, the woman gave me this testimony: "We went home and laughed. I don't work and my husband works for the Post Office. We knew he wasn't due for another raise for a year and a half. We knew that it was impossible." Then she added, "You know, within two weeks, a major policy change suddenly came through at the Post Office. My husband got a raise, and it was enough that within six months that financial burden was gone!"

As you keep building yourself up in faith and stay in a faith-filled environment, you can be certain that God is going to make sure you have the answers you need. And isn't it sweet when the Spirit of God begins to move, and the Lord tells you beforehand, "This is taken care of."

THE FIVE INFALLIBLE STEPS OF FAITH

- Meditation
- Illumination
- The Prayer of Faith
- Confession
- Possession

CHAPTER NINE

ABRAHAM:
THE FATHER OF OUR FAITH

WE CAN SEE A GREAT EXAMPLE of how a person grows from faith to faith by looking at the life of Abraham, whom God calls the "Father of our Faith." God spoke to Abraham and gave him a covenant promise. Abraham heard the Word of God, but then he let it slip. We think of Abraham as being full of faith, but as we study Abraham's life, we will see places where he had struggles and displayed doubt and unbelief. There were times when, just like us, he did some foolish things. We will see how accommodating God was to appear to Abraham over and over and over again and speak the promises to him. Just like us, Abraham had to keep hearing the Word of God. And just like us, Abraham had to learn to hold fast to the promises of God.

HOLD FAST! THIS THING IS ALIVE!

In Hebrews 10:23 we are told to **"hold fast the confession of our hope without wavering, for He who promised is faithful."** In the original Greek, the word translated "hold fast" gives a picture of just how we do this. The idea here is to grab hold of something that's alive and squirming, to hold it down, pressing down on it with all your weight, and keep it from getting away. What a powerful picture!

The Bible tells us that the Word of God is living and powerful and sharper than any two-edged sword (Hebrews 4:12). In the same way, the covenant promises of God are alive. When a covenant promise of God comes "alive" to you, when it becomes *rhema,* you need to hold fast to that word. You must seize that promise, wrap your arms of faith around it, hold it down, grasp it tightly, and place all of your weight on top of it. Pin it down!

Please note: the promise is not the slippery part – the verse continues on to assure us **"He [God] is faithful that promised."** The slippery part is our confession! We must tame our tongue to say only what God says about our situation. We can say, "This is a covenant promise of God and I'm not letting it go. I am going to hold on to my confession of this promise until the Word starts doing what I know it's supposed to do in my life."

We have seen that there's a period where we meditate on the Word of God, speaking it to ourselves, over and over again, in order to get into faith. Again, some people call this phase "the confession unto faith." We saw this pattern in the Old Testament, when God told Joshua, **"This Book of the Law shall not depart from your mouth, but you shall meditate in it day and night"** (Joshua 1:8). You meditate on the Word by putting it in your mouth.

After a season of meditation, illumination comes. God's Word is dramatically revealed to you personally, and you are no longer speaking it in order to believe it – now you are speaking it having believed it. You embrace the promise and you pray the prayer of faith. Then between

the time you say, "Amen" and the time you see the fulfillment of the promise standing there before you, you are
going to continue to confess the Word of God, now having
totally embraced it. You have spoken the Word concerning a covenant promise to yourself over and over again.
Suddenly, the lights are turned on and you realize, "It's
mine! I'm going pin it down and hold onto it until it's
manifested in my life."

COMING INTO ALIGNMENT WITH GOD'S WORD

This word "confession" comes from the Greek word
homologia which is commonly translated, "to say the
same thing as." And that's a good definition. But there is a
deeper meaning to this as well. A more complete translation would be: "to say the same thing as and to come into
complete agreement and alignment with."

We must learn to align ourselves with the words that
God speaks to us. We may hear someone proclaiming
Scripture or we read it in the Bible for ourselves. We may
hear someone explain their understanding of a verse or we
may read something in a book. Suddenly, we know we are
hearing the thoughts of God. The lights start turning on.
We start embracing the promise, saying, "I can put my life in
alignment with this, I agree with this spirit, soul, and body."

In other words, we get the heartbeat of God and suddenly our heartbeat is beating completely in rhythm with
the rhythm of God's heartbeat. He has put His Spirit in us
and we have the mind of Christ (1 Corinthians 2:9-16). By
the Spirit and by the Word we can know the mind of the
Lord and we can be in complete alignment with it. When we
hold fast to the confession of that total alignment, our hearts
beating in unison with God's, then we are in a solid place.

HOLDING ON WITHOUT WAVERING

In such a place, we can hold on to our confession "without wavering." This Greek word translated "without wavering" really means "without laying down." In other words, don't go to bed on your faith. A lot of people start off okay. They say, "Man, this is going to work! This is the answer to all the problems in my life!" They start confessing the Word, they start believing it, and they receive a few things from the Lord. Then all of a sudden, they come up to a big obstacle to their faith. If they don't seem to be getting their faith to work there, they just throw their hands up and say, "You know, that whole faith message is delusional. I think it gives people false hope."

I submit to you that any hope that comes from the Word of God is not false hope. The Word of God is the truth, and whatever else you experience is false: it's the lie. Amen! The problem is never with God. It's with us finding out how to cause His promises to be manifested in our lives on a regular basis. We don't lie down and go to bed on our faith. Instead we pin down our confession – we sit on it so it doesn't squirm away from God's Word. Even if we have a sympathetic ear, we don't complain about our symptoms, our debts, or our relationships! We say what God says and nothing else!

Hebrews 11:1 is a very familiar passage: **"Now faith is the substance of things hoped for, the evidence of things not seen."** Earlier, we learned that substance means "solid foundation": our faith is the solid foundation of things that we hoped for. The Greek word translated "substance" comes from two root words *hupo* which means "under or alongside," and *stasis* which means means "to stand" or "to stand by."

Have you ever seen a bulldog who has been given the

soup bone of his dreams? He starts chewing on that thing and discovers he's in soup bone heaven. He finally lays it down, but he keeps watching to see if anybody is going to challenge him for the bone of his dreams. He's "standing by" that bone.

What a great picture of faith! Faith stands by a covenant promise of God just like that bulldog. Faith says, "I'm not going to let this thing go. I'm going to clamp my jaws on it and keep it in my mouth. The Word of God will be to me like a soup bone to a bulldog." Once you are ready to be that vigilant, that determined to stand guard over the things God has promised you and to protect them like a bulldog protects his soup bone, you will be ready to move into all the covenant promises God wants you to have.

Verses 2 and 3 continue the thought:

For by it the elders obtained a good testimony. By faith we understand that the worlds were framed by the word of God, so that the things which are seen were not made of things which are visible.

In the middle of talking about the elders having a good testimony, the writer seems to suddenly throw in a sentence about how God created the universe by faith. While it is absolutely true that God spoke this universe into existence, this is not the subject of this verse. The Greek word translated here as "worlds" is not the Greek word for universe or for the planet Earth. The Greek word used here means "a period of time, an age," which speaks of a definitive epoch of time, such as a decade, or a century, or a millennium. It's measurable. It has a beginning and an end. With that in mind, let's take another look at these verses. The writer says that through faith we have certain determined periods of time framed by the Word of God, so that things which are seen are not made of things which are visible. Then he starts describing these great men of faith.

The picture here is this: these men got a word from God and they changed the course of history. They changed their predetermined epoch of time, realigning it to line up with God's plan.

Even though we are going to look at these great men of faith, I want you to see that any person who gets a word from God can change their world. Perhaps you've heard the saying, "One word from God can change your life forever." Usually that word is not some long, flowery prophecy that goes on and on. It's usually something like Brother Oral Roberts heard from the Lord after he was healed of tuberculosis: "Take My healing power to your generation." Or like the word Brother Hagin heard: "Teach My people faith." These men of God did not let go of that commission from heaven — they hung on to it their entire lives.

In the early days of Life Christian University, I was pastoring a small church as well as teaching University courses and establishing University campuses across the United States. Dr. Dan Coflin, a close friend and the Vice President of LCU, invited me to share his large, new church building and offices. He was thinking both churches would have services - just at different times. When I prayed about his offer, I heard God say, "Merge your church and do what I have called you to do." I obeyed that word, and since that time, the University began to explode around the world.

When you get that one word from God, you don't have to be anything special. You don't have to think of yourself as some special person in the category of Noah,

Abraham, Jacob, or Moses. It's one person with one word from God that changes the history of the world.

God wants us all to be history makers, so you'd better get used to the idea! First of all, you are changing your history, and when you do so, you change the history of many people around you. You may touch the lives of millions – you don't know what chain reaction a life of serving God may have.

THE FATHER OF OUR FAITH

Abraham was a man who heard a word from God – and it changed his life forever. He became a history-maker. Hebrews 11:8-12 – the "Faith Hall of Fame" – has this to say about Abraham:

> **By faith Abraham obeyed when he was called to go out to the place which he would receive as an inheritance. And he went out, not knowing where he was going.**
>
> **By faith he dwelt in the land of promise as in a foreign country, dwelling in tents with Isaac and Jacob, the heirs with him of the same promise; for he waited for the city which has foundations, whose builder and maker is God.**
>
> **By faith Sarah herself also received strength to conceive seed, and she bore a child when she was past the age, because she judged Him faithful who had promised. Therefore from one man, and him as good as dead, were born as many as the stars of the sky in multitude – innumerable as the sand which is by the seashore.**

Praise God! Those innumerable descendants include

you and me because we are Abraham's descendants of faith.

Now, it often happens when we read about the lives of the great men of faith that we say, "That was Moses" or "That was Abraham" as though they were not just regular people. As though they didn't stink, even if they didn't use deodorant. We think they were something special.

I've got news for you: they didn't have deodorant back then, and they did stink! And they had bad breath too, because they didn't have toothpaste and toothbrushes like we have. The people in the Bible were regular people, just like you and me.

As we take a closer look at the life of Abraham, you will be greatly encouraged. You will no longer worry about moments when your faith wavers or when you feel double minded. When the Spirit of God opens your eyes to see how the Father views our journey from faith to faith, it is going to make you more receptive than ever to follow the move of the Spirit to accomplish your God-given purpose.

"LEAVE YOUR FATHER'S LAND"

Abraham received his first word from God in Genesis 12:1-3:

> Now the Lord had said to Abram: "Get out of your country, from your family and from your father's house, to a land that I will show you. I will make you a great nation; I will bless you and make your name great; and you shall be a blessing. I will bless those who bless you, and I will curse him who curses you; and in you all the families of the earth shall be blessed."

When God first spoke to Abraham, he was called "Abram" and he was living in Ur of the Chaldeans. He was a moon-worshiper. God intervened in Abram's life because He saw something about his integrity. God didn't choose the nation of Israel to bring forth the Messiah; He chose this one man, because of his integrity, and raised up a nation through him. Out of this nation, God planned to bring forth the Messiah and bless the whole world. God saw something worthy in Abram and spoke to him about a new direction for his life. God said, "Get out away from your father and all of your family, and come to a new land that I have given you."

The first time God spoke this covenant promise to Abram, He also told him, "Get out of your father's house, and leave your father's land." But Abram did not obey what the Lord told him to do. We read in Genesis 11:31:

And Terah took his son Abram and his grandson Lot, the son of Haran, and his daughter-in-law Sarai, his son Abram's wife, and they went out with them from Ur of the Chaldeans.

After a supernatural experience with the God of glory, Abram informed his family that he would be leaving his country and his family. All of a sudden, his father, Terah, puts himself in charge of the whole expedition and invites his nephew to come along.

How do you get that out of "Leave your father"?

"Dad, the Lord told me to leave and go to a new country."

"Good! I'll lead the parade, and we'll all go with you."

Does that look like exact obedience to God's instructions? Now you may think it wrong for me to beat up on poor old Abram, but I want to point out that he was not perfectly obedient in his walk of faith. I want Abraham to appear a little more human to you – to take some of the mystique out his story, because once you see how gently God worked with a very-human Abram, it will build your faith that God will work with you, despite your human flaws and failings. In fact, as we read through Abram's story, there will be several times that you'll just have to say, "What were you thinking, Abram?"

Genesis 11:31b-32 says, **"They came to Haran and dwelt there. So the days of Terah were two hundred and five years, and Terah died in Haran."**

The whole family moved to Haran and lived there. They didn't move any further because that was where Abram's father wanted to stay. Abram couldn't go on with God toward the land of promise until his father died.

LEARNING TO OBEY GOD

Didn't God say, "Get out of your country, From your family And from your father's house"? So why did Abram's kindred go with him? As we will see, Abram would face problems because he didn't do it God's way. Many of us have discovered that obedience always carries with it blessing and miracles, while disobedience carries with it everything but blessing and miracles. Abram learned this as he went along.

After Terah's death, Abram remembered the Word of the Lord to him and prepared again to leave his kindred. Genesis 12:4 says, **"So Abram departed as the Lord had spoken to him, and Lot went with him."** The same mistake is repeated again – Abram left the place, but not his relatives.

Later in that same verse we read, **"And Abram was seventy-five years old when he departed from Haran."** Have you ever heard someone say, "You've got to have faith like Abraham's; you've got to have twenty-five-year faith"?

They are implying that sometimes God gives you a promise and it doesn't come to pass for twenty-five years, even though you are standing in faith the whole time.

There are reasons for delays in receiving God's promises. But I want to point out that Abram wasn't really in faith for twenty-five years. He was in the process of hearing the Word, over and over again, and of overcoming his doubt and unbelief. He was growing in faith the entire twenty-five years, because nobody gets it all at once.

Abram was seventy-five at this point, yet he had this word from the Lord that He was going to make him a great nation, which meant that Sarai, his wife, who was 65, was going to have a son.

After Terah's death we begin to see how, little by little, God started moving to make sure the things He promised Abram would come to pass.

"I WILL GIVE YOU THIS LAND"

After Abram and his family entered the land of Canaan, the next step in God's plan for him, God spoke to Abram again. Genesis 12:7 says, **"Then the Lord appeared to Abram and said, 'To your descendants I will give this land.' And there he built an altar to the Lord, who had appeared to him."**

This was the second time God stated His covenant to Abram. What does the Bible say about faith and how it comes to us? **"So then faith comes by hearing, and hearing by the word of God"** (Romans 10:17). When we're talking about spiritual hearing, many have found that they have to hear it and hear it and hear it. That's why we meditate on the Word and speak it out of our mouths until it becomes real to us, until we get that illumination. Then we pin down our confession so it can't wander off. That's when we are going to see something happen.

After God had promised to give Abram the land of Canaan, a famine struck that was so severe that Abram and his family travelled to Egypt. Before they left, Abram made a covenant with Sarai (who was also his half-sister).

He told her, "Everywhere we go, people are going to want to kill me so they can take you for their wife, so we'll just tell everybody you're my sister." God had already told Abram, "I'm going to give you and Sarai this land as part of My covenant promise to you. You are going to be a great nation." Abram didn't need to fear that someone was going to kill him, because God said he was going to live.

In the same way, God tells us He's going to satisfy us with long life (Psalm 91:16) and He will fulfill the number of our days (Exodus 23:26). That's the very basis of believing God for divine healing. His plan for me doesn't include my getting killed by some disease, a car wreck, an airplane crash, or a terrorist attack. If He said He would satisfy me with long life, then my faith is hooked up to making it to that destination, to reach "long life" – however I define it.

To me, long life is living to be well over a hundred years old. It's got to be that for me. I had a grandmother who lived to be a hundred and one – and she didn't get saved until she was ninety-six! She only served God for five years. I got saved at twenty-three. I believe since I started serving the Lord early, then He certainly will give me at least a hundred and one years! I feel like it is going to take that long to get my job done. Then I'll be satisfied.

Abram heard the covenant promise, but fear came, and he immediately started to doubt that God's Word was absolutely true. This covenant promise was obviously too much for him to believe.

In Genesis 12:14, it says, "So it was, when Abram came into Egypt, that the Egyptians saw the woman, that she was very beautiful." It is interesting to note that at sixty-five, Sarai was still so beautiful that Pharaoh's servants came to him and said, "You should see this one, boss! What a fox! Sixty-five or not, I am telling you, she is fine!"

Pharaoh sent for Sarai, and just like that, Abram sent his wife off to Pharaoh's harem! Can you imagine? Aren't you impressed with Abram's faith so far? I don't know what Sarai was thinking, but I don't think she was thinking great faith thoughts about her husband. Her thoughts were probably more like, "You dirty dog. If I get out of this, I'm going to make you pay."

The wild thing is, as we will see in chapter 13, God blessed Abram anyway. In exchange for Sarai, Pharaoh gave Abram sheep, oxen, donkeys, camels, and servants. God made sure Pharaoh gave Abram all these things.

The story continues:

> But the Lord plagued Pharaoh and his house with great plagues because of Sarai, Abram's wife. And Pharaoh called Abram and said, "What is this you have done to me? Why did you not tell me that she was your wife? Why did you say, 'She is my sister'? I might have taken her as my wife" (Genesis 12:17-19a).

Apparently Pharaoh pressed Sarai for that information, and she admitted she was Abram's wife. Pharaoh now tells Abram, "Here's your wife, take her, and go your way." Verse 20 says, "Pharaoh commanded his men concerning him; and they sent him away, with his wife and all that he had." In other words, Abram got to keep everything Pharaoh had given him. He was blessed in spite of his doubt and unbelief. He had heard and obeyed the voice of God saying, "Get out and go to the land that I promised you." Abram was blessed for the faith and obedience that he demonstrated, but he was not yet walking in the level of faith necessary to receive the full promise of a son, which was his heart's desire.

In Genesis 13:5-7, it says:

Lot also, who went with Abram, had flocks and herds and tents. Now the land was not able to support them, that they might dwell together, for their possessions were so great that they could not dwell together. And there was strife between the herdsmen of Abram's livestock and the herdsmen of Lot's livestock.

Lot was also greatly blessed. Between the two of them they had so much livestock they couldn't share the same land. A conflict erupted between their herdsmen. Abram knew they should separate from each other and told Lot to choose where he wanted to live.

Lot told Abram, "I like the looks of the well-watered plain over by Sodom and Gomorrah. Plus we heard that it was a swinging place. We'd kind of like to hang out over there close to the swinging stuff." Little did he know how swinging it was!

Abram and Lot separated. God had originally told Abram to leave his relatives, and it seems the Lord was not able to do very much in Abram's life until they finally parted ways. It's interesting to note that at this point, Abram was hearing the word from the Lord and had faith that God would bless him financially no matter where he went, even if he got stuck with the driest sections of the land. He was probably thinking, "After the mess with

Pharaoh, what worse thing could I do? And yet God blessed me!"

Finally Abram was in position to receive God's full blessing. His father was no longer with him, Lot was no longer with him, and God could speak to him again.

Can anybody testify? Sometimes you've got to get some things in order in your life before God can speak to you again. One of the keys to obtaining unwavering faith is to go back to the last thing God told you to do, clean it up, and get it in order. Then God can speak to you again.

God spoke to Abram again in Genesis 13:14-17:

> **"Lift your eyes now and look from the place where you are – northward, southward, eastward, and westward; for all the land which you see I give to you and your descendants forever. And I will make your descendants as the dust of the earth; so that if a man could number the dust of the earth, then your descendants also could be numbered. Arise, walk in the land through its length and its width, for I give it to you."**

So the covenant was spoken to Abram the third time. Faith comes by hearing, and hearing and hearing: three times now, Abram has heard from God. God promised Abram, "I'm going to make you the father of a great multitude, an almost innumerable company."

Verse 18 says, **"Then Abram moved his tent, and went and dwelt by the terebinth trees of Mamre, which are in Hebron, and built an altar there to the Lord."** To Abram's credit, whenever God spoke to him, he would stop and build an altar to the Lord and would worship God there.

In chapter 14, we find how Abram was used by God to defeat four kings who attacked Sodom. They took the families living in the city into captivity, including Lot and his family. Abram had 300 men of faith, mighty men of valor, as part of his entourage. (It is amazing how many times God takes about 300 men and does incredible exploits!) Abram's men went into battle, and the anointing was on them to defeat the four kings and rescue all the people and goods that had been stolen.

On the way back home, Abram encountered Melchizedek, who was the priest of God. When Melchizedek met with Abram, he bowed before Abram, which means symbolically, "God is bowing everything that He has and rendering it to you, Abram." And then on behalf of Abram, Melchizedek turned and bowed before God, symbolically saying, "Everything that Abram has is Yours, Lord."

This is a picture of covenant, where both parties share everything. The closest thing we have to a blood covenant today is marriage: all the assets of the husband become the wife's and all the assets of the wife become the husband's.

After Abram and his men won this great deliverance, what did Abram do? He gave tithes of everything he had to the Lord. As soon as Abram tithed, fear must have come upon him, because the very next thing the Lord told him was not to be afraid. In Genesis 15:1 it says, **"After these things the word of the Lord came to Abram in a vision, saying, 'Do not be afraid, Abram. I am your shield, your exceedingly great reward.'"**

I have seen this happen again and again. People come to the fear barrier concerning their tithe. The devil usually says, "You can't tithe, you're going to go broke." Everyone who tithes has to pass through the tither's fear barrier. Abram found out that God was his shield and his exceeding great reward. This is what you will find when you go through the tither's fear barrier as well.

When the Lord said, "I am your shield and your exceeding great reward," He was saying, "I am your constant, never-ending supply of everything that you are going to need." This is the same thing that the Lord speaks to us as tithers in Philippians 4:19: **"My God shall supply all your need according to His riches in glory by Christ Jesus."**

After God spoke to Abram this fourth time, Abram expressed his doubts that God would fulfill the rest of the covenant. In verse 2 and 3, he says:

"Lord God, what will You give me, seeing I go childless, and the heir of my house is Eliezer of Damascus?" Then Abram said, "Look, You have given me no offspring; indeed one born in my house is my heir!"

Abram is basically saying, "Lord, what do I care about all this stuff? All I want is a family. But if You don't give me a son, Eliezer is going to be my heir."

God answered him in verses 4 and 5:

"This one shall not be your heir, but one who will come from your own body shall be your heir." Then He brought him outside and said, "Look now toward heaven, and count the stars if you are able to number them." And He said to him, "So shall your descendants be."

This was the fourth time God repeated His covenant promise, saying, "You're going to have a son. He's going to come out of your own body" – even though Abram was over seventy-five.

ABRAM BELIEVED GOD

Four times now Abram had heard this covenant promise. This time, he believed the Lord and the Bible says, **"And he believed in the Lord, and He accounted it to him for righteousness"** (Genesis 15:6).

Abram got a hold of a little bit more. His life was being transformed by the renewing of his mind. But he was not there yet.

In the same way, you don't need to beat yourself up just because you are not there yet. You are hearing the Word of God. It's coming to you. You are laying hold of it. It's going to take a little bit of effort, a little bit of work. You are going to have to hear it, and hear it, and hear it. Abraham had to hear God speak to him four times before he believed.

THE CUTTING OF COVENANT

What follows in verses 9-21 is an exchange that would be well-understood by anyone living in Abram's day and culture. Basically God had been speaking the covenant to Abram, but now He was going make – or cut – a blood covenant with him. Notice that the cutting of the covenant happened immediately after Abram believed and God could "count" him as righteous.

God said to Abram, **"Bring Me a three-year-old heifer, a three-year-old female goat, a three-year-old ram, a turtledove, and a young pigeon."**

When God said to get these animals, Abram knew what God had in mind. They were going to cut a blood covenant. Abram brought the animals, cut them in half, and laid them on the ground. When two men cut a covenant, they would walk between the slain animals in a "figure eight," meet in the place in the middle, and declare the covenant. I'm sure Abram was wondering how he would do the covenant walk with the invisible God who had been speaking to him!

In verse 12, we see that God first put Abram into a deep sleep. Then He told him:

> **"Know certainly that your descendants will be strangers in a land that is not theirs, and will serve them, and they will afflict them four hundred years. And also the nation whom they serve I will judge" (Genesis 15:13-14a).**

God already knew that Joseph would go to Egypt and then his brothers would join him there. God knew things would be hard for Abram's descendants, that they would be held in captivity in Egypt for four hundred years.

God continues to prophesy in verses 14b-16, saying:

> **"Afterward they shall come out with great possessions. Now as for you, you shall go to your fathers in peace; you shall be buried at a good old age. But in the fourth generation they shall return here, for the iniquity of the Amorites is not yet complete."**

God spoke forth all that would happen, but ended with the promise that Abram's descendants would come back to this land.

Verse 17 tells us, **"And it came to pass, when the sun went down and it was dark, that behold, there appeared a smoking oven and a burning torch that passed between those pieces."**

I believe that while Abram was in the trance-like sleep, he had a spiritual vision in which he saw what was happening and realized that God was cutting the covenant with him. Fulfilling the tradition of that time, two did walk the covenant walk through the slain animals that day, but it wasn't just God and Abram. The Bible tells us the Lord appeared as "a smoking oven [the power of God] and a burning torch [the Word of God]." God the Father walked the covenant with God the Son.

This is a good thing for you and me to know: we are in covenant with God the Father because Jesus cut the covenant for us, with His own blood. We are in a blood covenant cut by the High Priest of our confession, our *homologeo*. We have entered into this covenant. Just as Abram now had a blood covenant with God, we have a covenant with God. Abram still struggled with believing every word that God said was part and parcel of this covenant. Don't we also experience this from time to time? Some of God's promises seem too great to be grasped. And yet God says, "Watch! I'm going to keep fulfilling it."

After the Father and Jesus had walked between the slain animals, God once again spoke the promise of the covenant: **"To your descendants I have given this land, from the river of Egypt to the great river, the River Euphrates"** (v. 18). This was the fifth time God stated the covenant.

A HUMAN ATTEMPT TO FULFILL GOD'S PROMISE

God gave Abram a promise, sealed by a blood covenant, that he would have a son. This had long been the desire of Abram's heart. But years passed, and there was still no child. The story continues in chapter 16. Poor dear Sarai. Not only is she married to a guy who sold her into a harem, but she's getting older and older. In verse 2,

Sarai says, **"See now, the Lord has restrained me from bearing children."** It wasn't the Lord who restrained her from bearing, but Sarai didn't know that. She said, **"Please, go in to my maid; perhaps I shall obtain children by her."**

Sarai was probably thinking, "Poor old God! He can't make this thing happen. We've got to help Him out. Let's come up with a plan. I know! I'll just have an heir through my handmaiden."

When Sarai suggested a way to work around the problem of her barrenness, the Bible tells us **"Abram heeded the voice of Sarai."** Ladies, no matter how foxy you happen to be, it's not a good idea to tell any man, "Oh, you can go in and have my handmaiden and marry her as well." Notice how long Abram struggled with Sarai's suggestion. There was no argument on his part whatever.

At this point, it looks like Sarai and Abram are really messing up the plan of God. Abram went into Hagar and she conceived. And when Hagar saw that she had conceived, her mistress was despised in her eyes. Hagar taunted Sarai, saying, "I conceived and you couldn't. I'm more special to Abram than you are."

In Genesis 16:5, Sarai told Abram, **"My wrong be upon you!"** Or in other words, "This is your fault!" Sarai continued, **"The Lord judge between you and me."** All of a sudden, Sarai changed her mind about her plan to help God out. Now she's saying, "This is just great; this is all your fault, Abram. You didn't fight me on this one little bit."

Husbands and wives, you must understand this: Satan has a plan devised to break apart your marriage. This is especially true if you have any responsibility in the Body of Christ, because everyone is watching you. Satan wants to cause trouble in the very households where God is calling forth leadership. Satan tries to set up little traps, little wedges, to divide you and your spouse. Strife can come from those closest to you: for Sarai, her personal hand-maiden is suddenly this divisive figure. As leaders, we must be aware of how the devil's devices are arrayed against us, so we can uncover them and render them harmless by applying God's Word, His love, and His grace.

Sarai was so angry with Hagar that she told Abram, "Abram, you had better get her out of my sight." Abram gave Sarai permission to deal with Hagar as she saw fit. When Sarai dealt harshly with her, Hagar fled into the desert. The Angel of the Lord appeared to her, blessed her, and per-suaded her to go back and submit to her mistress. Hagar obeyed the angel and returned, and stopped despising Sarai.

Abram's decision to take a second wife and have a son by her created a lot of turmoil for Abram's family and for the entire world for thousands of years to come. We see the conflict between Ishmael's descendents (the Arabs) and the Jews in the news every single day.

Abram was 86 years old when Hagar bore Ishmael to him. The Lord did not appear to Abram again until he was ninety-nine (Genesis 17:1). It was thirteen years after Abram's faith fiasco – after Abram was hoodwinked by the devil's scheme – before God was willing to speak to him again. Have you felt like the windows of heaven have turned to brass? Have you felt like God was saying, "I've closed the windows and I'm not looking at you. Forget it." It's scary to live here on earth, totally dependent on heav-en to speak to you and not hear anything for thirteen years. But that's where Abram was.

"EXALTED FATHER OF A MULTITUDE"

Finally, the Lord appeared to Abram and told him, **"I am Almighty God; walk before Me and be blameless. And**

I will make My covenant between Me and you, and will multiply you exceedingly" (Genesis 17:1-2).

At this point in time, anyone reading Abram's story might not be confident that Abram was going to make it. They may be thinking, "God might have to pick Himself another boy!" But God knew what stock He had in Abram; He knew the course from the very beginning. But He also knew the struggles that Abram was going to face. Here, God is saying, "You can keep trying to do this your way, Abram. You always have that option. But if you will completely trust in Me, being finished with your own human attempts to fulfill your dreams, then I'll fulfill My covenant between Me and you and I'll multiply you exceedingly."

Abram made the best choice: he fell on his face!

God continued to speak to him, saying:

"As for Me, behold, My covenant is with you, and you shall be a father of many nations. No longer shall your name be called Abram, but your name shall be Abraham; for I have made you a father of many nations" (Genesis 17:4-5).

Over and over again, God had given Abram a covenant promise, but faith for the fulfillment of the promise was still beyond Abram's reach. In order to get Abram to agree with what God had already said about him, God changed Abram's name to "Abraham," which means "Exalted father of a multitude." God made Abram's name a faith statement. Whenever Abraham would say his new name, he would be calling himself, "Father of a multitude."

Can you imagine Abraham meeting a new group of people? He introduces himself: "Hi, I'm the father of a multitude."

They say, "Oh, you are? I see your three hundred men.

How many sons do you have?"

Abraham answers, "One."

They think to themselves, "I don't know if you can make that claim!"

But what had taken place in Abram's heart? He heard God's Word. God said, "Look, Abram, you're going to have to embrace what I have told you. You are going to have to say the same thing (*homologia*) out of your mouth and you are going to have to be in complete alignment with it. You must embrace this word with your whole heart."

Now Abraham is getting the picture of how this thing works. Now the meditation of his heart comes out every time he introduces himself; when he says his own name, he says, "I am the father of a multitude."

Faith's not going to work until you agree with God and say the same thing about yourself that God says about you. That's just the way faith works. First you put God's Word in your mouth to put it in your heart, and then once it's in your heart, you put it in your mouth again, to demonstrate that you believe it with all your heart.

In fact, it wouldn't hurt you to change your own name, to say what God has already said about you. What's your name? Healed by the stripes of Jesus. Above and not beneath. Blessed coming in and going out. Understand that is what God is saying about you!

When God called Abraham "the father of many nations," He was stating the covenant for the sixth time. Immediately after this, God gave Abraham a new sign of the covenant. He told him, "You are going to have to circumcise yourself and your whole household. This is the sign of the covenant."

Once I saw a great little cartoon of Moses standing

there with the two tablets, saying to God, "Let me get this right. The Arabs get all the oil and we have to cut off what?"

God was raising the bar on Abraham's faith. Abraham is wondering, "How clearly did I hear the word from the Lord and what am I going to tell my three hundred men? How do I explain what they are going to have to go through as a sign of the covenant?"

Although circumcision may seem odd, God always has a spiritual meaning behind His instructions. God makes pictures for us to see how His kingdom works. When you think about it, this was a picture of the covenant blessing being passed on from generation to generation, so the covenant sign was cut in the place of procreation. In effect, God was saying, "This covenant isn't just for you alone. You can sever curses from your family for generation after generation. You can cause the blessings of heaven to come into the lives of your children and all your descendants."

A MOTHER OF NATIONS

Next, God changed Sarai's name. As Abraham's partner, she would be the matriarch of the nation of Israel:

> **Then God said to Abraham, "As for Sarai your wife, you shall not call her name Sarai, but Sarah shall be her name. And I will bless her and also give you a son by her; then I will bless her, and she shall be a mother of nations; kings of peoples shall be from her" (Genesis 17:15-16).**

Sarah means "Princess." God said, "I am making Sarah a princess from which kings will come."

LAUGHTER

Have you ever been overcome with laughter at the wrong moment – and the more you tried to stop laughing, the more you laughed? God was speaking to Abraham about receiving the deepest desire of his heart, about his wife Sarah conceiving the promised child. In the midst of this, the Bible tells us:

Abraham fell on his face and laughed, and said in his heart, "Shall a child be born to a man who is one hundred years old? And shall Sarah, who is ninety years old, bear a child?" (Genesis 17:17)

It suddenly dawned on Abraham how ridiculous it was for them to have a child at their age. If Sarah couldn't have children during her prime, how far-fetched is it to believe she could conceive a child at ninety? Abraham fell on his face, laughing and said, "Yeah, right!"

Are you impressed with Abraham's faith? When God told him how He was going to work out His covenant promise, Abraham laughed out loud in God's face. That's not a great faith response!

Can't you see Abraham doubled over with laughter and rolling on the ground? He's thinking, "Hey, do you know how old Sarah is? Do you know how old I am? Thirteen years ago I could have pulled this off, but today I'm not so sure. I don't think this can happen now."

In verse 18, Abraham makes a counter offer, saying, **"Oh, that Ishmael might live before You!"** In other words, "Lord, I've got Ishmael. Why not use him? I can buy into this coming forth through Ishmael."

But God replied:

"No, Sarah your wife shall bear you a son, and

you shall call his name Isaac; I will establish My
covenant with him for an everlasting covenant,
and with his descendants after him."

God told Abraham to name his son "Isaac," which
means "laughter." In effect, God was saying, "Your son will
be named 'laughter' because you laughed in My face. For
the rest of your life, whenever you speak to your son, you
will be reminded not to laugh at My promises!"

After this, God stated the covenant a seventh time.
He told Abraham, "I'm going to establish an everlasting
covenant with Isaac's offspring." In verse 21, He told
Abraham when all this would happen: **"But My covenant
I will establish with Isaac, whom Sarah shall bear to you
at this set time next year."**

IS ANYTHING TOO HARD FOR THE LORD?

The eighth time Abraham heard the covenant promise repeated, it was by the Lord Jesus, Himself in a pre-
incarnate appearance, a "Christophony." In Genesis 18:1,
the Bible tells us, **"Then the Lord appeared to him by the
terebinth trees of Mamre, as he was sitting in the tent
door in the heat of the day."** Abraham immediately
offered water and a meal to the Lord and His two com-
panions. Abraham then ducked into the tent to ask Sarah
to bake some bread while he prepared meat for the men.
When the meal was ready, Abraham took the food to the
men and stood by while they ate. They asked him,
"Where's Sarah your wife?"

Abraham replied, **"In the tent."**

Then the Lord said, **"I will certainly return to you
according to the time of life, and behold, Sarah your wife
shall have a son."**

Sarah was standing behind the Lord at the door of the tent, and she overheard the Lord repeat the covenant promise. What Abraham had been telling her all these years she now heard for herself: Abraham was going to have a son! Not only that, it was going to happen through her! Like Abraham, she responded with great faith: she laughed! The Bible tells us:

> **Now Abraham and Sarah were old, well advanced in age; and Sarah had passed the age of child-bearing. Therefore Sarah laughed within herself, saying, "After I have grown old, shall I have pleasure, my lord being old also?" (Genesis 18:11-12)**

This story should be such an encouragement to us! It shows that you are not going to quench the anointing of the Spirit of God by your doubt and unbelief. God does not get offended by people laughing in His face at His faith promises. Guess what? He's tough enough to handle it. But things work a whole lot better once we get into agreement with God. He's not moved from His position of faith by our unbelief. He just wants everyone to join Him there!

The story continues in verse 13 and 14:

> **And the Lord said to Abraham, "Why did Sarah laugh, saying, 'Shall I surely bear a child, since I am old?' Is anything too hard for the Lord? At the appointed time I will return to you, according to the time of life, and Sarah shall have a son."**

Jesus, the Living Word of God, has no trouble believing that God has enough power to fulfill any word He speaks. He asked Abraham, "Is anything too hard for the Lord?" then stated the covenant promise once again.

PASSING IT FORWARD

A ninth and final time God repeated the covenant in Genesis 18:18, saying, **"Abraham shall surely become a great and mighty nation, and all the nations of the earth shall be blessed in him."** Then God states the reason why He chose Abraham from the very beginning:

"For I have known him, in order that he may command his children and his household after him, that they keep the way of the Lord, to do righteousness and justice, that the Lord may bring to Abraham what He has spoken to him" (Genesis 18:19).

The foundation of ethics and the development of Christian character is to know what God is looking for, to know what's important to Him. God knew Abraham was going to be a good father, that he was going to teach his son the ways of the Lord. God said, "I know Abraham will teach his children and everyone in his household to live according to My Word. I can entrust this man with the responsibility to bring forth the nation through which I will bring the Messiah."

Even though Abraham wavered in his faith, even though he struggled all along the way, God saw integrity in Abraham. God knew that whatever He imparted to Abraham, he would pass it on. We, also, must determine that whatever God imparts to us, we will pass it along, so that everyone who comes after us will benefit by it. That puts us in position where God will say to us, "You're the kind of person I can work with. I will keep bringing My Word to you, I'll keep bringing My covenant promises to you. Your life will indeed improve, and you're going to see some mighty and miraculous things happen."

STUMBLING AGAIN

Unfortunately, just before Abraham really gets it, where he reaches that solid place of faith where his heart is in total alignment with God and he is able to hold fast to God's promise, he stumbled and fell again. In Genesis, chapter 20, we see another major display of doubt and unbelief. Abraham and his family traveled south to Gerar. Once again, Sarah and Abraham told everyone they were brother and sister. Abimelech the King of Gerar, noticed Sarah's beauty and took her for his harem. Once again, Abraham just stood and watched.

Can you believe it? God has spoken to Abraham nine times, they have cut a blood covenant, Abraham's name was changed so he's speaking God's promise continually. You'd think he'd have this "faith thing" down totally. But when pressure came, he forgot that God could intervene, as He did with Pharaoh. Abraham fell back into his old, fearful pattern – he lied to protect himself instead of trusting God.

Once again, God protected Sarah:

But God came to Abimelech in a dream by night, and said to him, "Indeed you are a dead man because of the woman whom you have taken, for she is a man's wife."

But Abimelech had not come near her; and he said, "Lord, will You slay a righteous nation also? Did he not say to me, 'She is my sister'? And she, even she herself said, 'He is my brother.' In the integrity of my heart and innocence of my hands I have done this" (Genesis 20:3-5).

When God spoke to Abimelech, he immediately took

Sarah back to Abraham. He also chewed Abraham out, saying, "You have done deeds to me that ought not to be done!"

The next thing that happened is incredible. Despite the fact that Abraham and Sarah lied to him, and endangered his life and the lives of his whole family, Abimelech blessed Abraham:

> **Then Abimelech took sheep, oxen, and male and female servants, and gave them to Abraham; and he restored Sarah his wife to him. And Abimelech said, "See, my land is before you; dwell where it pleases you." Then to Sarah he said, "Behold, I have given your brother a thousand pieces of silver" (Genesis 20:14-16).**

The fear of the Lord was upon Abimelech, for God had told him, **"Abraham is a prophet, and he will pray for you and you shall live"** (Genesis 20:7). Abimelech loaded Abraham down with more sheep and more cattle and more goods and sent Abraham and his family on their way. Just as He had done in the situation with Pharaoh, God brought profit to Abraham even from his failures.

In verse 17, Abraham prayed for Abimelech and his wife and his maidservants, for they were not able to have children because God had closed up their wombs. This is the first recorded time Abraham ever prayed for anyone. When he prayed, God healed Abimelech and the women in his family, and they were able to bear children once again.

FAITH'S GESTATION PERIOD

Soon after this, the Lord also healed Sarah, and she and Abraham also conceived:

> **And the Lord visited Sarah as He had said, and the Lord did for Sarah as He had spoken. For**

> **Sarah conceived and bore Abraham a son in his
> old age, at the set time of which God had spoken
> to him.**
>
> **Now Abraham was one hundred years old when
> his son Isaac was born to him (Genesis 21:1-2, 5).**

Abraham was ninety-nine when the Lord changed his
name from Abram to Abraham. God had spoken to him
many times: he had been hearing and hearing and hearing
and hearing the promises, but he was double-minded –
struggling with it one minute and going with it the next.
But he finally got his mouth in agreement with what God
had said about him all along.

What's the gestation period for a baby? Nine months.
At age ninety-nine, Abraham gets it right, and at age one
hundred, Isaac is born. How long does faith take? Did
Abraham really have twenty-five-year faith? No. He had
three-month faith. He was in faith only a short period of
time before Sarah actually conceived.

It's important to see that we don't measure faith's
"gestation period" from the time when you first heard
God's Word and got an inkling, a mental assent about
something. No, it's once you've connected with God and
said, "That's it! I'm going to go after Your covenant promises. I'm going to say the same things that You're saying.
I'm going to hold onto this promise and receive this
Word." You keep speaking it to yourself.

Like Abraham, our timetable is before the Lord. He has
seen the years, the months, the weeks and the days we
have struggled to connect with faith. He assures us that
the fruit of our victory will be sweeter than we can possibly imagine.

When the child was born, Abraham named him Isaac ("Laughter"), just as God had instructed him to. Sarah was so delighted she said:

> **"God has made me laugh, and all who hear will laugh with me."**

> **She also said, "Who would have said to Abraham that Sarah would nurse children? For I have borne him a son in his old age" (Genesis 21:6-7).**

With the birth of Isaac, God changed Abraham and Sarah's mourning into joy. When their long-awaited son was born, there was great rejoicing and laughter in the house.

GOD FORGETS OUR WAVERING

Let's take a look at what God had to say about Abraham in Romans 4:16-22:

> **Therefore it is of faith that it might be according to grace, so that the promise might be sure to all the seed, not only to those who are of the law, but also to those who are of the faith of Abraham, who is the father of us all**

> **(as it is written, "I have made you a father of many nations") in the presence of Him whom he believed – God, who gives life to the dead and calls those things which do not exist as though they did; who, contrary to hope, in hope believed, so that he became the father of many nations, according to what was spoken, "So shall your descendants be."**

And not being weak in faith, he did not consider his own body, already dead (since he was about a hundred years old), and the deadness of Sarah's womb.

He did not waver at the promise of God through unbelief, but was strengthened in faith, giving glory to God, and being fully convinced that what He had promised He was also able to perform. And therefore "it was accounted to him for righteousness."

Wait a minute! Is God talking about Abraham here? Let's read these statements over again!

"Who contrary to hope, in hope believed." Yeah, right! He sold his wife twice, into two different harems!

"And being not weak in faith...." Yeah, sure! He fell on the floor and laughed in the face of God.

"He did not waver at the promise of God through unbelief." Hello? Are we talking about the same guy that we just read about?

"But was strengthened in faith, giving glory to God." Oh, my gosh!

"Being fully convinced...." Yeah, God persuaded him over and over again for twenty-four years!

"It was accounted to him for righteousness." God sure thinks differently than we do!

What this tells me is that once God gets a man or woman into a position of faith, He forgets everything that it took to get them there. The same thing happened when you were born again - God no longer remembered any part of your sin. Isaiah 43:25 says, **"I, even I, am He who blots out your transgressions for My own sake; And I will**

not remember your sins." God doesn't remember your sins once you are born again. Once you are in faith, that's all God sees. He doesn't see the struggle that it took to get you into faith. All the wavering, all the doubt and unbelief, all the laughing in the face of God's covenant are suddenly obliterated and all God sees is pure faith remaining.

That's really good news for us today! To know that God says, "If you'll just hold fast, you will see the glory of God." God is merciful to us just as Jesus was to the man in Mark 9:24, who cried out, **"Lord, I believe; help my unbelief!"**

The Lord says, "No problem, I'll work with that. You believe; I'll work with the little bit of faith that you have." So you just hold fast and watch God mold your faith, move your faith, and twist it around until suddenly you find yourself in the realm of the Spirit. From God's perspective every little bit of faith that comes into your heart counts. He says, "There's a person who is not double-minded. They are not wavering. I can answer their prayer of faith."

It's all by the anointing of the Spirit of God. It's all by God's grace. Very little faith could be seen in the life of Abraham while he struggled to prove that he had faith before God, but God could see into the realm of the spirit. God could see what was working in Abraham's heart. And when Abraham finally took hold of faith, that's all God remembered.

TODAY IS YOUR DAY!

Maybe you are struggling with a promise from the Lord. There are some things you are facing right now that you can't overcome. You've tried. You've been working at this thing, trying to build your faith, but you're just not there yet. You are tempted to just lie down and go to bed on your faith. You are beginning to think that maybe the whole idea was delusional, that it was just a dream that really wasn't a covenant promise from God.

I believe that, today, God wants to do something in your heart. He wants to couple the anointing of the Spirit of God with the words you just read. He wants you to be able to see His mercy and compassion. He is saying, "I am taking that Word that you have been putting into your heart. I am massaging it. I'm shining the light on it. I'm bringing it into your understanding in such a way that you will have something you can speak out loud.

"Once I get you to that place, I am going to release My Spirit into your faith and it's going to come alive. You will see something transformed in the Spirit. There's going to be a deposit of a miracle in your heart today. You have been working your faith. That's all I see once you come into faith. I'll forget everything else."

Isn't that good news to know that God has forgotten the struggles, the stumblings, the times you have laughed in disbelief at the promises of God?

He says, "Guess what? I'm going to make this promise so real to you that it's going to be like that soup bone of your dreams. You will lock your jaws on it. You are going to stand by that Word and pin down that covenant promise. You are going to hold onto your confession of faith until it comes to pass. That's the faith I'm working with, that's all I see. When I look into the realm of the Spirit from this day forward, I will only see you holding onto that promise – and it's going to come to pass."

CHAPTER TEN

FAITH AND THE INNER MAN

MOST PEOPLE ARE NATURALLY CURIOUS – we like to know how things work. As a child, I took broken watches apart. I wanted to learn how they worked so I could fix them. I never developed that skill, but I learned a lot about all the engineering needed just to make a watch work.

As a Christian, I've always been curious about how spiritual things work. I've asked, "Lord, how do You do that? I'd like to know!" Now, on certain things, we're just never, ever going to get an answer because God doesn't intend that we have an understanding of some things until we are in heaven.

We see this even in the natural realm. We've always called birth, "the miracle of birth." Like many parents, I had a discussion with my two sons about "the birds and bees" when they were eight and ten years old. I didn't want them to learn it the wrong way, from the wrong people. I explained about the human seed, a sperm, and how it goes into the egg. I could scientifically explain that part.

145

But how do the chromosomes from these two cells create this one new being that suddenly sparks off with cells multiplying and differentiating, some cells becoming organs, some bones, some skin? Generally, just one child comes into being, but sometimes twins or triplets or quadruplets are born. Why? And how does God take a human spirit and place it into this newly conceived life? There's no doctor or scientist who really understands this. Nowhere in the Word of God is there any explanation about how God does this.

And how does God raise somebody from the dead? We can talk about all the gifts of the Spirit being in operation and what would be necessary, but how God actually does it is something that's going to be a mystery to us until we see Jesus face to face.

There are going to be some unanswered questions, but, praise God, there are many things about life that God does want us to understand. I believe there are answers we can get now, while we are still on earth. For example:

- How does faith come alive on the inside of us?
- What is the difference between the heart and the soul?
- How does God work by His Word and by His Spirit within us?

Before we take a closer look at the three parts of man, breaking them apart to see how God works by His Word and by His Spirit in the inner man, let's look at what Adam and Eve were like before the Fall.

MAN IN HIS ORIGINAL STATE

Man was created in God's image. Genesis 1:26 tells us, **"Then God said, 'Let Us make man in Our image,**

according to Our likeness.'" The Hebrew word for God here is *Elohiym*, which is a plural word reflecting the triune being of God: Father, Son, and Holy Spirit. All three beings are saying, "Let us make man in our image, after our likeness." Genesis 1:27 continues, **"So God created man in His own image; in the image of God He created him; male and female He created them."** "Being made in His image" is really talking about the spirit of man being made in God's spiritual image, though I believe we must be similar in physical likeness as well. God will always deal with the primary thing first – God is a Spirit (John 4:24) and we're made in His likeness spiritually.

Genesis 2:7 says, **"And the Lord God formed man of the dust of the ground, and breathed into his nostrils the breath of life; and man became a living being."** The Hebrew word for "breath" in this verse is *neshamah,* which means "a vital wind or breath." It is also translated "spirit." And the Hebrew word for "soul" in this verse is *nephesh,* which literally means "a breathing creature." It refers to the conscious mind.

The Hebrew language is a very picturesque language. It's not detailed and precise like the Greek. God's plan for what He wanted to show us from examples in the Old Testament using the Hebrew language was different from what He planned to show us in the New Testament. His choice was to have the Greek language used at that point in time, because for the teachings in the New Testament, the language needed to be very precise.

Doing word studies in the original languages of the Bible is enlightening and often necessary to really understand the meaning of different passages. The Holy Spirit chose exactly the right words to express the thoughts of God, but they're not always translated exactly the way they should be. We need to look back at the most literal meaning of the words, and then God can enlighten us with other details and spiritual understanding.

Taking the literal meanings of the Hebrew words, Genesis 2:7 would read, "God breathed His vital, living Spirit into Adam's nostrils and the man became a breathing, conscious creature."

We know that after Adam was created in God's image and made alive spiritually, he later died spiritually. In Genesis 2:17, God told Adam and Eve, **"But of the tree of the knowledge of good and evil you shall not eat, for in the day that you eat of it you shall surely die."** Now, spiritual death does not mean "cessation of life." In spiritual death, a person doesn't cease to exist. Every single human being on the planet has a spirit that will be alive for all eternity. Spiritual death means "separation from God." When Adam and Eve sinned, they experienced spiritual death as separation from God.

Genesis 3:7 shows us what happened when Adam and Eve became sin-conscious: **"Then the eyes of both of them were opened, and they knew that they were naked; and they sewed fig leaves together and made themselves coverings."** Later, when God was walking in the garden in the cool of the day, they heard His voice, but they hid from Him. In Adam's conversation with God afterwards, he said that he was afraid because he was naked and he hid from God. Adam and Eve had suddenly become conscious of their sin.

An image of sinfulness became the normal state of man, as we know it now in the fallen condition. From Adam and Eve on, all the rest of us have had this "sin nature," and therefore, this consciousness of sin in our lives. It happened immediately with Adam and Eve, and they hid from God now knowing evil as well as good. We'll see more about this later, when we study righteousness and contrast an image of righteousness with an image of sinfulness.

MAN AS A THREE-PART BEING

Now let's take a look at man as a three-part being and take a moment to dissect these parts. Just like a kid taking apart a broken watch and seeing the complexity inside, it will give us a greater appreciation of all the intricate design work that God has done inside us.

In 1 Thessalonians 5:23, Paul said, **"may your whole spirit, soul, and body be preserved blameless...."** He's identifying our three parts – spirit, soul and body – and alerting us to a preservation of each part that can take place. Let's look at the Greek words for those three parts. "Spirit" is the Greek word *pneuma,* and it means "breath," but it's "a forceful breath." "Soul" is the Greek word *psuche* from which we get "psychology." It means "breath" also, but it's "a gentle and voluntary breath." There's a subtle difference between spirit and soul. While both of them mean breath, your spirit is forceful; it's like the breath of life being breathed into man, while your soul is like a gentle breath which just continues on in a natural state. "Body" is the Greek word *soma,* and it means "body – as a sound whole."

There are two other Greek words that I'd like to introduce here. The first is *kardia,* from which we get "cardiologist." It literally refers to the blood-pumping organ of the body, but in the Bible, it is used figuratively and refers to a person's thoughts and feelings. The second is the word for "mind," which is the Greek word *nous* and means "the thoughts, intellect, feelings, and will."

In Hebrews 4:12, we see a number of these parts of

man mentioned. It says:

> **For the word of God is living and powerful, and sharper than any two-edged sword, piercing even to the division of soul *[psuche]* and spirit *[pneuma]*, and of joints and marrow, and is a discerner of the thoughts and intents [literally "in, by or with" plus *nous*] of the heart *[kardia]*.**

We see spirit and soul in this verse, as well as the thoughts and intents of the heart. Hebrews 4:12 tells us that the Word of God is able to reveal this to us, to help us dissect our parts.

Modern translations make this function of God's Word even more clear.

> **For the word of God is full of living power. It is sharper than the sharpest knife, cutting deep into our innermost thoughts and desires. It exposes us for what we really are (Hebrews 4:12 NLT).**

> **For the Word that God speaks is alive and full of power – making it active, operative, energizing and effective; it is sharper than any two-edged sword, penetrating to the dividing line of the breath of life (soul) and [the immortal] spirit, and of joints and marrow [that is, of the deepest parts of our nature] exposing and sifting and analyzing and judging the very thoughts and purposes of the heart (Hebrews 4:12 AMP).**

When we understand how God has made us, and how we are designed to function, we will be better able to understand how we can grow in faith.

EXAMINING THE SPIRIT OF MAN

We're not as conscious of our spirit as we are of our

soul. What you're used to knowing about yourself, how you express yourself, is from the realm of the soul. But the real you is a spirit being, made in God's image. The real you was separated from God because of sin and was reunited with God at the new birth.

The morning after you were born again, you woke up with a "knowing" that you confessed Jesus as your Lord. Maybe you felt saved that next day, and maybe you didn't. You certainly remembered who you were the day before, because you were used to operating out of the unsaved, soulish realm of your own thought processes. When you looked in the mirror, you didn't look any different, except maybe you were smiling more, because being born again does bring joy to your life. But, your facial features were still the same. Your mind and your body were not changed when you were born again.

What changed was your spirit-man. That part of you was disconnected from God, still in existence, but in a comatose-like state. Your spirit was actually crying out to your mind, trying to get across to you that it desired to be born again. It desperately wanted to be reconnected to God. You finally made a conscious decision with your mind to receive Jesus as your own personal Lord. Suddenly your spirit-man was satisfied because the Holy Spirit moved in and filled him. You became this entirely new living creature that didn't exist anywhere in space or time before. The real you, your spirit-man, was now born again.

THE SPIRIT OF GOD AND THE SPIRIT OF MAN

The same Greek word *pneuma* is used for "Holy Spirit" and "human spirit." In the King James Version we find *pneuma* translated both "spirit" and "ghost." It seems there were three universities chosen by King James to translate the Bible into common English in 1611: Oxford, Westminster, and Cambridge. Two of the groups used the word "spirit," and one used the word "ghost." There is no difference in the Greek. There are not two different Holy Spirits. The Holy Spirit and the Holy Ghost are one and the same.

We have seen that the second rule concerning the interpretation of Scripture states that specific words that could be translated in different ways must be interpreted by the context in which they are written. Since *pneuma* is used for both the Holy Spirit and the human spirit, the context of the verse shows whether it refers to deity or humanity. The translators capitalized "Spirit" when they believed it referred to the Holy Spirit. For example, in Romans 8:26, it says, **"Likewise the Spirit also helps in our weaknesses. For we do not know what we should pray for as we ought."** That's obviously referring to the Holy Spirit helping us in our weakness.

In 1 Corinthians 14:14 Paul writes, **"For if I pray in a tongue, my spirit prays."** It's a lower case "s" there, identifying that Paul is talking about his human spirit.

In some places we find both the Holy Spirit and the human spirit referred to in the same verse. Romans 8:16 says, **"The Spirit Himself bears witness with our spirit that we are children of God."** The Holy Spirit gives you a "knowing" in your human spirit that you are now a child of God.

As an aside, the King James translation here says "sons of God." One of the things that we have to get over as Christians is "gender identification." Yes, God made males and females different for specific purposes and reasons, and all those differences should be celebrated. But before the Lord and in ministry, He doesn't differentiate. In Christ there is neither male nor female (Galatians 3:28). When

God calls the real you to the ministry, He calls your spirit, not your body.

Ladies, do you know that in God's eyes you're not really a "princess" before Him? He sees all of us as "kings." When the King James Version calls us "sons of God" and "kings," it is referring to the rightful position of authority that God sees both genders in – equally! When we are born again, God considers us all His "kings and priests." Ladies, don't be offended that the Word calls you a king. It's not a negative thing. God is trying to exalt the position of honor in your understanding so you can see yourself as He sees you.

> You also, as living stones, are being built up a spiritual house, a holy priesthood, to offer up spiritual sacrifices acceptable to God through Jesus Christ (1 Peter 2:5).

> But you are a chosen generation, a royal priesthood, a holy nation, His own special people, that you may proclaim the praises of Him who called you out of darkness into His marvelous light (1 Peter 2:9).

> And has made us kings and priests to His God and Father, to Him be glory and dominion forever and ever. Amen (Revelation 1:6).

> "And have made us kings and priests to our God; And we shall reign on the earth" (Revelation 5:10).

Another place we find both the Holy Spirit and the human spirit in the same verse is in John 3:6 – "**That which is born of the flesh is flesh, and that which is born of the Spirit is spirit.**"

THE PROCESS OF THE NEW BIRTH

It's important to understand how the new birth takes place, because this is the beginning of our life of faith. In examining the new birth, we will find a step-by-step process that we can refer to as we go on to discover how to live a life of ever-increasing faith.

You were born again when the Holy Spirit took up residence in your spirit. This is a three-part process which includes cleansing, birthing, and joining.

CLEANSED BY THE WORD

First of all, your spirit was cleansed or washed with the Word of God. The Holy Spirit will not dwell in any place that's full of sin. So, the first thing God had to do is to cleanse your spirit with the washing of the water of the Word in order to make you a suitable habitation for the Holy Spirit. In one sense this is instantaneous, but in another sense, it is a process with specific steps that must happen for the whole process to be complete.

There are several places in Scripture where we see that the Word has the power to "wash." In John 15:3, Jesus told His disciples, **"You are already clean because of the word which I have spoken to you."**

Ephesians 5:25 and 26 compares this cleansing capability to washing with water: **"...just as Christ also loved the church and gave Himself for her, that He might sanctify and cleanse her with the washing of water by the word."**

Hebrews 12:22 paints a powerful picture of the way God sees us after we have been born again. It says, **"But you have come to Mount Zion and to the city of the living God, the heavenly Jerusalem, to an innumerable company of angels."**

Isn't that good to know? As soon as you were born again, you were suddenly in the presence of an innumerable company of angels. You've also come into **"the general assembly and church of the firstborn who are registered in heaven"** (Hebrews 12:23). That's your place in the Body of Christ. You've come into the Church of God, the Church of the firstborn, and your name is written in heaven. You've also come into the presence of **"God the Judge of all, to the spirits of just men made perfect."**

As a side note, I believe that the spirits of "just men made perfect" is a reference to the Old Testament saints who were in the holding place of Paradise, known as Abraham's Bosom. This is the group that Paul refers to in Ephesians 4:8, those in captivity that Jesus captured and took with Him to heaven. They were "just" before God, but could not enter heaven until Jesus paid the price for man's sin. After that, they could be born again, and the Holy Spirit could take up residence in their newly recreated "perfect" spirits.

Every person who is born again actually has a perfect spirit, just like these "just men." You may be sitting all alone in your room, and to your way of thinking, you are still far from perfect. But God sees you on Mount Zion, in the presence of God, surrounded by innumerable angels and the spirits of other born-again people. Just like them, your spirit, the real you, has been made perfect.

Your spirit had to become perfect, clean, and holy in order for the Holy Spirit to move in. We have already seen how this justification process takes place by faith in Jesus Christ (Romans 3:28 and 5:1 and Galatians 2:16 and 3:11).

BORN OF THE SPIRIT

The second step in the process of rebirth is that your spirit becomes "born of the Spirit."

In John 3, we find the story of Nicodemus, a Pharisee and a ruler of the Jews, who came to see Jesus one night. The miracles Jesus did had convinced him that Jesus was a teacher who came from God. Jesus could tell Nicodemus was looking for spiritual answers and was hungry for the kingdom of God.

Jesus told him, **"Most assuredly, I say to you, unless one is born again, he cannot see the kingdom of God."**

Nicodemus asked, **"How can a man be born when he is old? Can he enter a second time into his mother's womb and be born?"**

Jesus answered, **"Most assuredly, I say to you, unless one is born of water and the Spirit, he cannot enter the kingdom of God."**

Jesus said we must be born of water and of the Spirit.

Some have taught that being "born of water" refers the fact that in the natural birth process, a woman's water breaks. They say that when that happens, you are being born of water.

But I don't believe that's what Jesus is referring to. It's obvious that you've got to be born first. Jesus wasn't saying, "You have to be a human being first, and then you can get born of the Spirit." No, Jesus is not being that obvious or redundant here. When He says, "You must be born of water and of the Spirit," He's talking about being born again by the water of the Word.

We're born again by the Word of God that washes us, and the Holy Spirit as the agent that brings us into salvation. Unless these two things happen, a person can't enter into the kingdom of God.

Jesus continues His thought in verses 6-8:

"That which is born of the flesh is flesh, and that which is born of the Spirit is spirit. Do not marvel that I said to you, 'You must be born again.'

"The wind blows where it wishes, and you hear the sound of it, but cannot tell where it comes from and where it goes. So is everyone who is born of the Spirit."

We are born of the Spirit. We can't describe it exactly, because it happens in the invisible realm of the spirit. But we know that the Holy Spirit is the agent who brings us into salvation as He comes into our spirit.

God wants to do this work in the spirit of every person. He wants to cleanse them and then move in, by the Holy Spirit, giving them the new-birth experience.

But this goes a whole lot deeper.

The actual born-again experience possesses within it everything that we will ever need with God. Everything we will ever need to experience a totally fulfilled life with God comes to us at the moment of the new birth. It's just that we're not conscious of it and we don't understand what happened. We can't perceive it with our senses because it all happens in the invisible realm of the spirit.

Actually, the whole process of growing in faith, getting baptized in the Holy Spirit, learning all the things that we're learning today is, basically, discovering what really took place at the new birth. Potentially, everything you ever needed was given right at that time, because, suddenly, within your spirit, the Holy Spirit is present. Remember, this is the Holy Spirit who created the entire universe that you and I dwell in. Not only that, this is the

Holy Spirit that raised Jesus from the dead! That was the greatest display of God's power ever, even greater than the creation of the universe.

The Holy Spirit, Who wrote the Word of God and Who knows all of the mind of God, dwells in your spirit. We're not conscious of the mind of God available to us; we're not conscious of all the power that created the universe and raised Jesus from the dead – yet He's still in there. The secret is, we must constantly learn how to allow His knowledge and His power to break forth through our lives, transform us, and then use us for God's kingdom. Potentially, it's all right there at the time of the new-birth.

JOINED WITH THE SPIRIT

The third step in the rebirth process is that you become joined with the Holy Spirit. Your spirit actually becomes one with the Holy Spirit. 1 Corinthians 6:17 says, **"He who is joined to the Lord is one spirit with Him."** In context, Paul was warning Christians about sexual sin, saying, "Men, don't join your body to a harlot, because you'll become one flesh with her." He was referring to God's plan for marriage between a man and a woman. In God's eyes, He sees husband and wife as joined together, the two becoming "one flesh" (Genesis 2:24).

In passing, Paul adds that in the realm of the Spirit, once you are born again, you become one spirit with the Holy Spirit. In the invisible realm of the Spirit, the Holy Spirit moved into your spirit, which is the real you. When God looks at you now, He sees the Holy Spirit. It's as if He doesn't distinguish the difference between your spirit and the Holy Spirit. Paul is using the illustration of marriage to help us see this truth. In both cases, God knows you are still an individual, whether a husband and wife or a believer and the Holy Spirit. Yet in His sight, He says the two have become one.

GOD'S PURPOSE: RESTORING
UNITY WITH MANKIND

We need to understand this positional truth because it is the key that unlocks our access to the throne of God. When we finally realize that when God sees us, He sees the Holy Spirit and us – so joined together that He cannot tell where one stops and the other begins – we will see that when we pray the prayer of faith, we're coming from am amazing position of strength.

Satan can't win against the combination of you and the Holy Spirit in your spirit. When you're in agreement with the Holy Spirit, you suddenly become the majority: now it's Father, Son, Holy Spirit, and you all in agreement. That unity cannot be overcome by any demon from hell.

This is what God has been working on ever since Adam and Eve fell. This is what His purpose has been for all those thousands of years: He wanted to live inside human spirits once again. Before Adam and Eve fell, the Holy Spirit had been dwelling in their spirits, but once they sinned, He had to leave. That was their spiritual separation from God, their spiritual death.

Although spiritual death happened immediately, just as God had said it would (Genesis 2:17), it took almost a thousand years for Adam and Eve to die physically. Their bodies were originally designed to be indestructible. Even after the Holy Spirit left them, and the whole universe went into a state of decay and "groaning" (Romans 8:19-22), even after they'd become sinful and separated from God, it still took almost a thousand years for the devil to kill them.

Over time, man's expected years on earth dwindled down. God finally said, **"My Spirit shall not strive with man... his days shall be one hundred and twenty years"** (Genesis 6:3). God gave that word to Noah before the flood. Then 120 years later, the flood really did take place.

From that point in time, there was a limit on man's life expectancy, which dropped drastically from 969 years for Methuselah to Joseph who lived to be a 110. (In my book *Divine Healing & Health* I present a complete teaching on longevity.)

When Moses was writing the book of Genesis, he heard the prophecy God had given Noah in the realm of the spirit and wrote it down. Moses knew what God had said – and it's interesting that Moses lived 120 years.

I believe that the covenant promise is still 120 years. Some people say, based on Psalm 90:10, that the covenant promise is 70 to 80 years. But if you read that verse in context, you'll see that it is referring to a life of disobedience or rebellion. That's part of the curse, to live only to be 70 or 80 because of disobedience or rebellion. But if you do things God's way, you can live to be 120 and fulfill all your days.

When Moses, the author of Psalm 90, was 120, his eyes were not dim nor his natural vigor diminished in any way (Deuteronomy 34:7). God had to remind him the time was up. He was in perfect health when God took him home. He walked to the top of the mountain of God and died.

REVERSING SPIRITUAL DEATH

The first disciples were born again when they believed the Word and received the Holy Spirit. In receiving the Holy

Spirit, they reversed spiritual death, the separation from God caused by Adam and Eve's sin.

After Jesus' resurrection, Mary was the first one to visit to His tomb. John 20:16 tells us what happened next: **"Jesus said to her, 'Mary!' She turned and said to Him, 'Rabboni!' (which is to say, Teacher)."**

Mary was the first one to see Jesus in His resurrected state and know that it was Him and to believe that God had raised Jesus from the dead. Mary was the first one to be born again. Remember the requirements to be saved found in Romans 10:9-10? Mary believed in her heart that God raised Jesus from the dead and she called Him Master (or Lord).

In verse 17, Jesus said to Mary, **"Do not cling to Me, for I have not yet ascended to My Father; but go to My brethren and say to them, 'I am ascending to My Father and your Father, and to My God and your God.'"**

Verse 18 says Mary Magdalene came and told the disciples that she had seen the Lord, and that he had spoken these things to her. Isn't it interesting that the first person to be born again was a woman, and the first one sent out as an evangelist was a woman? Don't let anybody tell you that God doesn't call women to preach. Jesus set the pattern right here, if we'll just get it straight: women are called. They can go preach and proclaim the good news.

FULFILLING ALL SCRIPTURE

Something interesting happened between verse 17 and 19, because first, Jesus told Mary, "Don't keep clinging to Me." Later, when He appeared to His disciples in verse 19, He said, "You can touch me now." Between verses 17 and 19, while Mary went and told the disciples, Jesus ascended to the heavens and presented Himself before the

Lord, just as He told Mary He would. Why did He do that? He was fulfilling all Scripture.

When God told Moses to build the Tabernacle, He showed him the heavenly pattern (Exodus 25:9 and Hebrews 8:5). The Tabernacle of Moses gave a picture of the redemptive work of Christ. God wanted the children of Israel to rehearse the redemptive work of Christ year after year, so that when the Messiah came, they wouldn't miss Him. Unfortunately, by the time the Messiah came, they had their eyes on the rehearsal and the ritual, rather than on Jesus, the fulfillment of it.

Moses saw a vision of the heavenly Tabernacle and of Jesus going through the redemptive work of God in heaven. Then Jesus came to earth to literally fulfill it all Himself. The Bible says in John 1:14, **"He dwelt** [tabernacled] **among us."** He was the Tabernacle itself. A full study of the Tabernacle gives us such wonderful symbols as we see that Jesus was every article in the Tabernacle, literally every part from the entrance at the gate to the mercy seat in the Holy of Holies.

Not only was Jesus the Tabernacle itself, Jesus was also the High Priest as well as every offering. What Jesus did, as the High Priest, was to present His own blood before the mercy seat of God the Father in heaven. I don't believe that He had to take it in a bowl, as the earthly High Priest had to. Jesus simply showed up in His resurrected state: His blood was in Him and all the redemptive work that was necessary was done. Divine justice was satisfied.

By the time we get to John 20:19, Jesus had finished presenting Himself to the Father and placing His blood before the mercy seat. He had descended back to the earth and now presents Himself to His disciples. Verse 19 says, **"Then, the same day** [this was still Resurrection Day] at evening, being the first day of the week, when the doors were shut where the disciples were assembled, for fear of the Jews." The disciples are still afraid. They've heard Mary's report, but they're all still locked up in a room, scared as little rabbits. Then Jesus walked right through the walls in a glorified body, stood in the midst of them, and said, "Peace be with you."

Verse 20 continues, "When He had said this, He showed them His hands and His side. Then the disciples were glad when they saw the Lord." I like to picture the events in the Bible as I read them. What would you do if you were one of the disciples in that despairing state? You'd seen Jesus suffer horribly at the crucifixion. For three days you'd been hanging around, moaning and groaning together. All of a sudden, Jesus appears and shows you His hands and His side. Suddenly, you now believe Mary's crazy story that He was no longer dead, but risen.

Sometimes the Bible doesn't fully describe what really takes place, but I know human beings well enough to know how the disciples would respond. They didn't just quietly say, "Oh, Hallelujah. Glory to God, Jesus is risen." No! They jumped all over Him, clung to Him, and worshiped Him. I'd be down kissing His feet and thanking God that He was raised from the dead, and that He really was who He said He was: The Son of God! My goodness! They were thronging Him and rejoicing!

THE RETURN OF THE HOLY SPIRIT

Verse 21 and 22 finish the story:

So Jesus said to them again, "Peace to you! As the Father has sent Me, I also send you." And when He had said this, He breathed on them, and said to them, "Receive the Holy Spirit."

Now, I ask you, when Jesus says, "Receive the Holy Spirit," which spirit are you going to receive? The Holy Spirit! Some people have said, "The Church doesn't receive the Holy Spirit until the Book of Acts."

No, the disciples were born again in John 20. Everything necessary to be saved has taken place: they believed in their hearts that God raised Jesus from the dead and confessed with their mouths that Jesus is Lord. Jesus breathed on them and they received the Holy Spirit. They were now born again.

The Church didn't begin on the day of Pentecost: it was empowered on the day of Pentecost. There is a whole separate experience.

John 20 reveals when the new birth - the greatest miracle anyone could ever receive - happened in the lives of these men and women. Suddenly, God transformed them. Even though they had walked with Jesus, they were still sinners, doomed in their sin. Jesus had told them their sins were forgiven (John 15:3) and their names were written in heaven (Luke 10:20), but the reality is, they couldn't be born again yet. They were a little like the righteous Jews who had died before the Messiah had come, who had to go to Abraham's Bosom and wait.

But now that Jesus had opened the way into the very presence of God, the disciples were able to be born again. They experienced the exact same thing that Adam and Eve had enjoyed in the Garden of Eden. For the first time since the Fall, humans could be complete again. The Holy Spirit had returned to man and was now available to dwell in him and to be one with his spirit. Praise God!

It was on Resurrection Day that the disciples got a chance to receive the Holy Spirit and the new birth. For ten years, the Gospel was preached - but only to the Jews.

Then God revealed to them, "Hey guys! This is for the whole world. It's for everybody!" Praise God for the day it was revealed that you and I were welcomed in to receive the same miraculous experience.

BORN AGAIN OF INCORRUPTIBLE SEED

In 1 Peter 1:23 it says our spirit is **"born again, not of corruptible seed but incorruptible, through the word of God which lives and abides forever."** The Holy Spirit comes into your spirit as an incorruptible seed. This seed is holy, it cannot be defiled, it cannot perish. Instantly, the Holy Spirit is so joined with your spirit that no one can tell where one starts and another stops. Since the Holy Spirit is incorruptible, your spirit instantly becomes incorruptible. It is now holy, it cannot be defiled by sin, it cannot perish.

YOUR BORN-AGAIN SPIRIT CANNOT SIN

This helps us understand two passages of Scripture that seem to contradict each other and have confused some believers. In 1 John 1:8 - 2:2 we find a familiar passage. John writes:

If we say that we have no sin, we deceive ourselves, and the truth is not in us.

If we confess our sins, He is faithful and just to forgive us our sins and to cleanse us from all unrighteousness. If we say that we have not sinned, we make Him a liar, and His word is not in us.

My little children, these things I write to you, so that you may not sin. And if anyone sins, we have an Advocate with the Father, Jesus Christ the righteous.

165

And He Himself is the propitiation for our sins, and not for ours only but also for the whole world.

John is writing to believers here. Basically, he's saying, "Hey, you believers! If you're saying you're without sin, you are deceiving yourselves. Even as born-again believers, you still do some wrong things every now and then. But when you confess that sin to the Lord, He is faithful and just, and will forgive your sin and cleanse you from all unrighteousness."

Later in this same letter, John wrote the passage that seems to contradict this:

He who sins is of the devil, for the devil has sinned from the beginning. For this purpose the Son of God was manifested, that He might destroy the works of the devil.

Whoever has been born of God does not sin, for His seed remains in him; and he cannot sin, because he has been born of God (1 John 3:8,9).

Now, how can John say, "If you say that you're without sin, you're a liar and the truth is not in you," and at the same time say, "If you're born of God, you can't possibly commit sin because His seed remains in you"?

John could say that because he understood that man is a three-part being: spirit, soul, and body. Your soul and body can – and will – sin. No one's soul or body has ever become perfect yet, so it's guaranteed that you will sin again, sometime between now and the day you step over into glory.

Later, in 1 John 3:8, John is talking about the soulish man and the physical body when he says, **"He who sins is** of the devil, for the devil has sinned from the beginning." Then John says, **"For this purpose the Son of God was manifested, that He might destroy the works of the devil."** Your mind and body were once slaves to sin (Romans 6:16-19), but Jesus broke the power of sin and destroyed the works of the devil.

In verse 9, John addresses the real you, the spirit-man. John goes on to say, **"Whoever has been born of God...."** What part of you is born of God? Your spirit. Your spirit-man is the "whoever." You are not just your soul, you are not just your body, the real you is your uniquely individual spirit-man.

The three parts of you are still so connected that they can't be separated. If you've ever accidentally hit your thumb with a hammer, your body suffers and your soul suffers. Every part of you suffers! The parts are interconnected, but the "whoever" that was born again is your spirit.

When John says, **"Whoever has been born of God does not sin,"** he is saying that it's impossible for your spirit-man to sin. If your spirit-man were able to sin, the Holy Spirit would have to move out, and you'd lose your salvation.

Guess what? The Holy Spirit does not move in and out of your spirit every time your soul or your body does something wrong. Your soul may think an unholy thought; your soul and body working together may do a wrong deed; but the Holy Spirit will not leave your spirit. The work that Jesus did on the cross was so complete, so perfect, so sound, that once the Holy Spirit moved in, you are saved for as long as you want to be saved.

Some people say, "Once saved, always saved." I like to add "as long as you want to be saved." How did you get saved? You believed in your heart that God raised Jesus from the dead and you made a decision to receive Jesus as

Lord. You would have to reverse that decision to become unsaved. You would have to decide that Jesus is not Lord, that it is all a lie, and that Jesus was not raised from the dead. You would have to decide that you don't want to have anything to do with God, because you don't believe that there is a God or that Jesus is Lord.

No man can pluck you out of God's hands (John 10:29). No man can pluck you out of Jesus' hands (John 10:28). Your salvation is a permanent, perfect work. The Holy Spirit, an incorruptible seed, remains in you. The real you cannot sin because you're born of God. The spirit-man has been taken care of, made holy forever. From this moment forward, you can be sure there is nothing wrong with your spirit. Your spirit is perfect. It's the vessel where the presence of the Holy Spirit of the Living God dwells – all the time! If that doesn't make you confident in your position with God, nothing will!

Understanding this positional truth is not easy, but keep meditating on these verses, and let the truth that your spirit is already made perfect just keep seeping in. Illumination will come! This is a truth that God wants you to know and understand.

In fact, all of your faith walk is based on allowing this truth to be manifested in every area of your life. You see, we can't live the Christian life by imposed outward rules and regulations. It can't be done from the outside-in. It's done from the inside out.

I believe this truth is so powerful and strong that as we exercise our faith in the work of the Lord Jesus on the Cross, we can be radically transformed by the renewing of our minds. We can keep our bodies under and walk out of sin's grasp. The power of God is there to keep us from sinning.

But if we were to take the credit for our victories

ourselves and not give glory and honor to the Lord, that would be a sin.

When you have experienced the new birth, and the Word of God is working in your life, it becomes a joy to live before the Lord. You allow Him – by faith – to create a life of righteousness and holiness in you. The Holy Spirit dwells in your spirit as incorruptible seed, working from the inside out. This sinless life dwells within you and can be increasingly expressed in the natural realm of everyday existence.

God sees you in Christ and He sees the Holy Spirit inside you. It's a wonderful position to be in. As we come to the Lord, asking things in prayer, it gives us great confidence and increased faith.

YOU ARE COMPLETE IN HIM

As we look into this concept of being complete in the realm of the Spirit, we come upon Colossians 2:9-10 that says, **"For in Him dwells all the fullness of the Godhead bodily; and you are complete in Him, who is the head of all principality and power."** In other words, in Jesus dwells all the fullness of the Godhead bodily, and we're complete in Him. What part of us is complete? We know that our soul and our body are not yet complete: we really have to work to bring them into subjection, to put them under, to take thoughts captive and renew our mind. This verse has to be referring to our spirit-man.

YOUR SPIRIT KNOWS GOD'S WORD

The Holy Spirit, who holds all the thoughts of God and knows every scripture in the Bible, dwells on the inside of us. He lives in our spirit – in a union so complete that we are one spirit with Him. We have in our spirit access to all the Word and counsel of God available to man, everything we need for life on this earth. Because the Holy Spirit knows it all, so can we!

I'd like to clear up some confusion here about the term "feeding your spirit the Word of God," and "getting the Word down in your heart." We hear people say these things. And in several places the Bible does mention hiding the Word of God in our hearts:

> **Your word I have hidden in my heart, That I might not sin against You! (Psalm 119:11).**

> **The law of his God is in his heart; None of his steps shall slide (Psalm 37:31).**

> **I delight to do Your will, O my God, And Your law is within my heart (Psalm 40:8).**

> **Receive, please, instruction from His mouth, And lay up His words in your heart (Job 22:22).**

If you use the word "heart" and "spirit" as synonymous terms, these verses would mean that you would be hiding the Word in your spirit. But the reality is, the word "heart" does not always refer to the spirit. Most of the time "heart" refers to the soul, which means that when we hide the Word in our heart, it's actually placing the Word of God into our thoughts, our understanding, allowing God to bring a spiritual revelation of what that Word means.

One of my professors at Rhema Bible Training Center would say, "We need to mine our spirits for the Word that's already down in there." He spoke in terms of finding a "golden nugget." He had "golden nuggets" that he had discovered in the Word in every one of his sermons, and they were fantastic.

Another way of saying it: you are going fishing for the knowledge that is already in your spirit. It's already there;

your spirit-man possesses it. Technically speaking, you do not "feed your spirit." Even though we consider God's Word to be spiritual food, you don't need to feed your spirit, because your spirit is already complete in Him.

We do, of course, need to renew our minds, and we need to bring our bodies into subjection. The Bible tells us in Romans 8:13 that we're to **"put to death the deeds of the body."** In 1 Corinthians 6:20 it says, that we are to glorify God in our bodies. In 1 Corinthians 9:27 Paul says, **"I discipline my body and bring it into subjection."** Paul brought his body under subjection to the counsel of God and to God's will.

Paul wrote in 2 Corinthians 4:16, **"Even though our outward man is perishing, yet the inward man is being renewed day by day."** In other words, our outward man is growing older. That's part of the curse of the Fall; we can't change that part. We can overcome the curse of the Law; not the curse of the Fall. We are going to grow older, we are going to die. Certain things can't be changed. Hebrews 9:27 says, **"It is appointed for men to die once, but after this the judgment."** Each one of us will die, unless we're still here when the Lord Jesus returns – then we'll get transformed in the twinkling of an eye.

The outward man grows older, yet the inward man – that's the soul of man – is renewed day-by-day. We can be continually transformed by the renewing of our minds.

TRUE WORSHIP COMES FROM THE SPIRIT

In John 4:23-24, Jesus said,

"But the hour is coming, and now is, when the true worshipers will worship the Father in spirit and truth; for the Father is seeking such to worship Him.

"God is Spirit, and those who worship Him must worship in spirit and truth."

Your spirit-man is the part of you that comes into union with God and truly worships God. This started right after you were born again, at the very beginning of your new life in Christ. The reality is, your spirit-man was dead, but he was crying out to be re-united with God. There was a huge void, an emptiness in your spirit.

Adam and Eve were not created with that void – God breathed the breath of life into them. The Holy Spirit dwelled inside them. But when they sinned, both individually and as the corporate head over the human race, the Holy Spirit left them and couldn't return. Jesus is referred to as the "second Adam" because when He came, He gave the Holy Spirit back to man. After the Resurrection, the Holy Spirit could come and dwell in our spirits again. When we experience the new birth, we're back in the same position that Adam and Eve were in. We are alive to God. The only difference is, we are still subject to the curse that came into the human race as a result of the Fall.

A lot of people wonder if forgiveness was granted to Adam and Eve. Will we see them in heaven? Of course! God is a merciful God. He's not going to condemn them to an eternal hell. He loved them. After they sinned the original sin that caused death and destruction to go through the whole human race, He immediately came in to cover over their sin. He sacrificed animals and covered Adam and Eve with the animal skins. This was His first blood covenant with them – the final blood covenant was through the sacrifice of His own Son, Jesus Christ, the Second Adam.

And so, true worshipers, again, worship the Lord in the Spirit.

SPIRITUAL PERCEPTION OCCURS IN THE SPIRIT

The Bible tells us many times that Jesus "perceived" or "knew" the thoughts of others "in His spirit." As a born-again person, you too now have a means of perception that you didn't possess before.

Before you were saved, you might have experienced a "knowing," an almost prophetic warning of something that later came to pass. Unbelievers are crying out for spiritual knowledge and, of course, Satan comes along with all kinds of counterfeits. Once people go down the path of deception and start experiencing spiritual power, they are easily seduced. They get pulled over into a counterfeit usage of the un-regenerated human spirit.

This is a tremendous trap. Satan has completely convinced people of every kind of lie under the sun. Unbelievers caught in false religions are convinced they're serving God while they are really serving Satan, the author of their religion. He's a thief who comes to steal, kill, and destroy. But Satan's demonstrations of counterfeit power are no match for the miracles the Lord is doing all over the world.

In Mark 2 we find an example of how Jesus perceived the thoughts of others in His spirit. This is the story where the four men took their paralyzed friend to Jesus to be healed. We hear sermons about the faith of the "four friends," but I say all five had faith together. The paralyzed man had to have some faith, or he would not have allowed his friends to drop him down through the roof. That's dangerous, especially if you can't hold onto the bed because you are paralyzed!

I believe this event happened in Jesus' own house. He had His headquarters in Capernaum, where this story occurred, so it would make sense that He would be teaching in His own place. Besides, I don't think Jesus would allow the men to tear apart someone else's tile roof. Since it was His own place, he didn't mind.

Jesus was teaching the doctors of the law, the scribes, and the Pharisees, and the power of God was present to heal every single person there. But, the doctors of the law and the scribes were doubters and unbelievers. Even in the midst of the power of God, they didn't plug into what Jesus had to offer.

Jesus saw the totally paralyzed man who was let down. He knew He would wrinkle the theology of the Jewish leaders immediately when He told the paralyzed man, "Son, your sins are forgiven you."

Some of the scribes thought to themselves, "He blasphemes! Who can forgive sins but God alone?"

Verse 8 tells us, **"But immediately, when Jesus perceived in His spirit that they reasoned thus within themselves, He said to them, 'Why do you reason about these things in your hearts?'"**

The scribes didn't come out and openly ask that question, but Jesus perceived their question in Himself, in His spirit. He knew the doubts they had, He knew what they were thinking. Jesus asked them, **"Which is easier, to say to the paralytic, 'Your sins are forgiven you,' or to say, 'Arise, take up your bed and walk'?"** Then He said, "But so that you'll know that I am the Son of Man who has the power on earth to forgive sins, watch this!" Jesus told the paralyzed man, **"Arise, take up your bed, and go to your house."** Instantly the man was healed. Jesus healed him to prove that He also had the power to forgive sins.

Just as Jesus "perceived in His spirit," you too could

have that happen. With a gift of the Spirit – the word of knowledge – operating in your life, you can perceive things in the realm of the Spirit and know what others are thinking, what their reactions are.

To summarize this section on the spirit of man, we have seen that your spirit is the real you. It was once dead, but is now alive to God, having been washed by the water of the Word and born again of the Spirit of God. The Holy Spirit now lives in your spirit, so joined together with your spirit that the two are one. Your spirit is now complete, holy, and perfect. It cannot sin. God's Word – all of it – is already deposited in your spirit. You have complete access to all the wisdom you will ever need. Your spirit is the part that enters into true worship. And the gifts of the Holy Spirit operate in your spirit.

EXAMINING THE SECOND PART
OF MAN: THE SOUL

Now let's examine the soul of man. The soul includes every mental faculty that you possessed before you were born again. It's your mind (your thoughts), your will, and your emotions.

Note that your will – your decision-maker, the volitional faculty to choose – is also part of your soul. Some people think that it's part of your spirit, but it's not. Your will does impact your spirit, because as soon as you make the decision in your soul to be born again, your spirit can come to life. Your spirit always wanted to be saved. There's a void there, that causes mankind to want to know the Creator, to be connected and united with God.

Before salvation, you operated in the soulish realm only. What you know about yourself is all in the soul – all your thoughts about yourself, whether they're good or bad, your insecurities as well as your self-confident thoughts. All the emotions that you've ever experienced are also in the realm of the soul.

Once you are born again, though, the process of renewing your mind to God's Word begins. You begin to go through a great soul transformation. The Word of God is going to have a profound effect on your soul. It starts in your emotions. Many experience a great emotional change as soon as they are born again. It's a wonderful thing to experience this freedom, when you feel like you've been carrying the weight of the world. After I got saved, I felt like a thousand-pound weight was lifted off my back. Suddenly, the search was over. I had discovered God, I had discovered the one way to heaven for all eternity.

A SOUL CAN BE FILLED WITH THE SPIRIT

We've seen how your spirit-man was filled with the Spirit at the new birth. All you had to do was believe in your heart that God raised Jesus from the dead, confess Jesus as Lord, and receive Him as your own Savior, and you were filled with the Spirit in your spirit.

But, in order to release the fullness of the power of the Holy Spirit that's now in your spirit, you also need to have your mind completely transformed. You need to think completely in line with God. Essentially, you need to get your soul filled with the Spirit.

In the Old Testament it says that God filled individuals with His Spirit. For example, in Exodus 31:3 and 35:31, God filled Bezalel with the Spirit. Bezalel was the skilled craftsman who was anointed by God and filled with the Spirit to build the Tabernacle of Moses. Bezalel was a great worker of metal, who constructed all the furnishings of the Tabernacle. He made the Ark of the Covenant, the

Table of Showbread, the Altar of Incense, the Altar of Sacrifice, and the Laver. Bezalel was the one who hammered out the Golden Candlestick and all the other ceremonial utensils for the priests to use. Bezalel hammered the golden cherubim on the Mercy Seat from a single, solid piece of gold.

It took the mind of God to be able to know how to do all the things that God had told Moses to create for the Tabernacle, so God filled Bezalel with the Spirit for that particular task.

There are other examples of individuals in the Old Testament being filled with the Spirit. In Numbers 27:18, God told Moses that He had filled Joshua with His Spirit. And then Ezekiel 2:2 and 3:24 says that God filled Ezekiel with His Spirit.

Since this is the Old Testament, these men were obviously not born again. Christ had not yet come and died and been raised from the dead. We have seen that the Holy Spirit could not enter a person's spirit until Jesus' work of redemption was complete and the human spirit could be cleansed and made into a suitable habitation for Him. So, obviously, these were filled with the Spirit in one of two other areas: either the soul or the body.

Hebrews 11:13 says the Old Testament saints **"all died in faith, not having received the promises."** What promise did they not receive? The amazing spiritual promise of total redemption.

Under the Law of Moses, the best that you could have was "atonement" or the "covering over" of your sins. That's all the Old Testament sacrifices for sin could do: they could cover your sin, they couldn't remove it.

That's the big difference between "atonement" in the

Old Testament and "remission" in the New Testament. "Remission" is when your sins are absolutely removed completely away. The Old Testament gave us a picture of this in the ceremony of the "scapegoat" (Leviticus 16:10, 20-22). Once a year, the High Priest would lay his hands on the head of the scapegoat while confessing the sins of the nation, thus putting the sins on the head of the goat. Then the goat was taken out into the wilderness and let go. This picture or "type" was fulfilled as the Lord Jesus carried our sin away from us, out into the wilderness.

Hebrews 11:39 says that the Old Testament saints **"obtained a good testimony through faith,"** although they **"did not receive the promise."** In other words, they obtained a good testimony or report in the presence of God. Like Abraham, they believed God, and it was accounted to them for righteousness (Galatians 3:6). Not every Jew in the Old Testament went to Abraham's Bosom and later to heaven. Even if they fulfilled the requirements of the Law, if they didn't do it by faith, believing that these acts of obedience would take care of them, then all their religious acts were of no effect. Faith always had to be involved.

One constant throughout all of the Word of God is that God has always required faith. The Old Testament saints were obedient to the Lord, they did the things that were required of them under the Law, and then God was able to bless them. He took sickness from the midst of them; He gave them divine provision; their families stayed together, they lived free from opposition, their enemies were not able to overthrow them because they were blessed by the Lord. They had the kind of peace on Earth that so many people are seeking for and can't find – all because of the presence of the Lord.

MINDS FILLED WITH THE WORD OF GOD

Many of the patriarchs of old were raised up by God to write the Bible. Now, to be able to write something down, they had to go through a conscious thought processes. They had to be able to think God's thoughts. They had to hear exactly what God wanted to say. Where did they hear God's words? They heard them in their soul as God filled their minds with His Spirit and His thoughts. As He superimposed His thoughts on their minds, they were able to write those thoughts down.

Did they always know what they were writing? Absolutely not. They just knew they were under the anointing, and they were being obedient to what God was showing them. They had the mind of God and wrote what God told them to write down. Many of them didn't see their prophecies fulfilled in their lifetime. For some of them, it's been thousands of years - and their prophecies are still being fulfilled today.

As New Testament believers, God wants to fill our souls with the Holy Spirit. This infilling was first recorded in Acts 2. We have seen how Jesus' disciples were born again when Jesus came into their midst, breathed on them, and said, **"Receive the Holy Spirit"** (John 20:22). Jesus then instructed them to wait in Jerusalem for the "Promise of the Father" (Acts 1:4). In Acts 1:5,8, Jesus said:

> **"For John truly baptized with water, but you shall be baptized with the Holy Spirit not many days from now.... You shall receive power when the Holy Spirit has come upon you; and you shall be witnesses to Me in Jerusalem, and in all Judea and Samaria, and to the end of the earth."**

Jesus didn't say that they would witness, He said, "You

will be witnesses." The power that He promised was the power to be a living witness. Now, of course, we do want to speak up to give a defense for the great things God has done in our lives, but we are living witnesses when we are walking in the power of God.

In obedience to the Lord's instructions, a group of 120 born-again disciples had waited for 10 days, until the Day of Pentecost. They had gathered for a prayer meeting in the upper room. Acts 2:1-2 tells us:

> **When the Day of Pentecost had fully come, they were all with one accord in one place. And suddenly there came a sound from heaven, as of a rushing mighty wind, and it filled the whole house where they were sitting.**

The Greek word for "filled" in verse 2 is *pleroo,* which literally means "crammed full." The Holy Spirit literally crammed as much of Himself into this room as could possibly be contained. He filled the room completely with His presence until it was "crammed full" of the presence of God.

Verses 3 and 4 tell what happened next:

> **Then there appeared to them divided tongues, as of fire, and one sat upon each of them. And they were all filled with the Holy Spirit and began to speak with other tongues, as the Spirit gave them utterance.**

The Greek word for "filled" in verse 4 is *pletho,* which means, literally, "to be fulfilled." The disciples were fulfilled when the Holy Spirit came upon them. In other words, God designed it from the beginning that you would operate with both the Holy Spirit dwelling in your spirit, and a consciousness of the Holy Spirit's presence in your soul.

You would be able to speak the Word of God, to declare the thoughts and the mind of God to others, and to proclaim the goodness of God. You would be able to glorify Him with your mouth, speaking from an understanding in your soul, and have it be in alignment with the anointing of God in your spirit.

On the day of Pentecost, the disciples were actually "fulfilled" and empowered. This same experience is available to every believer today.

The Bible says once they were all filled with the Holy Spirit, they **"began to speak with other tongues, as the Spirit gave them utterance."** The Holy Spirit is the one who provides the sounds, the "utterance." When you are filled with the Spirit, with the evidence of speaking with other tongues, you hear tongues in your mind before you actually speak those tongues out of your mouth. The Holy Spirit provides the utterance, but He doesn't make you speak. He impresses syllables and words from an unknown language upon your mind. At the time it's happening, you're in a state of euphoria and ecstasy, so, you're not consciously thinking, "This is an operation of my soul, because I can hear these words in my mind, so I'll go ahead and speak them out." No, it's all happening so fast, you don't really know what's going on. But this is the way the sequence has to be: you cannot speak with your mouth something that doesn't transfer and process through your mind.

Here's a quick illustration of how your mind processes thoughts and images by virtue of words, and how very hard it is to pull your mind away from what you are hearing. I can say, "For the next few seconds, whatever you do, don't think about elephants." Then I can tell you, "Don't think about their gray, wrinkly skin. Do not think about their long, flexible trunks. Don't think about how huge they are, or about their giant feet or their long, skinny tails. Do not think about elephants, please! Get all thoughts of elephants out of your mind!"

Even though you haven't thought about elephants for weeks and weeks, as soon as you hear my words – first in your ears and then in your understanding – it is almost impossible not to think about elephants. When you are bombarded with words about something, that's what you will be thinking about.

When you were baptized in the Holy Spirit, the Holy Spirit bombarded you with languages of heaven, and you heard these syllables in your mind. Of course, the devil was quick to tell you, "Oh, you're making those words up, that's just gibberish. That's just you." Actually, it was you – it was the Holy Spirit and your spirit. The Holy Spirit was providing the language (the tongue), but the sound you heard was the voice of your spirit-man starting to talk. You heard that new language – in fact, your mind was bombarded with it. The person ministering to you should have told you, "The Holy Spirit is going to provide the utterance, but you have to be obedient to speak it out of your own mouth. He's not going to grab your mouth and pop it open and wag your tongue around and vibrate your vocal chords and make these words come out." You had to speak out those words that you heard in your head as somebody laid hands on you and prayed for you to be filled with the Spirit.

The utterance in tongues processes through your mind first, before you can speak it out of your mouth. Your mind is part of your soul, proving that your soul can be filled with the Spirit. Once your mind has processed it and you've spoken it out, you're suddenly in a flow with something new that's taken place in your soul. You now have a "direct line" from the Holy Spirit (who now lives in your spirit) to your mind. You are now "networked," and information can flow quickly and easily from His mind to your mind.

We have seen that once you were born again, your spirit-man was filled with the Holy Spirit. A deeper understanding is that at the new birth, only one part of you was filled with the Spirit. There is so much more available to you, because once you are baptized in the Holy Spirit your mind can also be continuously filled with the Spirit.

Some have asked, "What is it exactly that you get when you get baptized in the Holy Spirit?"

When you experience the baptism of the Holy Spirit, you receive the Holy Spirit in a very personal way. He was living inside your spirit, but now He can come into a whole other area of your life, into the realm of your soul. Suddenly you have a chance to know Him as a person, to know Him more intimately than you can know any other person on the planet. You can know Him even more intimately than you can know your spouse. For example, you can't really know every single thing that your spouse is thinking. If that were the case, you'd never, ever have to communicate again!

But after you are baptized in the Holy Spirit, you can instantly know what the Holy Spirit is thinking at any moment. Not only that, the Holy Spirit certainly knows more about you than your spouse does. In fact, He knows everything about you. So you see, there is the potential for a far deeper relationship with the Holy Spirit than with any other human being. We want to honor the fact that He's a person who lives inside us.

There have been times when I am praying to the

Lord, when I am so conscious of the presence of the Holy Spirit on the inside of me that I actually look down, right at my belly, and speak to the Holy Spirit in me. In John 7:38 KJV, Jesus said, **"He that believeth on me, as the scripture hath said, out of his belly shall flow rivers of living water."** I am so aware of Him inside me that I look down at my belly when I talk to Him. There have been times, even as a Word-of-Faith, Spirit-filled Christian, that I was in such need of the Lord's presence that I physically walked along with my hand held out beside me. His presence would be so strong that I felt Jesus was taking me by the hand. It is a great comfort to know that, whatever trial or situation I'm walking through, I'm going through it hand-in-hand with Jesus!

It might seem a little odd to some people, but talking to the Holy Spirit inside me and walking along, hand-in-hand with Jesus works for me, and it builds a closer, more intimate relationship with the Lord. I like to honor the Holy Spirit: He's become my greatest friend.

Along these lines, I get a little offended when people say, "I've received the baptism in the Holy Spirit."

You haven't received the baptism in the Holy Spirit, because that's just an experience. When you were baptized in water, do you tell people, "Oh, I received the baptism in water"? No, you say, "I was baptized in water."

No, you've received much more than an experience. You've received the person of the Holy Spirit, someone you can develop a relationship with. We want to give total credibility and honor and glory to the Holy Spirit for all of His work in our lives.

When you receive the Holy Spirit with the evidence of speaking in other tongues, you are empowered by the Holy Spirit to become a living witness. It's the beginning of being totally transformed by the renewing of your mind. Your consciousness of the Word and the presence of God and the power of God becomes greater than at any other time in your life.

After you are born again, it is so important to be baptized in the Holy Spirit. This is the most powerful beginning step of being transformed by having your mind renewed. As a matter of fact, if people do not go through the process of being baptized in the Holy Spirit, they are limited in their ability to fully understand the things of God.

You may hear preachers say, "Oh, this experience is not for you today." That tells me they are limited in their area of expertise. You can listen to them concerning salvation, but they don't qualify to teach you about anything beyond the importance of being saved, the same way your kindergarten teacher doesn't qualify to teach you quantum physics. They simply aren't qualified to teach you about the spiritual gifts available to you and how powerfully God wants to use them in your life.

Being baptized in the Holy Spirit is the gateway into the supernatural. My life changed miraculously after I was baptized in the Holy Spirit. I had been saved for a week and totally delivered from drugs and alcohol for a week. I'd been experiencing the supernatural, but I really wanted the power of God in manifestation in my life. After I was baptized in the Holy Spirit, I suddenly had a hunger for the Word like I'd never even imagined. When I read my Bible, all the lights came on. Maybe the same thing happened to you after you were baptized in the Holy Spirit. You suddenly had a greater understanding of spiritual things. All the pieces of the puzzle began falling into place, and it all started to make sense to you.

That's because the baptism in the Holy Spirit is the

great tool God uses to transform you by the renewing of your mind. The next step is immersing yourself in the Word: reading the Word, meditating on the Word, speaking the Word to yourself, reading about the Word, hearing teaching about the Word. As you retrain your mind to stop thinking as the world has taught it to think and to begin to think like God thinks, it starts to have a profound effect on your life.

It's interesting to do a word study in the Strong's Concordance, looking up the Greek words for spirit (*pneuma*), soul (*psuche*), and mind (*nous*). You will find that the Bible has more to say about your mind and your soul than about your spirit. That's because Jesus has taken care of your spirit with the new birth. But we have all the responsibility to take care of our minds, and live according to the Word of God. James 1:21 says, **"receive with meekness the implanted word, which is able to save your souls."** James was addressing believers, so he's talking to people who are already "saved." But it was their spirit that was saved; now he's talking about how to get their souls saved. James is talking about getting saved continuously.

James lets us in on an important secret when he says, **"Receive with meekness the implanted word."** The Word of God actually becomes a part of our soul. James is encouraging you to go through this process of receiving the Word so that your soul can be continually transformed by the renewing of your mind.

EXAMINING THE HEART OF MAN

As we begin our examination of the heart of man, it is important to see that every scriptural reference to the heart is not always a reference to a person's spirit-being. Sometimes the word "heart" in the Scripture refers to the soulish part, sometimes it refers to the spiritual part.

Let's look at some verses that refer to the soulish part of the heart.

Proverbs 6:18 speaks of a heart, **"A heart that devises wicked plans."** A heart can devise plans, which is a function of the mind, not the spirit.

Proverbs 15:28 says, **"The heart of the righteous studies how to answer, But the mouth of the wicked pours forth evil."** The heart can study, which is also a function of the mind, not the spirit.

In Psalm 73:7 it says, **"Their eyes bulge with abundance; They have more than heart could wish."** The heart can desire or wish, which is a function of the mind, not the spirit.

Proverbs 3:5 says, **"Trust in the Lord with all your heart, And lean not on your own understanding."** The heart can choose to trust the Lord. Choice is a function of the soul, not the spirit.

Hebrews 3:12 says, **"Beware, brethren, lest there be in any of you an evil heart of unbelief in departing from the living God."** This verse says a believer can have an evil heart of unbelief. We have already seen that a believer's spirit is perfect, so this verse must be referring to the believer's soulish parts.

Luke 6:45 says, **"A good man out of the good treasure of his heart brings forth good; and an evil man out of the evil treasure of his heart brings forth evil. For out of the abundance of the heart his mouth speaks."** We have seen how words are processed through the mind before they come out of the mouth, so "heart" in this verse must be referring to the mind.

Sometimes, the Bible mentions heart and spirit in the same sentence, and you can tell that the two are not being used interchangeably. For example, Ezekiel 36:26-27 says:

"I will give you a new heart and put a new spirit within you; I will take the heart of stone out of your flesh and give you a heart of flesh. I will put My Spirit within you and cause you to walk in My statutes, and you will keep My judgments and do them."

"Heart" here is obviously a reference to more than just the spirit.

Another example is found in Romans 2:28-29:

For he is not a Jew who is one outwardly, nor is circumcision that which is outward in the flesh; but he is a Jew who is one inwardly; and circumcision is that of the heart, in the Spirit, not in the letter; whose praise is not from men but from God.

When Paul speaks of the circumcision of the heart in the Spirit, he is talking about bringing your soulish parts into covenant agreement with the Spirit of God.

There are also scriptures that speak of having a double heart or a double mind.

Psalm 12:2, speaking of the ungodly says, **"They speak idly everyone with his neighbor; With flattering lips and a double heart they speak."**

Hosea 10:1-2 says that the heart can be divided:

Israel empties his vine; he brings forth fruit for himself. According to the multitude of his fruit he has increased the altars; according to the bounty of his land they have embellished his sacred pillars.

Their heart is divided; now they are held guilty. He will break down their altars; He will ruin their sacred pillars.

Sometimes Scripture uses heart to refer to the spiritual part of man. For example:

In 1 Peter 3:3-4 KJV, Peter encouraged the women to adorn themselves spiritually and to not let their adorning be only in natural things:

Whose adorning let it not be that outward adorning of plaiting the hair, and of wearing of gold, or of putting on of apparel;

But let it be the hidden man of the heart, in that which is not corruptible, even the ornament of a meek and quiet spirit, which is in the sight of God of great price.

In this passage Peter wasn't condemning the women for adorning themselves with gold or braiding their hair, because he also mentioned the putting on of apparel. If it were unspiritual to wear any gold or braid your hair, then it would also be unspiritual to put on any apparel! We know that's not what Peter was teaching the Church! Rather Peter is saying, "Let your adorning be something besides just the outward adorning; let it be a meek and quiet spirit which is very precious in the sight of God." When he speaks of "the hidden man of the heart," he is referring the spirit.

The bottom line is, your heart is comprised of both your spirit and your soul. That's why references to the heart sometimes refer to the spirit, but most often to the soul. The day your body dies and you cease to be able to carry on with life in your human flesh, your spirit and part of your soul will go into the presence of God. Only the part of your soul that has been renewed to the Word of God, the part that has been transformed by the renewing of your mind, is actually going to go into the presence of God. Everything else that is carnal, that is of this world, is going to die on this side. You can't carry that part of your soul into the kingdom of God; it's not welcome there. All the lies you've believed, the sinful thought patterns, the temptations and negative emotions, those are not acceptable in heaven. All of these negative things are going to be wiped away as you go into the presence of God.

For somebody who's been born again, but never matured in the Lord, everything in heaven will be a complete and total shock. For those who have been transformed by the renewing of their minds, it's going to be an exciting time. You'll be able to recognize and know a lot of the things in heaven. You'll say, "Hallelujah! I knew it was going to be like this!" And you're not going to be shocked because that part of your soul has been in communion with God long enough to be able to recognize heavenly things.

ILLUMINATION TAKES PLACE IN A RENEWED MIND

Earlier we discussed illumination as one of the five infallible steps of faith. Now that we have an accurate picture of the inward parts of man, let's take a look at where illumination actually takes place. Because the Holy Spirit lives in our spirit, our spirit is already complete and has full knowledge of God's Word. It is our mind that needs to be renewed and transformed. And that is where illumination takes place.

Romans 12 give us insights into the renewing of the mind. Verse 1 says, **"I beseech you therefore, brethren, by the mercies of God, that you present your bodies a living sacrifice, holy, acceptable to God, which is your reasonable service."**

Paul addresses the body first. He says to present your body as a living sacrifice. Your body is the temple of the Holy Spirit (1 Corinthians 6:19) by virtue of the fact that He lives in your spirit and can fill your soul – and both of those are in your body. They can't be separated until the time of your physical death.

Then Paul says that presenting your body is a reasonable thing for you to do. Jesus died on the cross for you. He went through a separation, spiritually, from God the Father and became sin for you, exchanging His righteousness for your sin. After you start examining all that He's done for you, isn't it just the reasonable thing to do, to present your body a living sacrifice? The least that we could do is live in a way that is holy and acceptable to Him.

The power to be able to do this comes in verse 2: **"And do not be conformed to this world, but be transformed by the renewing of your mind, that you may prove what is that good and acceptable and perfect will of God."**

We must come to a place where our mind and our spirit begin to agree. Since your spirit already has full knowledge of the Word of God, once you start getting your mind to line up with that Word, and the two come into agreement, a great, dynamic, powerful force is unleashed.

THE FORCE OF AGREEMENT

The Bible has some interesting things to say concerning agreement. Amos 3:3 asks, **"Can two walk together, unless they are agreed?"** Two people can't even walk

191

together down the road unless they agree on where they're going. Matthew 18:19 says, **"If two of you agree on earth concerning anything that they ask, it will be done for them by My Father in heaven."** There's power in the prayer of agreement.

This is one of the greatest untapped resources available to us today. If two people can find the place of spiritual agreement on something, you suddenly unleash the power of God to be able to get it. It's going to be given to any two of you who can agree on it. The power of the prayer of agreement is a tremendous tool for married couples, yet so few couples are willing to do the work it takes to really come into agreement.

A lot of people will say they are agreeing with you when you pray together about something – and you may think that they're agreeing with you – but that's no guarantee that you are both really, truly believing exactly the same thing. One person may just be giving mental assent and not be in faith at all.

You need to "locate" people when they ask you to pray a prayer of agreement with them. Ask them what they are believing for and what scriptures they are standing on.

Pastor Bob Yandian in Tulsa, Oklahoma, told an amazing story that really happened to him. A man came to him in the prayer line and asked, "Would you agree together with me, in prayer?"

Pastor Yandian asked, "What is it we're praying about?"

"It's just an unspoken prayer request."

"We don't allow unspoken prayer requests in this church. I need to know what you're praying about before

I can spiritually agree with you. I'll pray in faith over the things that you're praying for in faith. But we have to both be on the same page of faith, or else there's no reason for us to even pray together. I can't pray for an unspoken prayer request. I can ask the Lord to bless you, but that's about it. What is it you want me to agree with you about?"

The man said, "I want you to agree with me that my wife will die so that I can marry another woman I've met."

The pastor was amazed! He said, "I'm sorry. I will never agree with that, because God won't agree with that. That's insane! That's a sin. The woman you want to die is one flesh with you. You're in total error." The pastor then drew the man into a counseling session to get his thinking straightened out.

It's so important that you know what people are thinking before you say, "Sure, I'll agree with you," concerning some unspoken prayer request!

Agreement is a spiritual force that makes great power available. And in a renewed mind, the spirit and the soul agree.

BEING SINGLE-MINDED

We need to be single-minded. Once our mind is renewed in a certain area, we are fully persuaded that what God has said about that area is true, even if our senses tell us differently. At that point, we are being single-minded. We are no longer double-minded and unstable: we are now in a position to receive from God.

James 1:6-8 says this:

But let him ask in faith, with no doubting, for he who doubts is like a wave of the sea driven and tossed by the wind. For let not that man suppose

193

that he will receive anything from the Lord; he is a double-minded man, unstable in all his ways.

You can't be double-minded and receive from God.

Mark 9:17-27 tells the story of a father who came to the Lord on behalf of his son. The son was possessed by an evil spirit who often threw him into the fire. The father begged Jesus, **"If You can do anything, have compassion on us and help us"** (v. 22).

Jesus said, **"If you can believe, all things are possible to him who believes"** (v. 23).

Immediately, the father of the child cried out, and said with tears, **"Lord, I believe; help my unbelief!"** (v. 24). The father was acknowledging, "I've got some belief, Lord, but I've also got a lot of pre-programmed thoughts in my head. I've been told so much stuff over the years, that I've got this unbelief, too. Please, could You help my unbelief?"

And of course, Jesus immediately ministered to his son and set him free.

Like this father, we often have some belief and some unbelief. We must allow the Lord to help our unbelief, to help us overcome it by faith. As we renew our minds, we are tapping into the resources of the Spirit of God so that we can be in complete faith and not be double minded and wavering and unstable in all of our ways.

THE POWER OF AGREEMENT

When the Spirit and the soul agree, great power is released because there's no more doubt in your heart. Mark 11:23-24 says:

"For assuredly, I say to you, whoever says to this mountain, 'Be removed and be cast into the sea,'

and does not doubt in his heart, but believes that those things he says will be done, he will have whatever he says. Therefore I say to you, whatever things you ask when you pray, believe that you receive them, and you will have them."

The key issue is to not doubt in your heart. Remember, your heart contains both the spirit and the soul. The spirit is the hidden person of the heart. Even once you're born again, you're not conscious of everything about your spirit. You're not conscious of all the Word that your spirit contains. You're not conscious of all the power that your spirit contains, even though it's there, it's resident, it's available to you.

Our spirits are filled with the Holy Spirit of the living God. Our desire is to be conscious and to be tapped into all of the power that is there and that is available to us.

TRANSFORMED!

Throughout this book, we've pointed to the necessity of the renewing of our minds if we are going to have the God kind of faith. In Romans 12:2, Paul uses the word "transformed" to describe the magnitude of the change that will take place in us: **"Do not be conformed to this world, but be transformed by the renewing of your mind."** The Greek word translated "transformed" in this verse is only used four times in the New Testament. It is the Greek word *metamorphoo,* and it means "to change into another form." The same Greek word is translated as "transfigured" in two passages of Scripture, Mark 9:2 and Matthew 17:2.

We find a tremendous picture of everything *metamorphoo* means in Matthew 17:1-2:

Jesus took Peter, James, and John his brother, led them up on a high mountain by themselves; and He was transfigured before them. His face shone like the sun, and His clothes became as white as the light.

In this familiar passage of Scripture, Jesus took His three closest disciples apart, and He was transfigured before them. They saw the Shekinah glory of God upon Jesus. After a moment, they noticed Moses and Elijah (v. 3) in the Spirit, talking with Jesus.

I'm sure that Moses and Elijah were very excited to be there. They had come from Abraham's Bosom, or Paradise, where they had been waiting for the Messiah to come. Now they were standing with Him, talking with Him about His upcoming death at Jerusalem (Luke 9:31). I believe they were encouraging Him as He prepared to pay the ultimate price for all mankind.

Think about it: Moses was never born again while on the planet. Neither was Elijah or King David. They lived under the Old Covenant. They never experienced rebirth, never became a new creation. As the Messiah, Jesus would become sin for all mankind, experience separation from God, and then be made alive again by the Holy Spirit. Once this happened, Moses, Elijah, David and all the other Old Testament saints could be redeemed from Abraham's Bosom and go with Jesus to the presence of God (Ephesians 4:8). They could go directly into the throne room of God and see God face to face, which they'd never been able to do before.

You and I have a completely different experience in both life and death than all the Old Testament saints. Since the Cross, every single believer who dies goes immediately into the presence of God and sees Jesus face to face, directly after leaving this earth.

REALITY REVEALED

When Jesus was "transfigured before them," He was radically changed in appearance. That's the picture of the Greek word *metamorphoo*. It's where we get the English word "metamorphosis."

A great illustration of metamorphosis is something you and I have all seen as kids. We've seen little caterpillars weave themselves into little cocoons and then go through metamorphosis. Inside the cocoon, they're transformed into another form. When they pop that cocoon open, these gorgeous, beautiful wings suddenly unfold and they take off and fly. That nasty, little worm that was crawling around was transformed into this glorious, flying creature. We see the true picture of what a butterfly is.

On the Mount of Transfiguration, Jesus revealed to His disciples, for the first time, His true nature. In other words, He revealed on the outside what was really on the inside - just like the caterpillar inside the cocoon is transformed, and then suddenly reveals to the outside world what he really is.

We find Luke's account of this same event in Luke 9. It doesn't use the word *metamorphoo,* but it does say this, **"As He prayed, the appearance of His face was altered"** (Luke 9:29). The word "altered," here, literally means "to be changed from the disguise." In other words, Jesus' flesh was His disguise. It's as though Jesus said, "When people look at My flesh, they're going to think that I'm just another man. But I'm in disguise. I'm really God in the flesh, walking the earth."

Now, the reality is, we can carry this same thought

over to the new birth which you have experienced. The natural body, the earth-suit that you wear on the outside, is simply your disguise. Even your soul and personality – the things you think and say on a regular basis, that are so tied to this world because we have responsibilities in this world – even that is the disguise of the real you on the inside.

But God's plan is for us to be able to reveal our true selves to the outside world, by letting the glory break forth, like Jesus did. As we do, it will transform even our soul and the way we appear to those around us. God has a process for this glory to be revealed on the outside. Our flesh is a veil that blinds us to who we really are. We see only our flawed earth suits. As we renew our mind, we begin to realize that those in the spirit-world see us the same way that they see Jesus – radiant with the light of God and walking in the same spiritual authority that Jesus had.

I'm sure that both the angels and the demons often wonder, "Why don't they pick up those mighty weapons and end it all?" The demons *have* to be concerned that we might suddenly discover who we really are and take the Sword of the Spirit and destroy them. The angels are surely wondering, "Why don't they just whip those demons? Don't they know who they are? Don't they know what's been given to them?"

To the extent that we receive the revelation of who God has made us to be, we will be like Him in this world. To the degree that we renew our minds, we can come with confidence to God, knowing that we have a position of strength, power, and authority through the righteousness given to us by Jesus Christ.

If we allow this process, which begins at the time we are baptized in the Holy Spirit, to continue to transform us, we will be so changed that we will walk with a great boldness of faith.

I know people with the boldness and courage to jump on an airplane, go to a foreign land, and schedule a crusade. They have the boldness to declare that if the people bring all their sick, every one of them will be healed by the Lord. They have the boldness to challenge the witch doctors, saying, "Oh, you think you have power? Come to this meeting, and watch the demonstration of the Spirit of God. Jesus is going to heal every single sick person who is at this meeting. If He does, then you need to receive Him as your Lord and recant your false gods and the demons that you're worshiping."

That's boldness!

How do you get the faith to do that? You allow the Holy Spirit to keep transforming you by the renewing of your mind until you begin to see yourself doing those kinds of things. When you do these things by faith, you find out God backs you up – as you do your part, He does His part over and over again. More and more, you continue to move out in what God has called you to do.

IT'S A PROGRESSIVE THING

There is one other passage where the Greek word *metamorphoo* is used. Second Corinthians 3:18 says, **"But we all, with unveiled face, beholding as in a mirror the glory of the Lord, are being transformed [metamorphoo] into the same image from glory to glory, just as by the Spirit of the Lord."**

We are changed into the same image that we see in the mirror – the image of the glory of the Lord. We keep looking in the mirror of God's Word until we see what God sees. God sees us looking just like Jesus – transfigured and glorious.

God is going to cause us to have experience after experience; we're going to be changed from glory to glory. In the next chapter, we're going to see that the righteousness of God is revealed from faith to faith to faith to faith. In other words, by faith, you'll get a greater revelation of how you've been made the righteousness of God. It's a progressive thing. God will continually work that in you over and over and over again to bring up your level of faith.

First John 4:17 says, **"Love has been perfected among us in this: that we may have boldness in the day of judgment; because as He is, so are we in this world."** As Jesus is right now, so are we in this world. In the realm of the Spirit, what is Jesus like right now? He's the resurrected, exalted, glorified Son of God. That's how God sees us in the realm of the Spirit right now. That's the potential. Is there any sickness in Jesus in heaven right now? God says that's what we have available to us. Is there any poverty with Jesus? Is He concerned about going bankrupt or having to hock the Pearly Gates just to be able to pay the mortgage on the throne? No. There is no poverty in God's kingdom – and "as He is, so are we in this world."

THE SPIRIT-SOUL CONNECTION

God often uses natural things to explain spiritual things. One day He used something that, over the years, has given me great confidence in His ability to help me get my mind into position so it can be in agreement with my spirit – and I can see my prayers answered.

As a young believer, I had heard so many people say "To be in faith, you've got to feed your spirit." I knew I was studying the Word constantly, but there were times I knew I was still wavering in my soul. I wanted to be sure I had enough faith. I would wonder, "Has my spirit-man been fed enough? Is he strong enough?" I told the Lord, "I'd like to know what goes on inside me. What really takes place?"

The Lord reminded me of a time in Biology class when we were studying the differences between the right and the left hemispheres of the brain. Between the two hemispheres, there's a thick band of connective nerve tissue called the "corpus callosum." It is exactly like the tissue of your spinal cord that goes down through the vertebrae of your spine, but it connects the two hemispheres of the brain.

For a long time, doctors had studied a number of different things about the two hemispheres of the brain and had found that the right hemisphere of your brain motors the left side of your body, and the left hemisphere of your brain motors the right side of your body.

They wondered, "Could one side of the brain learn separately from the other side?" They couldn't answer that question because everybody had a corpus callosum connecting the two sides. Then a farmer had a freak accident. Someone had taken an axe up into the hay loft of the barn to cut the bands off the hay bales and accidentally left it up there. Later, someone else accidentally knocked the axe over the edge of the hayloft while the farmer was working down below. The axe fell, hitting him on the top of the head. It split his skull and went all the way between the two hemispheres of his brain and severed the corpus callosum.

You would think the farmer would have bled to death, but it didn't hit anything vital on either hemisphere of the brain. His doctor was able to remove the axe and sew him up, and he recovered.

The doctors doing brain research asked the farmer if they could study him. They said, "This is the first case we know where somebody has the two hemispheres of their brain completely separate from each other." They devised an experiment to find out if the two sides of his brain could learn independently of one another. They covered one eye and plugged one of his ears, then they brought a painting into the room for him to look at and played music that he had never heard before. He had this wonderful experience of viewing this new artwork and listening to this new music. Then, they took the artwork out of the room, and turned off the music. After that, they covered his other eye and plugged his other ear. When they brought the same painting in the room and turned on the same music, he said he'd never seen that painting before and never heard that music before. In other words, one hemisphere of his brain had learned completely separately from the other hemisphere. Without the corpus callosum, one hemisphere could know something that the other hemisphere didn't know.

After the Lord reminded me of this experiment, He said, "This is what takes place between the spirit and the soul. Every time you go through a process of renewing your mind, I make a new connection between the spirit and the soul."

Suddenly I saw how it all works! The day you confessed Jesus as Lord, the Holy Spirit completely filled your human spirit and gave you full knowledge of the Word of God. Then God made a connection between your spirit and soul, much as the corpus callosum connects the two sides of your brain. Suddenly, the two could communicate. The knowledge of salvation that He put in your spirit was duplicated – suddenly you had matching knowledge in the realm of the soul. On the day you were baptized in the Holy Spirit, God was able to establish a lot more connections between the spirit and the soul. All of a sudden, the fullness you had in your spirit was duplicated in your soul. Instantly, your soul was really energized and conscious of the presence of God and the power of God.

Then someone told you there were nine gifts of the Spirit available to believers. You said, "Hallelujah! I believe that! I'd like to have them all now!"

Your faith level increased incredibly; your soul was hungry for the Word. You started speaking the Word to yourself, you started meditating on the Word. As you did, the lights turned on, and illumination came – that's the renewing of the mind. Every time another scripture is illuminated to you, God is able to establish new connections between your spirit and your soul. Another area of your soul is suddenly conscious of the same information that's been residing in your spirit-man.

As we keep speaking the Word, meditating on the Word, and spending time with God, we learn to walk in the Spirit in total consecration to the Lord, living in absolute great faith.

The covenant promises of God include a long life. I believe that He's going to require some of us to live to be well over a hundred years old. At that advanced age, we will still be preaching this message and living this way, to prove that the Word of God works. The world will get to see it manifested in our lives. I'm a work-in-progress just like everybody else, but I don't feel I've even hit middle life yet. I'm still too young at fifty-nine to have a mid-life crisis! Because mid-life is really sixty. I'm shooting for well over a hundred. I feel like I'm going to need that to accomplish all God has given me to do.

It's a wonderful thing to know that you can have a conscious knowledge of everything that's in your spirit.

CONNECTING THE SPIRIT AND SOUL

The corpus callosum connects the left and right hemispheres of the brain and allows information to flow between the two.

In a similar way, once you are born again, there is a connection between your recreated human spirit (where the Holy Spirit now lives) and your soul. This connection grows tremendously when you are baptized in the Holy Spirit, which allows information to flow more freely between the two.

HEART (before New Birth)

HEART (after New Birth)

The Holy Spirit moves into your spirit and begins to enlighten your soul.

HEART (baptized in Holy Spirit)

Rapid increase in the number of connections between your spirit and your soul.

HEART (with renewed mind)

As you continue to study, your mind comes to understand what your spirit already knows. Your life is transformed.

You'll never tap into it completely. The thoughts of God will never be as available to your mind as they are to your spirit and you'll never think all the thoughts of God one hundred percent of the time. But having multiple areas of these "connective fibers" between your spirit and your mind is certainly going to improve your life. It's going to cause you to be victorious. To those called to the ministry, you realize, "Hey, it's not an option. I have to be victorious in life. I've got to walk in health. I've got to walk in the provision of what I need in order to fulfill what God's called me to do."

We are going to be the standard-setters and standard-bearers in what God has for us. We're all still works in progress, but God wants us to be completely filled up with the Holy Spirit – spirit, soul and body – and to go through this process of being transformed. As you continue to harness your attention onto the Lord and His Word, God puts these "connective fibers" between your mind and your spirit so that your soul can know what your spirit knows.

You are in a journey of life, and God sees the integrity of your heart; He sees that you're making the effort.

One of the key things to keep in mind at all times is that we are to judge no one but ourselves. We need to look after ourselves and purpose to grow ourselves. We are not in a position to judge anybody else's faith or lack thereof. The Lord says, "Every other believer is my servant as well. I'm able to find out what's wrong with them; I can make them stand. I'm able to cause them to be able to walk in faith. Don't you criticize any of my servants...or anybody else" (Romans 14:4 paraphrased).

And so, I'm not critical of people who don't believe God for as much as I do. I just wish that they wouldn't teach against this message saying, "These things are not available, they're not from God." I wish they would just be private with what they believe, and not drag down so many other people with them. They absolutely destroy people's hope.

They think we're giving people "false hope." The reality is, we're giving people "God's hope." I wouldn't teach or preach anything that was contrary to the Word of God. It's not an issue of being divided against other people with different beliefs. It's a matter of saying, "No, we're all believers. They believe to a certain level, and you and I are going to believe as far as we possibly can. God has put all these covenant promises out there, and we've determined we're going to believe and receive every single one of them."

Our faith is going to be constantly growing in order to receive all that God has for us. We don't believe that God is limited or that we have to be limited in our growing and stretching, all the days of our lives. Praise God!

A POSITION OF STRENGTH

There are times when all of us feel weak in faith, like the father who said with tears, "Lord, I believe; help my unbelief!" In those times, it's wonderful to know that your spirit man is fine. Your spirit is already one hundred percent in agreement with God. You're actually saying, "Lord, I'm meditating on the Word, and trying to bring my soul in complete subjection to Your Word."

I experienced a major breakthrough in my faith when I realized that as I come into the throne room of God's grace, one part of me is already complete in Christ Jesus. My spirit-man is absolutely, totally acceptable to God; completely redeemed, completely changed and transformed. I'm taking with me the very glory of God's presence.

Now I come and say, "Lord, I believe that I've received

understanding and knowledge and faith in this area. I am in agreement with my spirit, the real me. I'm asking You, right now, in Jesus' name, to answer this prayer request." We have this position of strength and authority, because we know that our spirit-man is fine.

God is so gracious when He sees you making the effort to study and meditate to renew your mind on a regular basis. When you come to Him and say, "Lord, I believe. Would you help me with this little bit that I'm struggling with?"

He'll say, "Absolutely. I'll do a miracle for you. I'll take care of this."

Or He'll say, "Absolutely. I'll take care of this." And He makes a new connection between your soul and your spirit. Suddenly your soul is illuminated with the truth you need, the truth your spirit-man already knew. Suddenly you are in faith, and a promise from God that moments ago looked impossible, now has substance. You know it's yours now – it will come, it's just a matter of time.

CHAPTER ELEVEN

RIGHTEOUSNESS: HEAVENWARD & EARTHWARD

WHY STUDY RIGHTEOUSNESS? When building a solid foundation for faith, a full understanding of righteousness is one of the key elements. It is essential that you understand righteousness if you want to go into the upper stratosphere of the miraculous – which is where God wants to take you. He really wants you to soar in faith like an eagle, but you can't unless you understand your right-standing with God.

If you think God is mad at you or that He is disgusted with your sinfulness, you will cower from His presence. When you sin, you will run away from Him and hide. Many Christians live this way because of a misunderstanding of righteousness. The Apostle John wrote 1 John 1:9 to believers: **"If we confess our sins, He is faithful and just to forgive us our sins and to cleanse us from all unrighteousness."** Any Christian who sins can run to God and get washed afresh and anew. But if you are afraid to go to God, you will stay under the burden of guilt and shame.

SOMETHING IS MISSING

In the beginning, Adam and Eve were given dominion over everything on the earth (Genesis 1:26, 28). When Adam and Eve sinned, they did not lose dominion. No, what they lost was the presence of the Holy Spirit and access to God's throne. For thousands of years, mankind stayed in that state, not having the Holy Spirit dwelling within them and not knowing that every single person could have the same access to God's throne of grace that the Lord Jesus has.

Anyone who is unsaved and living without the Holy Spirit has a big empty place inside – they are missing the most important ingredient. They are hugely lacking, as humans were designed to have the Spirit of God (Genesis 2:7). Without Him, they are almost subhuman! No wonder we see lower and lower levels of behavior, acts of sin and degradation that man has been pushed down into. Mankind has lived with an image of sinfulness all these years.

By the work of the Cross, by His own blood, Jesus made it possible for every human being to be completed. Then, on the Day of Pentecost, we read that the disciples were "filled with the Holy Spirit" (Acts 2:4). As stated before, the Greek word translated "filled" also means "fulfilled." Not only did God design us to have the Holy Spirit dwelling inside us, He also designed us to have the same empowering of the Holy Spirit that they received on the Day of Pentecost. We now have a "hotline to heaven" and a supernatural prayer language. Now we can always pray the perfect prayer: we pray according to our understanding, then bathe that prayer by praying in the Holy Spirit. He adds whatever is missing!

Completed and empowered, we humans can once again be all that God created us to be. We can walk in the realm of the miraculous and demonstrate God's will on earth, just as Jesus did – once we are free from an image of sinfulness and fully grasp our righteousness.

AN IMAGE OF SINFULNESS CAME WITH THE FALL

An image of sinfulness came with the Fall. When Adam and Eve sinned, they immediately made aprons out of leaves to cover themselves because they were suddenly aware that they were naked. Nobody told them they were naked, they just had a knowing, a consciousness. They had disobeyed God's command – and now they were hiding from God. They were aware that something terrible had happened to them. Their fellowship with God was broken – the Holy Spirit had departed from their spirits. They felt the emptiness, the longing within. They now knew evil as well as good.

The future of the whole earth had suddenly changed, because they had believed a lie. Satan had told Eve, "If you eat of the tree of the knowledge of good and evil, you'll be like God." What a lie! Adam and Eve were already like God – as much like God as they were ever going to be – except for this one issue: they did not know evil. They only knew God and the earth He had created, and it was all good. God, on the other hand, knew the difference between good and evil. God had seen Satan cause a great war in heaven, where one-third of the angels followed Satan in his rebellion against God (Revelation 12:7-9). If Adam and Eve had known the difference between good and evil, they would have known that Satan was evil. Unfortunately, they were tripped up by his terrible lie and fell into disobeying God's command. Eve thought, "Yeah, if I could know more and be more like God, I'd like that."

One thing to remember about the above scene in the

Garden of Eden is that when Satan appeared to Eve, he did not look like the serpents we now know. Serpents didn't start slithering around until after God pronounced judgment on them in Genesis 3:14. No, Satan did not slither up to Eve. As far as I know, the response of most women if a snake started talking to them would not be, "Oh, what was it you wanted to say?" Usually they just scream, "Aahhhh!" and run! That response is a normal, natural response. No, I believe that Satan came to Eve like a serpent in his cunningness, but that he looked the way the Bible described him in Ezekiel 28:13, covered over with every jewel and with pipes and timbrels (tambourines) built into his body. He was the most fantastic creature that Eve had ever seen face to face. All the rest of God's creatures paled in comparison.

Eve was completely dazzled by this amazing being, sure that whatever he said had some weight and merit. Eve wasn't just enticed by a snake in the dirt, but by the most powerful angel that she and Adam were ever going to encounter. Eve was very impressed.

This beautiful creature told Eve a terrible lie. Eve was deceived and she ate. Obviously, Adam was just standing there listening the whole time she was being deceived because Eve then turned and offered the fruit to Adam. Once Eve ate, Adam felt compelled to eat too. He was so in love with Eve that he was willing to go along with whatever Eve wanted to do.

God made Eve for Adam, to complete him, because God saw that Adam was alone. None of the animals were a suitable companion for him. God took a rib bone from Adam and – in the Hebrew – the Bible says he "cautiously, meticulously formed and built her." Eve was different from Adam: she was his perfect complement. When Adam saw her, he said, "You are bone of my bone and flesh of my flesh," which is the equivalent of going "Wow!" He was blown away, he was madly in love. It was easy for him to do whatever she said.

Obviously, Adam was in love with Eve more than he was in love with God.

I remember reading this passage about the Fall for the first time after becoming a Christian. I had always thought that the account of Adam and Eve in the Bible was just a fairy tale or a myth. Suddenly illumination came and I was able to believe that this was actually a true story: this was exactly the way it happened.

I was angry at Adam. I thought, "Lord, I'm not sure Adam could have repented and gone to heaven. But if he's up there when I get there, I've got some questions to ask him, because I'm really angry. I look at the sinful condition of the world and all the problems because of sin, and I know this is all his fault. I'm angry that man is locked in this state down here. I wish we were all saved and we could all just go to heaven right now."

I was very critical of Adam. The Lord spoke to me immediately and said, "If you'd been him, you'd have done exactly the same thing." That shut my mouth! I learned not to judge, because we're all the same, and each one of us would have done exactly the same thing that Adam and Eve did. We don't know what this temptation was really like.

The first result of an awareness of sinfulness was that fellowship was broken between God and mankind. The next thing that happened damaged the relationship between Adam and Eve. Blame entered the world. Adam and Eve both blamed someone else, saying, "It wasn't my fault!" When God came to the Garden, He asked, "Adam, where are you? Why are you hiding from Me? Have you eaten of the tree that I told you not to eat from?"

Adam immediately said, "It was the woman You gave me!"

In just a few words, Adam was able to blame both Eve, and God who had made Eve, for the tragedy that had just occurred.

Next, God asked Eve, "What happened?"

Eve did not want to carry the blame alone. She said, "It was the serpent who came and deceived me."

With an awareness of sinfulness came a shifting of blame. We do the same thing. When we're guilty of sin, we're quite willing to pass the buck to someone else. Blaming one another continues to damage relationships between people every day.

AN IMAGE OF SINFULNESS
KEEPS FELLOWSHIP BROKEN

It was an image of sinfulness that broke Adam and Eve's fellowship with God. They no longer enjoyed the closeness that they had experienced with God while walking with Him in the cool of the day.

An image of sinfulness keeps your fellowship with God broken, even if you are a believer. When you are conscious of how human and guilty you are, you want to hide, to try to fix things yourself, before you come to God.

We must understand that there is a major difference between relationship and fellowship. You establish your *relationship* with God once you receive Jesus Christ as Lord. That makes you a son or daughter of God for eternity, able to receive all the covenant blessings.

When you sin, that relationship is not broken, but your *fellowship* is. For example, when I discipline my children, sometimes our fellowship is broken! Feelings are hurt. It never lasts long at our house, but there is a time of broken fellowship. However, relationship is never broken. I'm still their dad, and they are still my children. We are just not hanging out together and snuggling on the couch until fellowship is restored.

As a believer, if you hold onto an image of sinfulness, your fellowship is always diminished, which robs you of your confidence. God wants you to feel like you are His favorite, that He waits for you to wake up every morning and greet Him for the day, saying, "Good morning, Dad! Good morning, Brother Jesus! Good morning, Holy Spirit!" He wants to help you set your course for the day, conscious of Him instead of your first thoughts being about what hurts in your body or the troubles of the day. You are His favorite! Expect His favor to be poured out to you!

It's absolutely vital to understand the righteousness of God and what Jesus did for us. It is the basis for being able to go to God - walking boldly into the throne room of grace and asking for help in time of need (Hebrews 4:16), knowing that God is going to answer. If people feel condemned, sinful and conscious of sin, they have a hard time walking boldly before the throne of grace, no matter how many of the covenant promises they've been meditating on. They still feel like they are unworthy - and the devil certainly is glad to accommodate them in feeling that way.

AN IMAGE OF SINFULNESS IS THE BASIS OF ALL RELIGION

God created us to be in fellowship with Him and to have the presence of the Holy Spirit in us. Yet every human born since Adam and Eve has experienced broken fellowship with God and the lack of the Holy Spirit in their lives. They keep trying to fix that void. The natural thing is to say, "I've got to earn my way back to God. I've got to somehow earn God's favor."

An image of sinfulness actually breeds all religion and philosophy. All religion is birthed out of trying to earn, by your own works, God's acceptance, God's love, and God's fellowship. Religions give a structure and a list of good works designed to sooth man's awareness of sinfulness and put him back in position with God. Religious works attempt to fill the void caused by man's yearning to be in the presence of God once again.

What God wants is not religion, but relationship. That's what we have through Jesus. It's so hard for people in the world to accept that Jesus did it all. There's nothing we could have possibly done to get rid of sin – yet it's sin that keeps us from fellowshipping with God. Jesus did it all. He removed all our sin. All we have to do is receive Him and, suddenly, we get the fellowship, the presence of God, restored to us as a free gift.

Because of their image of sinfulness, people in the world say, "There's no way. It can't come that easy. You have to earn it. We know how the world works." Well, they know how the world works under the devil's system, under the fallen system. But God created a new system – His system – that supercedes the fallen system. His system is based on the free gift and mercy of God. It operates by the grace of God. We are able to receive all restoration by virtue of the work of Jesus Christ.

"YOUR FATHER THE DEVIL"

Satan is the author of all false religion and the father of unsaved and fallen men. We find an interesting passage showing this in John 8:41-47. Here, Jesus is speaking to the religious rulers and hypocrites. He said:

> **"You do the deeds of your father." Then they said to Him, "We were not born of fornication; we have one Father – God."**

> **Jesus said to them, "If God were your Father, you would love Me, for I proceeded forth and came from God; nor have I come of Myself, but He sent Me. Why do you not understand My speech? Because you are not able to listen to My word.**

> **"You are of your father the devil, and the desires of your father you want to do. He was a murderer from the beginning, and does not stand in the truth, because there is no truth in him. When he speaks a lie, he speaks from his own resources, for he is a liar and the father of it. But because I tell the truth, you do not believe Me. Which of you convicts Me of sin? And if I tell the truth, why do you not believe Me? He who is of God hears God's words; therefore you do not hear, because you are not of God."**

These religious Jews were sure they were serving God. But Jesus declared to them, "No, you've been deceived. By virtue of rejecting Me - God in the flesh - you're serving your father, the devil." Jesus pointed out that these men, who were trusting in their religion, had been deceived by Satan, the father of all lies, the father of all sin.

Even though Judaism is the root through which Christianity came, it is no longer valid today. In other words, you can't go to heaven by being a good, practicing Jew, or a proselyte of Judaism. Essentially, Jesus told the religious Jews, "You have so changed what God originally intended that you've created a false religion." Every attempt on man's part to have God cover their sin and to have some sort of relationship with the Father will fail.

As Jesus was ushering in the New Covenant, the Old Covenant was passing away. The Law was a way by which the Jews could enter into covenant with God. As descendants of Abraham they had favor with God, and they were the people through whom God would bring the Messiah. But the Law was never intended to be "the way" into God's presence – it could never restore the fellowship that had been broken. When Jesus came, the Law of Moses was completely done away with, abolished. That doesn't mean, of course, that all the immutable laws of God were done away with. What became obsolete were all the rituals found in the Law of Moses, all the things designed to be a rehearsal of what the Lord Jesus was going to do when He came to complete the whole plan of redemption.

Some people are confused on this point and ask, "Shouldn't we still observe the parts of the Law found in the Old Testament? I mean, it is still the Bible."

Yes, it is still the Bible, but no one today, neither Jew nor Gentile, is going to be saved by observing the Law of Moses. God's not going to have two different standards: there's one rule. Once Jesus came, He became the way, the truth, the life and no one can come to the Father, except through Him (John 14:6). Even though the Jews serve the same one true God that we serve, they must come to Him through the only access that we have to God and that's through Jesus, Himself.

It is critical that the Church be the Church that we're supposed to be. The Bible says that we're going to provoke the Jews to jealousy (Romans 11:11) as they see the blessing of God upon us. It will become apparent that we are truly the family of God, that we were grafted in

(Romans 11:17). As the Church becomes that living, powerful witness, it will demonstrate to the Jews that Jesus is the true Messiah. Although most missed Him when He was first sent to them, in the last days, many Jews will receive Jesus and be saved.

There is only one true God, and He manifested Himself in the flesh only one time and that was in the Lord Jesus. He is the one true way.

In America today, you can get in trouble by saying you've discovered the one true way – because the gospel is politically incorrect. Political correctness says, "You must embrace all religions and say, 'Whatever you want to believe is fine.'" But it's not fine. Every false religion is a tremendous deception that will keep people lost for all eternity.

God has called us to communicate the gospel to people – with love and demonstrations of power. Today, all over the world, the Body of Christ is winning people from false religions because of the demonstration of the Spirit and power in the name of the Lord Jesus Christ. He was the only head of any religion who was raised from the dead as proof that He was God in the flesh, the Son of God paying the price for our sins.

AS DIFFERENT AS LIGHT AND DARKNESS

God sees those who have accepted His Son and those who have not as totally different. We find God's perspective in the following passage from 2 Corinthians 6:14-18.

Do not be unequally yoked together with unbelievers. For what fellowship has righteousness with lawlessness? And what communion has light with darkness?

And what accord has Christ with Belial? Or

219

what part has a believer with an unbeliever? And what agreement has the temple of God with idols? For you are the temple of the living God. As God has said: "I will dwell in them and walk among them. I will be their God, and they shall be My people."

Therefore "Come out from among them, and be separate, says the Lord. Do not touch what is unclean, and I will receive you. I will be a Father to you, and you shall be My sons and daughters, says the Lord Almighty."

Here Paul, writing to believers under the anointing of God, refers to believers as "righteousness," "light," and "the temple of God." That's how God sees us. On the other hand, unbelievers are referred to as "lawlessness," "darkness," and devil worshipers ("Belial" means "worthless or wicked" and is another name for Satan).

God sees the difference between saved and unsaved people as the difference between black and white. Paul asks, **"For what fellowship has righteousness with lawlessness? And what communion has light with darkness?"**

It is amazing to me how many born-again people come to their pastor and say, "Pastor, I'm getting married. Would you please do the ceremony?"

Their pastor asks, "Who are you marrying?" And it turns out the believer is planning to marry somebody who's not saved. Did they never read this verse? Or do they think it doesn't pertain to them? Maybe they think, "I know they're going to get saved after we get married."

No, there is no guarantee that they will ever get saved. The believer is going to suffer great anguish because he or she was disobedient to the Word. Not only will there be difficulties in this life, but if their spouse doesn't get saved, then one will go to heaven for eternity, and the other will go to hell for eternity. It has to be tough to know that someone you love will be in that place of torment, forever.

Paul is talking here about the division, the great difference between the saved and the unsaved. There's no fellowship between righteousness and unrighteousness. They are completely, diametrically opposed to each other.

Then Paul quotes several Old Testament scriptures, proving what God had been saying all along, that He was creating a new, holy nation - a group of people who would come out of all nations, all creeds, and all religions, from all over the earth. They would be one people, and they would be separate, and they would be His people, through receiving Jesus as Lord.

THE CURE FOR AN IMAGE OF SINFULNESS

In 2 Corinthians 5:21, we find the cure for an image of sinfulness. It says, **"For He** [God] **made Him who knew no sin to be sin for us, that we might become the righteousness of God in Him."** According to God, here's what took place: Jesus became sin and we became righteousness. He was willing to take on our sinfulness in order to impart His righteousness to us. Because of this miraculous exchange, God now refers to us as "righteousness."

Those redeemed by Christ are now the definition of "righteousness" in God's dictionary. In fact, if you asked Him the meaning of the word "righteousness," He would say, "It's My people who've been made righteous with the righteousness of My Son, Jesus. It's what I've done in their lives. They are My standard of righteousness. I have taken all the sin away and made them completely holy, acceptable in the Beloved. I've put them in complete right-standing before Me, just as if they had never, ever sinned." That's the definition of "righteousness" in God's dictionary. We are His righteousness.

We are a display of what His righteousness will do. God likes to showcase the miraculous, transformed life: a person who was on the way to hell, who had experienced all the negative things of life because of serving the devil. We hear testimonies all the time: drug addicts saved, Mafia hit men serving the Lord, former witch doctors now in the ministry. God delights in shining the spotlight on someone who was once darkness, but is now light. He calls them "the righteousness of God in Christ."

THE RESULTS OF AN IMAGE OF RIGHTEOUSNESS

God wants us to put on His image of righteousness. As we do, we will become increasingly aware of what the Bible says about God's way of gaining righteousness. We will begin to see new things in the Word of God that will result in many far-reaching changes in our thought patterns.

First, we will be cleansed from an image of sinfulness. While religion seeks to keep us ever conscious of our sinfulness, God forgets our sins, cleanses us, and wants us to experience having our hearts cleansed from the sense of sin as well. This point comes through loud and clear in the Williams translation of Hebrews 10:16-23.

"This is the covenant that I will make with them in those last days," says the Lord: "I will put my laws into their hearts, and write them on their minds."

When you meditate on God's Word with *understanding*, it's as if He's downloading it, imbedding it, encrypting it onto your hard drive – the devil can't understand it! God embeds His Words in your mind in encrypted code. Williams continues:

"I will never, never, any more recall their sins and deeds of wrong."

God has the perfect mind, so of course, He *could* remember our sins. But He chose to absolutely forget and eradicate them from His memory forever. If we try to remind Him, He will say, "What are you talking about?"

For when these are forgiven, there is no more need of an offering of sin.

If we are walking in an image of sinfulness, we are dishonoring the offering of Jesus' blood to cleanse us from all unrighteousness and from the awareness of sinfulness. We dishonor the fullness of what His blood can really do, according to the Word of God. And when we reject God's Word, it's like rejecting Him. As Dr. Fred Price says, "Why don't you just spit in God's face and be done with it?" That's pretty strong! But in a sense, that's what believers who continue to walk in an image of sinfulness are doing.

Since then, my brothers, we have free access to the real sanctuary, through the blood of Jesus, the new and living way...

We have access into the real sanctuary, the heavenly sanctuary. And the access, the door into the sanctuary, is a "living way." God is so alive, and so much the source of life, that even the door into His presence is alive. If you touch the door, power comes out. The walk-way emanates the life of God.

...which He opened for us, through the curtain, that is, His physical nature....

The curtain in Solomon's temple was overlaid with gold thread on a regular basis. Some historians say the curtain had been overlaid so many times that it was one-foot thick! That curtain was seriously heavy! But God ripped it in two from top to bottom when Jesus died. The way was made! God was symbolizing, "I'm done with this veil that kept you from coming into My presence. You see the natural one ripped, because in the spirit, My Son was ripped asunder. He was the living way, and His soul was ripped in two." How can we deny the fullness of that inner sanctuary and what God has placed in there for us, when Jesus' own flesh was ripped apart like a curtain that we might have access?

...and since in him we have a great High Priest over the house of God, let us continue to draw near to God with sincere hearts and perfect faith;

When you have a sincere heart, you receive the work of the Cross, which provides an absolute image of righteousness. With an absolute image of righteousness, there is no fear of God. And where there is no fear of God, there is perfect faith. You know you are in the presence of the One who wants you to be with Him in the inner chamber even more than you want to be there! That has been His plan all along – to give each one of us a seat on His throne along with the Lord Jesus. He says, "Come on in. Be seated in My presence."

...with our hearts cleansed from the sense of sin, and our bodies bathed in clean water;

We've got this notion that because we are a three-part being – spirit, soul, and body – and that nothing good dwells in our mortal flesh, that we must get our spirit and soul in agreement then drag our bodies along to where

God wants us to go. It's as though our bodies are hating it all the time: "I hate laying hands on people and seeing them healed by the power of God." No, our bodies have been washed with the pure water of God's Word. He makes it so our bodies can carry the glory.

You become that suitable vessel of honor, fit for the Master's use. With your hands, you do the regular stuff all day long, but those same hands, washed by the water of the Word of God, can be the carriers of divine healing. It's a radical thing to think that you carry the anointing of God in your earthly body, and all you have to do is pray in faith, lay hands on somebody, and God can heal them of anything.

I refuse to think negatively about my body. We must have our minds transformed and our mouths in sync with what God is teaching us about our bodies. One of our professors in Stockholm, Sweden, has made this covenant: "I will never speak negatively about the body God has given me to dwell in on this earth. Instead, I will glorify Him with my body." We can be quick to complain about our bodies; but the best way to gain victory is to speak highly of what God has given us - spirit, soul, and body. An image of righteousness results in pure faith and an understanding that we are acceptable to God.

...let us without ever wavering, keep on holding to the hope that we possess....

Hope has to do with the future, but Bible hope always has to do with an anticipation of good based on God's character and His revealed covenant promises.

...for He is to be trusted who has made the promise.

The Father in heaven has made all the promises - He's behind it all, and we can trust Him.

As you passionately pursue God's plan for your life, you get used to clearly hearing what the Holy Spirit is saying and how He's leading you in your life as well as in ministry. He gives you the directions given to Him by the Head of the Church, the Lord Jesus Himself. And when Jesus gives directions to the Holy Spirit, it's because He received directions from the God who created the entire universe and everything in it. We can't even imagine how big it is, and He's way out beyond that. We will never know how huge God is. This God, who defies all description and stupefies our imagination, knows us so well. When He initiates the prompting to minister to someone, He says, "I've got someone who will do what I've asked them to do. Watch this, Son. Tell the Holy Spirit to have them do this."

We are called to a critical time - and God knows what we are capable of. It's important that we learn to hear and obey, but it always takes trust to step out in faith. Hebrews 10:23 reminds us: **"He is to be trusted who has made the promise."**

One time while I was ministering, I felt my body go completely numb and pain free. I thought, "What is this? I'm always used to something hurting a little bit!" Then I realized God had done it: He had anesthetized me to any of my own pain so He could talk to me about other people's pains. It was a word of knowledge with physical impressions in my own body. When I started feeling a blinding headache, I stepped out in faith and called out, "Somebody here has a terrible headache - and the Lord wants to heal you." The anointing began to flow, and healings manifested in that meeting.

God gave me a spiritual empathy, invited me to "eavesdrop" on His kingdom. He invites all of us to do that. He wants His people listening to what's going on in the spirit: God the Father speaks to the Son, who speaks to the Holy Spirit; the anointing comes on you and you obey that word. God knows what He's doing, Jesus knows what He's doing, and the Holy Spirit knows what He's doing – and you've been invited in.

But you won't enter in if you cower in the presence of the Lord all the time, if you are constantly aware of the wrong things you did twenty years ago. You must accept His image of righteousness! The fact that you attempt to walk uprightly before the Lord delights Him. He can work with that! He's looking for people who will attempt to keep walking in righteousness and holiness, listening and obeying His voice. He knows we can't minister in our own power and strength. It requires the anointing. He knows you well, and He's got you passionately striving after what He wants to do in your life. As you do, He keeps matching you with the ability to walk uprightly before Him.

DELIVERED FROM THE POWER OF DARKNESS

Colossians 1:13-14 KJV is a powerful verse that describes several other realizations that we will begin to see when we put on an image of righteousness:

Who hath delivered us from the power of darkness, and hath translated us into the kingdom of his dear Son: In whom we have redemption through his blood, even the forgiveness of sins.

You've been translated from the kingdom of darkness into the kingdom of God's dear Son. In the twinkling of an eye, when you said, "Jesus! Come into my heart; forgive my sins; I take You now as my Savior and Lord," all of a sudden, you were snatched out of the kingdom of darkness. The devil's stronghold on your life and all of his ability to hold you there, captive, was instantly released. Suddenly you're in the kingdom of God's dear Son.

Acts 8 tells of the time when Philip the Evangelist was having a great revival in Samaria. In the middle of the revival, God sent an angel to tell Philip to leave the revival and travel south on the desert road from Jerusalem to Gaza. God wanted Philip to witness to an Ethiopian eunuch who was traveling along that road. This eunuch held a powerful position under Candace, the Queen of Ethiopia, and was in charge of her treasury (v. 27). He went back to Ethiopia and preached the Gospel. History tells us that northern Africa became Christian at this time – I believe it was because of this one Ethiopian's witness.

God knew it was vital for this influential Ethiopian to hear the Gospel preached; that's why God said, "Philip, I want you to leave this revival in Samaria. I know you think it's the greatest thing on earth, but wait until you see how much impact you're going to have when you get this one man saved." Philip obeyed God and witnessed to the eunuch, who believed on Jesus and asked to be baptized. As soon as they came up out of the water, the Spirit of the Lord caught Philip away (v. 39). The Bible says, **"the eunuch saw him no more; and he went on his way rejoicing. But Philip was found at Azotus."** Philip was instantly translated from one location to another location ten miles away!

When Colossians 1:13 tells us we were translated out of the kingdom of darkness, it means we were suddenly and completely removed and taken to our new dwelling place – the kingdom of God's Son, Jesus. We were delivered out of Satan's authority; our new citizenship is in God's kingdom. We were re-created and born into God's kingdom, into God's own family. This positional truth from God's Word tells us where we rightfully belong.

Colossians 1:13 also says we have redemption through His blood. Satan has no legal right to reign over us – we are no longer slaves to sin. God has restored our ability to rule and reign. Jesus ruled and reigned when He walked on earth. He was fearless; He was confident; He was bold; He was the master over evil. There was no limit to His faith. We live in His kingdom now, and He transfers His fearlessness, His confidence, and His boldness to us. We are masters over every force and power of hell, because Satan is defeated through the Blood. Boldness, fearlessness, and confidence with God becomes part of our nature. Just as a branch flows with sap from the vine – we absorb boldness from the Lord as we continue to fellowship with Him.

Some may say, "I worry about looking arrogant if I have too much faith." You know, people are going to criticize you anyway, so you might as well go all the way! Just keep pursuing the Lord and getting better and better results!

I've been hanging out with Jesus. He has eradicated all my fears. I'll go anywhere He says to go, do anything He says to do, and say anything He says to say, even if it will get me in trouble! I am fearless enough to be what He wants me to be. The only thing I fear is not fulfilling what Jesus has called me to do. I can't think of a greater tragedy than this: God had a plan to use my life, to make me a beacon light to impact people all around me, but I got off track and missed what Jesus called me to do.

A third thing Colossians 1:13 says we have is "forgiveness of sins." The Greek word *aphesis* is translated "remission, forgiveness, deliverance and liberty." It means "letting sins go as if they had never been committed, remission of the penalty." Remission infers a total and complete removal of sin, not just a covering as in the Old

Testament. Back then the priests, once a year, would make atonement with the sin sacrifice. But Jesus' sacrifice for sin was once and for all. All your sins are constantly, permanently, irrevocably removed. No sin is attached to you.

Even if your mind is constantly bombarded with temptation, that is not an indication that you are still sinful. It's an indication that you are still human! You are going to face the human frailty of having temptation crouch at your door every single day of your life. But the power of God, the authority in the name of Jesus, and the anointing on your life pulls you through. Most of you reading this book have walked away from ninety-seven percent of the temptations that would have dragged you down and ruined your life. You may still be struggling with that three percent and feel you are still sinful. Here's what the Bible says about sinful thoughts: "Cast down that imagination." In other words, keep the thought from taking root.

Brother Hagin explained it like this:"You can't keep the thoughts from coming into your mind any more than you can keep a bird from flying over your head. But you can keep a bird from making a nest in your hair!" The secret is constantly turning to God. When the smallest temptation comes, run to Him and tell Him, "I can't live without Your presence!" Walk addicted to the presence of God.

REDEMPTION: THE HEAVENWARD SIDE VS. THE EARTHWARD SIDE

The Bible tells us we are re-created and born into God's kingdom, into God's own family. We know this is true even if we don't "feel" it's true for us. To better understand God's perspective, let's take some time to explore what I call the heavenward side and the earthward side of our redemption.

A great exchange has taken place. God took the most righteous Man that could ever live, who was born of the Heavenly Father and not of an earthly father, who was totally sinless. God took that Man's righteousness and made a miraculous exchange for our sin, putting our sins on Him and imparting His righteousness to us. This great, miraculous exchange is almost inconceivable to mankind. Those who are bound by religion cannot imagine that it could be so easy: that they could simply receive Jesus as Lord and gain the right-standing with God that guarantees their position in heaven for eternity. Their mind is bound by an image of sinfulness which says, "Somehow I must earn my way."

Our righteousness is a fact of heaven. Isaiah 53:9 says, **"And they made His grave with the wicked – but with the rich at His death."** In this verse, the Hebrew word for "death" is in the plural form, which should actually be translated "deaths." This fact has caused a lot of controversy with some in the Church because they've not stopped to understand what is being said.

When we say that Jesus died two deaths, one being the physical death and one the spiritual death, we are not saying that He ceased to exist. The definition of "death" is not "the cessation of life or existence."

The human spirit is eternal, so it does not cease to exist when the body dies. The death of our physical body means that our spirit and soul get separated from our physical body. "Spiritual death" means to be spiritually separated from God. So, Jesus suffered both physical death on the Cross and spiritual death, in that He was separated from God the Father.

This miraculous exchange happened as Jesus hung

on the Cross. Let's look at Matthew's eye-witness account of what happened that day.

And about the ninth hour Jesus cried out with a loud voice, saying, "Eli, Eli, lama sabachthani?" that is, "My God, My God, why have You forsaken Me?" (Matthew 27:46).

All His life, Jesus had experienced unbroken fellowship with God the Father and God the Holy Spirit. I believe Jesus was crying out, "My God, the Father! My God, the Holy Spirit! Why have You both forsaken me?" I believe that when the great exchange was made and our sins were put on Jesus, both the Father and the Holy Spirit turned their backs on Him and walked away, because Jesus had become sin, and God cannot have any fellowship with sin.

Jesus knew in advance this was going to happen. He knew in advance that He was going to have to pay this kind of price. It was no surprise to Him. But He was still one-hundred percent human. His physical body and His earthly mind and spirit cried out with the weight of what His spirit was going through, being separated from the Father and the Holy Spirit. Suddenly, the communion was broken and Jesus was all alone – for the first time ever. Right there, He started paying the price.

And Jesus cried out again with a loud voice, and yielded up His spirit.

Then, behold, the veil of the temple was torn in two from top to bottom; and the earth quaked, and the rocks were split, and the graves were opened; and many bodies of the saints who had fallen asleep were raised; and coming out of the

graves after His resurrection, they went into the holy city and appeared to many (Matt. 27:50-53).

An earthquake happened as Jesus yielded His spirit, and the graves were opened. However, the Old Testament saints did not come out of their graves until after Jesus was resurrected. Something else had to take place first.

WHAT HAPPENED BETWEEN THE CROSS AND THE RESURRECTION?

Jesus knew that the end result of his life was to go to the Cross. He had to wait until He was thirty years old to enter into His ministry. Then for three-and-a half years, He walked throughout Israel, ministering by the power of the living God. He showed us God's plan for man and God's plan for ministry: heal everybody, provide for everybody, and raise people from the dead if necessary. He taught us what the Father was really like, saying, **"He who has seen Me has seen the Father"** (John 14:9). The Old Testament concepts of judgement no longer apply, because for us, the Father looks just like Jesus.

In John 19:28-30, we see that Jesus was finally satisfied with all that His life had accomplished:

After this, Jesus, knowing that all things were now accomplished, that the Scripture might be fulfilled, said, "I thirst!"

Now a vessel full of sour wine was sitting there; and they filled a sponge with sour wine, put it on hyssop, and put it to His mouth.

So when Jesus had received the sour wine, He said, "It is finished!" And bowing His head, He gave up His spirit.

Many Christians think that when Jesus said, **"It is fin-ished,"** that all of His work was done, that He died and went to hell and suffered there for three days. Many believe that Jesus paid the price for our sins down in hell, where the devil beat Him until the Father was satisfied. I don't believe that's what the Bible says. The Bible says that Jesus suffered for us on the Cross, bearing our sicknesses, disease, and sin, and everything that separated us from God **"in His own body on the tree"** (1 Peter 2:24). He became sin for us on the Cross – the great exchange was made there, not in hell. There was no reason for Jesus to suffer in hell for three days.

Yet He was not raised from the dead until the third day. What was He doing in hell all that time? I believe He still had a little "mopping up" to do. "It is finished" per-tained to His earthly ministry and work, but He had a devil to take care of and defeat totally. He did some things in the spirit before He picked up His earthly body. Let's trace this out through the Scriptures.

JESUS TRIUMPHED OVER THE KINGDOM OF DARKNESS

Colossians 2:9-15 gives us a great picture of what real-ly happened. It begins with the fact that we are made complete "in Him," because of what Jesus did on the Cross. It paints a vivid picture of how all our sin was nailed to the Cross. That's where the great exchange took place.

> **For in Him dwells all the fullness of the Godhead bodily; and you are complete in Him, who is the head of all principality and power.**
>
> **In Him you were also circumcised with the cir-cumcision made without hands, by putting off**

the body of the sins of the flesh, by the circumcision of Christ, buried with Him in baptism, in which you also were raised with Him through faith in the working of God, who raised Him from the dead.

And you, being dead in your trespasses and the uncircumcision of your flesh, He has made alive together with Him, having forgiven you all trespasses, having wiped out the handwriting of requirements that was against us, which was contrary to us. And He has taken it out of the way, having nailed it to the cross.

Verse 15 then tells us what Jesus did next:

Having disarmed principalities and powers, He made a public spectacle of them, triumphing over them in it.

The word "triumphing" in this verse is from a Greek root word meaning "a hymn sung in festive processional parade." Jesus was having a victory march, much as the ancient Romans did. After a great victory, the Romans brought back the kings of the lands they had conquered along with any exotic animals they had captured. The defeated king was draped in chains of defeat, put in a cage on a cart and paraded before all the people. The defeated king symbolically represented everyone the victorious army had overthrown. Jesus had completely defeated the devil and all the demonic forces, and now He was parading the "loser" king before all the hosts of heaven, making "a public spectacle."

You may ask, "If the devil is so completely defeated, why is he such a problem today?" The Bible says, **"Your**

adversary the devil walks about like a roaring lion, seeking whom he may devour" (1 Peter 5:8). Satan can take advantage of those who don't know enough about their dominion and what has been purchased for them.

But when we understand that Jesus defeated him completely along with all the forces of hell, and now Jesus gives us dominion over them, we can live victoriously. We can dwell and operate in two kingdoms at the same time – heavenly and earthly. According to the kingdom of heaven, where our true citizenship is, we can rule over this earthly life, where we have temporary citizenship.

JESUS LED CAPTIVITY CAPTIVE

In Ephesians 4:8-12, we see a second thing that Jesus did between the Cross and the Resurrection.

Therefore He says: "When He ascended on high, He led captivity captive, And gave gifts to men." (Now this, "He ascended" – what does it mean but that He also first descended into the lower parts of the earth? He who descended is also the One who ascended far above all the heavens, that He might fill all things.)

"Led captivity captive" is in reference to the Old Testament saints who were in the holding place of Paradise, known as Abraham's Bosom. They could not go to heaven when they died, even though they were righteous believers in God under the Law of Moses. Before Jesus came, they could not be born again. They were waiting for a promise from afar off.

Once the "great exchange" had been made in the realm of the Spirit, Jesus descended to the lower parts of the earth to gather these righteous believers, then ascended to heaven and deposited them there. As nice as Paradise was, they were glad to go. Now they could see God face to face!

JESUS GAVE GIFTS TO MEN

After Jesus took all authority away from the devil, He gave all authority to the Church. Everyone who is born again has a ministry. Here Jesus poured out the ministries onto the earth. In verse 8, we read He "gave gifts to men." These gifts and their purpose are further described in verses 11 and 12:

And He Himself gave some to be apostles, some prophets, some evangelists, and some pastors and teachers, for the equipping of the saints for the work of ministry, for the edifying of the body of Christ.

Jesus gives these ministry gifts to the Church to prepare every Christian to enter into the individual ministry God has for them.

JESUS BROUGHT THE WORD OF FAITH TO US

We find a third thing that Jesus did after the Cross in Romans 10:4-11.

For Christ is the end of the law for righteousness to everyone who believes.

Jesus ended the Law of Moses and the right-standing you could have under that Law. Now right-standing with God is only accomplished through Jesus.

For Moses writes about the righteousness which is of the law, "The man who does those things shall live by them."

> But the righteousness of faith speaks in this way,
> "Do not say in your heart, 'Who will ascend into
> heaven?'" (that is, to bring Christ down from
> above) or, "'Who will descend into the abyss?'"
> (that is, to bring Christ up from the dead).

Jesus doesn't need to do this work all over again. He
did it once and for all – forever.

> But what does it say? "The word is near you, in
> your mouth and in your heart" (that is, the word
> of faith which we preach): that if you confess
> with your mouth the Lord Jesus and believe in
> your heart that God has raised Him from the
> dead, you will be saved. For with the heart one
> believes unto righteousness, and with the
> mouth confession is made unto salvation.

> For the Scripture says, "Whoever believes on
> Him will not be put to shame."

Here in this whole discussion of righteousness, we
see an important sequence. The word of faith came into
your heart and you believed that Jesus was raised from the
dead. With your mouth, you asked Him to forgive your
sins, which He did. God immediately imparted His righteousness into your life upon your confession of Jesus
Christ as Lord. You suddenly stepped into a position of
right-standing with God. These heavenward things happened instantly – the earthward part is done over the
remaining years of your life on earth, as you continue to
take the steps of making Him Lord, of giving your whole
life over to Him. It all starts by believing and confessing.

This passage in Romans 10 was quoted from
Deuteronomy 30:11-20.

"For this commandment which I command you today is not too mysterious for you, nor is it far off. It is not in heaven, that you should say, 'Who will ascend into heaven for us and bring it to us, that we may hear it and do it?'

"Nor is it beyond the sea, that you should say, 'Who will go over the sea for us and bring it to us, that we may hear it and do it?'

"But the word is very near you, in your mouth and in your heart, that you may do it. See, I have set before you today life and good, death and evil, in that I command you today to love the Lord your God, to walk in His ways, and to keep His commandments, His statutes, and His judgments, that you may live and multiply; and the Lord your God will bless you in the land which you go to possess.

"But if your heart turns away so that you do not hear, and are drawn away, and worship other gods and serve them, I announce to you today that you shall surely perish; you shall not prolong your days in the land which you cross over the Jordan to go in and possess.

"I call heaven and earth as witnesses today against you, that I have set before you life and death, blessing and cursing; therefore choose life, that both you and your descendants may live; that you may love the Lord your God, that you may obey His voice, and that you may cling to Him, for He is your life and the length of your days; and that you may dwell in the land which

the Lord swore to your fathers, to Abraham, Isaac, and Jacob, to give them."

Old Testament saints had to have faith that the promises of God through the Law of Moses were going to bless them for eternity and give them dominion and victory on this earth, prolonging their days. They had to use faith, and so do we.

All this was accomplished according to this pattern that God gave. Why it took blood, only God knows. From the sacrifice in the beginning that covered Adam and Eve's sin, to the Blood of Jesus, that was God's pattern and the plan. Jesus fulfilled every single part of it.

Every claim of justice was met as deity suffered for humanity on the Cross. Second Corinthians 5:21 says God **"made Him who knew no sin to be sin for us, that we might become the righteousness of God in Him."** Jesus chose to be our sin-substitute. It was His will, His free choice.

I think of it as a conference in heaven between the Father, the Son, and the Holy Spirit. God said, "I created this universe by speaking the Word. Then, Holy Spirit, You were the agency that responded and caused everything to be created. But now mankind has sinned. I need a perfect man to shed His blood and die in their place. I need a perfect man to make this great exchange: their sin for our righteousness. Which of Us will become one of them?"

Jesus said, "I am the Word that created them out of the dust. Obviously I should be the one to go. I will become a man and be one of them." The Eternal Word of God was willing to take on human flesh. Once He was encased in a human body, He would be trapped there for all eternity.

He didn't get out of that body once He ascended to heaven. He's in a resurrected, glorified state, seated at the right hand of the Father. There is a human running the universe He created as the Word of God. He is one of us. That's why our identification with Jesus transcends all of our fears of trying to relate to God. Jesus is one of us, our elder Brother, who made the way for us to go and be with the Father for all eternity.

THREE BAD DAYS IN HELL

We have been searching out what really happened to Jesus between the Cross and the Resurrection. So far, we've seen that Jesus made a public spectacle of the devil and his demons, triumphing over them at the Cross (Colossians 2:15). Then Jesus led the Old Testament saints to heaven and gave gifts of ministry to the Church. He brought the word of faith to us, putting it in our mouths and in our hearts. It was a busy three days!

Based on Colossians 2:15, I don't believe Jesus suffered in hell – I believe He gave the devil three really bad days! I believe it went more like this:

As Jesus began to descend into hell, Satan and all of his demons were thinking, "That's it! We've done it! We've ruined God's only plan of redemption. We've killed the Messiah; we've killed Jesus, His only Son. That's it, we've won. He's on the elevator now, coming down to hell! When those doors open, we're going to grab Him and chain Him up. We're going to hold Him here forever, and all of humanity is going to have to die with us."

Did you ever wonder why Satan works so hard to get so many people to sin? Why does he keep trying to deceive people to stay locked in sin and reject Jesus as Lord and Savior? Satan is not stupid. He knows that God is a God of grace and mercy. I really believe with all my heart that this is the reason that Satan tries to keep so many people out of God's kingdom: he's trying to gain his own redemption. He's trying to get God to change His mind about judging so much of mankind, that the majority would be cast into eternal hell. He's trying to get God to say, "I just can't do it! I can't send billions and billions of people into a Lake of Fire for eternity."

Satan knows that if God changed His mind because there were so many people going to hell, then He would have to forgive every sin and give blanket amnesty for everybody - and that would include Satan himself. I believe Satan is trying to gain his own redemption by forcing God's hand into declaring a blanket amnesty.

The truth is, God has already judged Satan. The Lake of Fire is not man's hell, it is the devil's hell, and Satan deceived man into going there with him. God is not going to give Satan amnesty. God has already spoken the Word that Satan is eternally damned and judged. He's going to be in that Lake of Fire for all eternity.

As Jesus descended on the elevator into hell, Satan and his demons were ready. They were waiting for the elevator doors to open. They were getting ready to grab Jesus and imprison Him with their chains.

Satan did not know that while Jesus was descending into hell, God was infusing righteousness back into Him. All the claims of justice had been met on the Cross. God was now able to justify Jesus and cause Him to become alive in the spirit once again. First Peter 3:18 says, **"For Christ also suffered once for sins, the just for the unjust, that He might bring us to God, being put to death in the flesh but made alive by the Spirit."** Jesus was put to death in the flesh, but made alive again when the Spirit of God came upon Him.

The elevator doors started to crack open. All of a sudden, a powerful foot came out and "Ka-Boom!" With a mighty high-kick, Jesus pounded the devil right in the forehead, fulfilling the prophecy in Genesis 3:15 that His heel would bruise Satan's head.

Jesus whipped the devil and chained him up. Then He defeated all the fallen angels and demons. And for the next three days Jesus paraded in triumph all around the heavenlies – the spirit realm – showing the absolute and complete defeat of the kingdom of darkness.

Then, on the third day, Jesus' body was raised from the dead. He came back to earth to reveal Himself to His disciples. Hallelujah!

I haven't seen all this physically with my own eyes, but I've seen it in the realm of the Spirit. I've heard Jesus speak to me, and I know He's the Resurrected Savior. I know He went through that separation for me and created this righteous state that I could stand in. He gave it to me as a free gift. In the same way that Jesus was accepted into the Father's presence, we have the same acceptance, because we have His righteousness. He was justified, and therefore, we are justified.

First Peter 3:19-22 tells us another thing that Jesus did between the Cross and the Resurrection.

By whom also He went and preached to the spirits in prison, who formerly were disobedient, when once the Divine longsuffering waited in the days of Noah, while the ark was being prepared, in which a few, that is, eight souls, were saved through water.

The Greek word translated "preached" here means the simple proclamation of the Gospel. It's making an announcement of what God has provided for salvation. The "spirits in prison" mentioned here were not in Paradise or Abraham's bosom. These were the ungodly men and women who were alive in the time of Noah, who drowned because they would not get into the Ark. Jesus was not persuading them to be saved – they were already judged. Jesus simply made the announcement, "I've paid the price for everyone who was righteous. Noah and his family are going right into the presence of God."

There is also an antitype which now saves us – baptism (not the removal of the filth of the flesh, but the answer of a good conscience toward God), through the resurrection of Jesus Christ, who has gone into heaven and is at the right hand of God, angels and authorities and powers having been made subject to Him.

We can have an **"answer of a good conscious toward God"** because we have His righteousness imparted to us. This is designed to give us a clear conscious to stand before the Lord.

You may ask, "But what about the fact that I'm imperfect?" You have to live by faith according to the re-creation that you've become as the righteousness of God in Christ. No human will ever be perfect. Paul tried, but even he fell short.

Even if we are not perfect, we now can have a clean conscience before God because of the Resurrection of Jesus Christ.

JESUS ACTED AS OUR HEAVENLY HIGH PRIEST

After His resurrection and before meeting with His disciples, Jesus did one more thing. In the Book of Hebrews, we see how Jesus fulfilled the heavenly duties of the heavenly High Priest. When Moses had the vision on Mount Sinai, God told him to make a tabernacle according the pattern he saw in heaven. Moses saw Jesus, the Son of God and the Word of God, fulfilling the redemptive plan of God in heaven.

Moses then made an earthly representation of what he had seen in the Tabernacle of Moses. Jesus fulfilled every single part of it. Hebrews 9:24-28 tells us:

For Christ has not entered the holy places made with hands, which are copies of the true, but into heaven itself, now to appear in the presence of God for us; not that He should offer Himself often, as the high priest enters the Most Holy Place every year with blood of another – He then would have had to suffer often since the foundation of the world; but now, once at the end of the ages, He has appeared to put away sin by the sacrifice of Himself.

Jesus made the sacrifice to put all sin away, once and for all, for every human being who would receive Him as Lord. You may ask, "If Jesus permanently put away all sin, why is there still sin in the world?" Because man chooses to sin!

But if we, as believers, choose to impose the power of God on our lives and believe that Jesus has put away sin, then we can join those who have had sin put away out of their lives. That's the way God already sees us. He sees sin put away. So why don't we just get the blessing of having it all completely put away?

And as it is appointed for men to die once, but after this the judgment, so Christ was offered once to bear the sins of many. To those who eagerly wait for Him He will appear a second time, apart from sin, for salvation.

Jesus will come again a second time, not to bear our sins, but this time He will come back in total, complete holiness and righteousness, to deliver us and take us to heaven.

JESUS HAS PREEMINENCE

Colossians 1:15-19 says:

He is the image of the invisible God, the firstborn over all creation. For by Him all things were created that are in heaven and that are on earth, visible and invisible, whether thrones or dominions or principalities or powers. All things were created through Him and for Him. And He is before all things, and in Him all things consist.

Jesus is above all things – the heavenly, godly ones and the early, demonic ones, because He defeated them completely. Everything in the universe holds together by virtue of the One who created it, and that's the Lord Jesus, Himself.

And He is the head of the body, the church, who is the beginning, the firstborn from the dead, that in all things He may have the preeminence.

For it pleased the Father that in Him all the fullness should dwell.

Jesus now has the preeminence or the first place.

Praise God! That's what Jesus re-gained between the Cross and the Resurrection.

In Acts 13:30-37, Paul preached a sermon in Antioch that covered the history of the Jews from the days of their slavery in Egypt to the coming of Jesus, the Messiah, and His death and resurrection. In verse 33, Paul quoted from Psalm 2:7, in which God says of Jesus: **"You are My Son, today I have begotten You."** In other words, on this day, God raised Jesus up again into newness of life, justified in the Spirit, alive to God, a living Son, the firstborn of the dead.

A GREAT MYSTERY

First Timothy 3:16 says:

And without controversy great is the mystery of godliness: God was manifested in the flesh, justified in the Spirit, seen by angels, preached among the Gentiles, believed on in the world, received up in glory.

As wild as science fiction movies can get, this is wilder than any movie plot. The Creator of the known universe sends His only Son to save the populace of an entire planet. They kill Him, but He comes back from the dead and saves them anyway. Without controversy, it is a great mystery!

PROOF OF THE GOSPEL

Romans 4:25 says the Lord Jesus was **"delivered up because of our offenses, and was raised because of our justification."** If you think about it carefully, this one verse alone proves, first, that Jesus died for our sins and, second, that we are totally forgiven.

We know Jesus carried our sins, because as the Son of God, Jesus was not subject to death; death had no place in

Him (John 14:30). He didn't die because He was beaten and crucified. He died because our sins were put on Him and separated Him from the Father. It would have been impossible for Him to die, if He had not carried our sins. We know we are forgiven because Jesus could not have been raised from the dead unless our sins were forgiven. If our sins were not forgiven, our sins would continue to separate Jesus from God.

Jesus pointed out a passage from the Old Testament that gives a vivid picture of His death on the Cross as our sin-substitute. In John 3:14, Jesus said, **"And as Moses lifted up the serpent in the wilderness, even so must the Son of Man be lifted up."** This refers to Numbers 21 when the fiery serpents were biting the children of Israel. God told Moses, **"Make a fiery serpent, and set it on a pole"** (vs. 8). Why did God tell him to put a serpent up on a pole? The serpent represented sin. It was made of copper which represented sin being judged.

Jesus said, "I must be lifted up, just like the serpent was lifted in the wilderness," because on the Cross, Jesus became sin for us. That serpent on the pole was like sin on the Cross. Jesus, hanging on the Cross, had all our sin placed on Him. God made Jesus, who knew no sin to become sin for us, that we might become the righteousness of God in Him.

Jesus didn't personally ever commit any sin Himself. He was sinless. He was tempted in all manner like you and I are, yet He never sinned (Hebrews 4:15). But, when He took our sin on Himself, He became sin on the Cross. As Jesus hung on the Cross, He became sinful and was separated from God. He became unacceptable to God, because God can't fellowship with sin. God the Father and God the Holy Spirit had to separate themselves from Him.

The fact that Jesus died physically is proof that our sins were put upon Him. His body was sinless, which meant it was immortal, as death comes because of sin (Romans 5:12; 6:23). Jesus couldn't have died physically if He had not died spiritually first. He would have still been hanging on the Cross two-thousand years later. His body did not die until He took on our sin and was spiritually separated from God.

JESUS' RESURRECTION PROVES WE WERE FORGIVEN

Along these same lines, the fact that it was possible for Jesus to be raised from the dead proves that our sins were forgiven. If our sins were not forgiven, our sins would continue to separate Jesus from God. He would still not be able to enjoy fellowship with the Father and with the Holy Spirit. Jesus could be raised from the dead because He paid the price for the sin. He was raised because He completed the work. He was completely justified in spirit and made us justified as well.

That's good news! If He died for us, He was delivered for our sins; then He was raised because we have now been made just and righteous. Praise God! If He had not completed the work and provided righteousness for every person who would trust Him, God would not have been able to raise Him from the dead.

OUR RIGHTEOUSNESS IS A LEGAL TRUTH

We have been exploring what Jesus did for us on the Cross, looking at it in great detail from many different angles, because it is crucial that we really understand what happened and what this means for our lives. On the Cross, Jesus legally prepared the way for us to be declared righteous forever. Our righteousness is now a legal fact as far as

God is concerned. Our righteousness is not based on our feelings, but on the unchangeable truth of God's Word.

Your born-again spirit man knows God's Word. He knows you have been declared righteous. As you study these truths, a connection will be made between your mind and your spirit. Illumination will come to your mind – which will suddenly be able to agree with what your spirit knew all along: you are the righteousness of God in Christ. An image of righteousness will give you the boldness to be able to walk into the presence of God without having to cower or feel like God's going to condemn you or judge you in any way. More and more, you will begin to have the full assurance and great confidence that God desires to answer your prayers, your supplications, and your requests.

GOD HAS BOUND HIMSELF BY HIS WORD

We have seen that our righteousness is not based on a feeling or an experience, but on legal truth, on God's Word.

Did you know that God has legally bound Himself to His Word? All of God's heavenly creatures – both angelic and demonic – are observing how God handles Himself. He did everything so they could see that He lawfully eradicated sin for those who would receive the work that Jesus provided for us.

Psalm 138:2b says, **"For You have magnified Your word above all Your name."** Knowing this quickly dispels the notion that God is a sovereign God and He doesn't have to honor His Word if He doesn't want to.

There's a Pentecostal denomination whose official position is: "You have no business going to God and asking Him for something in faith." They believe you should ask the Lord, "If it is Your will, please heal me." But you can never know if He will heal you or not, because it just may not be His will for you to be healed. Never mind how many times He has promised us healing in the Bible. They believe God is sovereign above His Word, that no matter what He's promised, He can break His promises any time He wants to.

It's interesting that they do believe God's promises for salvation are guaranteed. Unlike God's promises for healing, provision, and safety, salvation is a "sacred" area. I want to ask them, "If God is sovereign over all of His Word, and He doesn't have to honor any part of what He's said, then why does He have to honor His Word concerning salvation? If God can break His promises, why do you think He has to honor His Word to save you just because you received Jesus as Lord?"

I know they would say, "Oh, no, brother! That's the *only* Word that God has to honor."

Why? It seems to me, it's all or nothing. God either honors every promise, or He has the option of canceling any or all of them.

That's why it is vital to know Psalm 138:2. When God says that He has magnified His Word even above His name, He's saying. "It's all or nothing!" He's saying, "What I've spoken is so important to Me, I exalt it and honor it even above My own holy, righteous name." That's how powerful the Word of God is.

You can receive just a small part of God's Word if you want, or you can receive all of it. Every promise is true and for us today. Psalm 119:89 asserts, **"Forever, O Lord, Your word is settled in heaven."** Jesus said in Matthew 24:35, **"Heaven and earth will pass away, but My words will by no means pass away."** In John 10:35, Jesus said, **"The Scripture cannot be broken."**

The message of faith is so important because it is all about God's Word. Is His Word solid? Is His Word valid? Did He mean what He said when He said it? Is His promise good for all eternity? Absolutely, His Word is perfect. Whatever He said, He honors it. What Jesus legally purchased is really ours – righteousness, healing, and provision as well as eternal life. He did this all legally, according to God's plan. He bound Himself to the plan and He legally fulfilled it all.

A question that often comes up when studying God's flawless plan of redemption for man is this: "If God knew from the beginning that man was going to fall, why did He go to all this trouble to make such an elaborate plan of redemption? Why didn't He just plan that man would never fall?"

God wanted a family who had the ability to love Him and walk with Him by choice, not because we were automatons or robots that He created to worship Him. In order to make us truly family, we had to have the same faculties of being able to decide that He does. We had to have a free will, because He wants us to know Him and desire Him by our own choice.

Because of what Jesus did, each of us can now go from being a lost sinner, separated from God, to being God's child. All Jesus purchased on the Cross is our possession, provided as a free gift. When you receive this free gift, you are as acceptable to God the Father as Jesus Himself. This is the heavenward side of our righteousness.

In the next section, we will look at the earthward side, the impact this truth has on our lives. How do we implement the fullness of what is legally ours? We will see that there are a number of things we can do to release the power that comes with being clothed with the righteousness of Christ.

THE EARTHWARD SIDE OF REDEMPTION: MAKING IT WORK FOR US

We cannot have divine faith and miracles without understanding righteousness. We are approaching the day when we will need to have "radical" faith. Potentially, we could all have ministries very similar to those of the early Church and the Apostles. It takes knowing that we are in the center of God's will, doing exactly what He wants us to do, continually hearing from Him, getting our marching orders every single day. When we are tuned-in, God can show us specific things, without distraction or confusion. What a difference when we see ahead of time what God is doing! That way, we can – like Jesus – do those things that we see the Father do (John 5:19). I look to do one thing really well every single day. It's a delight to see what the Lord will direct us to do.

We discussed just the heavenward side of righteousness, everything that Jesus purchased for us. The earthward side is the *personal application* of what is legally ours because of what Jesus did. In order to receive the full blessings that are legally ours, we need to activate what has been done. This is equivalent to a judge enforcing a law that is on the books. Though the law is totally legal, it's only operative once it's in force.

God set up the legal system of the universe. Part of God's legal system was that judgement has to come and someone has to pay for sin, because sin produces death. But it was not God's intent that man should pay the penalty of death for himself. Even under the Old Covenant, there was always a substitute. Look at Adam and Eve: God covered their sins with animal skins. Throughout the Old

Testament, the sin sacrifices were blood sacrifices. Sin produced death, but man did not have to pay for his own sin.

When Jesus came, His blood did not just cover our sin, it completely removed it from our lives. That same sacrifice redeemed us from all that sin brought with it: sickness, poverty, and death, as well as an image of sinfulness. When we really understand all that God has done, we taste the powers of the world to come (Hebrews 6:5). God superimposes the heavenly realm over our life, like a dome of His protection. Every single covenant promise is "Yes! And so be it!" He is more desirous to see these things fulfilled in our lives than we will ever be to receive them! He wants us to receive everything we need to do what He wants us to do.

ACTIVATING WHAT IS LEGALLY OURS –
STEP ONE: TRANSLATION

Paul wrote several wonderful prayers for the Church, which we can pray over our lives and be greatly blessed. One of these prayers is found in Colossians 1:9-12.

For this reason we also, since the day we heard it, do not cease to pray for you, and to ask that you may be filled with the knowledge of His will in all wisdom and spiritual understanding;

As soon as Paul heard of their faith, He began to pray that they would be filled with the knowledge of God's will. Such knowledge is spiritually challenging. It makes you realize you can't be happy gathering dust, sitting on the pew.

...that you may walk worthy of the Lord, fully pleasing Him, being fruitful in every good work and increasing in the knowledge of God; strengthened with all might, according to His

glorious power, for all patience and longsuffering with joy; giving thanks to the Father who has qualified us to be partakers of the inheritance of the saints in the light.

I once heard a true story that illustrates this point so well. There was an elderly woman who was living in poverty. She had once been a personal attendant of the Queen. She had served the Queen faithfully all of her life, but when the Queen got old and passed away, the new King came in with new servants and new personal attendants. Suddenly, this woman's life-long job as assistant to the Queen was over. Before she died, the Queen had given her servant a beautiful certificate. The servant woman was illiterate, so she couldn't read the certificate, but she treasured it because the Queen had given it to her. She had it framed and hung it on the wall above her bed.

No longer able to live in the Palace, she found a humble place to live. It was old and run-down, but it was all she could afford. She began working again for various other people and continued working until she became ill.

She called for a doctor, who came to her house. While he was attending to her, he noticed the royal certificate on the wall. As he started reading it, he said, "This looks like a real document."

The elderly woman said, "Oh, yes. I used to be a servant to the Queen, and she gave me that personally."

The doctor said, "Do you mind if I take it and have it examined by the courts?"

The woman replied, "Well, you can if you want, but take my word for it, it's official."

The doctor said, "I believe you, but I would like to get a lawyer's opinion on what this means."

The old woman agreed, so the doctor took the certificate to be examined. He came back in several days and announced, "Woman, you have no need to be living in this place of squalor. The Queen took care of all of your needs. It says on this certificate that she has provided a home for you and all the money that you'll ever need for the rest of your life. Everything that you could ever imagine has already been provided for you."

The woman was totally amazed and speechless. She had no knowledge of what was legally hers. As far as she knew, the Queen had given her a beautiful certificate, but being illiterate, she didn't know what it said.

Unfortunately, that's where many Christians are. They're illiterate concerning what God has actually provided for them.

We need to take the Bible off the shelf, find out what's legally ours, and start applying it to our lives. That's what the doctor did for this elderly woman.

Earlier in this chapter, we explored the heavenward truth that we've been translated (transposed, transferred, and removed) from the kingdom of darkness into the kingdom of God's dear Son (Colossians 1:13-14). That's our spiritual position. We've been seated in heavenly places with Christ Jesus (Ephesians 2:6). That truth is in the Word of God – it is legally ours – but we have to become aware of that reality and accept it in our lives.

Basically, we are enforcing God's laws against the devil. We can do this because the devil has been defeated by Jesus – and we know it! The fact is that Jesus provided salvation for all mankind nearly two-thousand years ago on the Cross. Every person born on earth has the opportunity to receive Jesus as Lord. Some wait awhile to seize what has already been purchased for them by the Lord Jesus. I did: I waited twenty-three years to accept Jesus as Lord and receive the salvation that was already legally mine. At any point in time I could have laid hold of that opportunity to be born again.

In the same way, the opportunity is available to every believer to accept the Word of God concerning their position of righteousness. Jesus has purchased righteousness for us. It is already legally ours, but it is up to us to apply the Word concerning our position of righteousness to our own lives.

The heavenward truth of righteousness doesn't do you any good until you say, "I'm going to act like that. I'm going to receive all that this position gives me." God wants to open our eyes, to bring us into a place where we understand what it means to be redeemed, what it means to be translated into His glorious kingdom.

ACTIVATING WHAT IS LEGALLY OURS – STEP TWO: ILLUMINATION

Translation, the first step to activating what is legally ours, is something that happens to us instantly when we confess that Jesus is our Lord. Our spirits are instantly made completely righteous, as righteous as we will ever be.

Illumination, the second step in this process, is not something that happens instantly, but is rather a progressive, divine revelation of righteousness. God wants us to get a constant infusion, a bigger picture every single day of how acceptable He has made us through the work of Jesus. We do not "grow in righteousness" but we do grow in the knowledge of that righteousness.

As we spend time with Jesus, the Word of God, He illuminates us. He *is* light. In John 8:12, Jesus said, "**I am the**

light of the world. He who follows Me shall not walk in darkness, but have the light of life."

In John's gospel we read:

In Him was life, and the life was the light of men. And the light shines in the darkness, and the darkness did not comprehend it. That was the true Light which gives light to every man coming into the world (John 1:4,5,9).

Jesus told His disciples, **"You are the light of the world"** (Matthew 5:14). It's an awesome responsibility to know that the world is totally dependent on the Body of Christ to show them who God is and what He does by being God's only light in the world.

A NEW PERSPECTIVE

As we are illuminated, we begin to see things from a new perspective, one not based on what we see on earth. In Ephesians 1:3 we read:

Blessed be the God and Father of our Lord Jesus Christ, who has blessed us with every spiritual blessing in the heavenly places in Christ.

It was in the heavenly places that Jesus fulfilled everything that was necessary for our redemption. We have seen how He devastated the kingdom of darkness and triumphed over all the power of Satan. Now God wants to bless us with all the spiritual blessings Jesus won for us, even while we are here on earth.

Ephesians 2:6 tells us that God has **"raised us up together, and made us sit together in the heavenly places in Christ Jesus."** We are sitting with Jesus in heavenly places. This was legally purchased for us. It is our lawful, rightful place. That is the perspective we should have. This is "mystery language." It's right there, printed in the Bible, but unless it is illuminated by the Spirit of God, people just read over these words. It doesn't dawn on them what the words mean.

Whenever I hear someone say they are doing "pretty good under the circumstances," I want to ask them, "What are you doing under there?" When we know where we are seated, we know that even the circumstances are under our feet! We must realize that we are already saved, delivered, and healed. We can say, "Keep watching! You will see the manifestation of God's Word upon my life!" We can stand our ground and see these things turn.

IT'S PROGRESSIVE

We get a progressive illumination of this. We see the progressive aspects of this divine revelation in Romans 1:16-17.

> **For I am not ashamed of the gospel of Christ, for it is the power of God to salvation for everyone who believes, for the Jew first and also for the Greek. For in it the righteousness of God is revealed from faith to faith; as it is written, "The just shall live by faith."**

This message of righteousness gets revealed to us **"from faith to faith."** You can't get it all in one sitting. That would be like trying to eat a whole steer in one meal! As you keep meditating on the promises of God, your faith level goes higher. The higher your level of faith, the more you realize righteousness has been imparted to you. You have all of the legal rights that Jesus Christ Himself has. This is only revealed to you "from faith to faith" – it's not something you have a consciousness of on the very first day you are saved. The knowledge of righteousness doesn't come automatically – you have to seek it, you have to strive for it, you have to hunger after the things of God (Matthew 5:6).

Seeking the Lord is so important. The reality is that you weren't born again until you sought after God. He didn't baptize you in the Holy Spirit until you sought after Him. All of these things are accessed by faith. It's the same with all the rest of His covenant promises – you must seek them by faith. Faith must become a life-style: as this verse says, **"The just shall live by faith."**

In Romans 3:21-28, we find a very powerful passage of Scripture:

> **But now the righteousness of God apart from the law is revealed, being witnessed by the Law and the Prophets, even the righteousness of God, through faith in Jesus Christ, to all and on all who believe. For there is no difference;**

> **For all have sinned and fall short of the glory of God, being justified freely by His grace through the redemption that is in Christ Jesus, whom God set forth as a propitiation by His blood, through faith, to demonstrate His righteousness, because in His forbearance God had passed over the sins that were previously committed, to demonstrate at the present time His righteousness, that He might be just and the justifier of the one who has faith in Jesus.**

> **Where is boasting then? It is excluded. By what law? Of works? No, but by the law of faith. Therefore we conclude that a man is justified by**

faith apart from the deeds of the law.

This is righteousness without the works of the Mosaic Law, even thought the Mosaic Law testifies of this righteousness coming. This is what Jesus purchased for us.

This righteousness is given to us – we receive it strictly by faith. We can conclude we are justified by faith without the deeds of the law. We can't earn it – no works would be righteous or holy enough to earn it – but the work that Jesus did was enough and it's given to us as a free gift.

We perceive this gift of righteousness gradually, progressively from faith to faith, as we hunger and thirst for it and seek after God.

ACTIVATING WHAT IS LEGALLY OURS –
STEP THREE: TRANSFORMATION

Transformation, the third step in activating what's legally ours, is also progressive. As we get a progressive illumination from the Scripture of our righteousness, we are progressively more able to walk in it.

Paul made it sound so simple in Romans 12:1-2:

I beseech you therefore, brethren, by the mercies of God, that you present your bodies a living sacrifice, holy, acceptable to God, which is your reasonable service.

Paul said all we have to do is present our body as a living sacrifice. He said it is our reasonable service – the least we can do, seeing that Jesus died for us. You may say, "Wow! I don't know if I want to do that! I want to be saved, but a living sacrifice? That's pretty intense!"

It takes faith. Abraham was able to offer Isaac as a

sacrifice, knowing that God was able to raise Isaac from the dead. In the same way, we know that God will raise up the part of us that needs to be raised up, even as He leaves the other part dead!

And do not be conformed to this world, but be transformed by the renewing of your mind, that you may prove what is that good and acceptable and perfect will of God.

It's hard to tell many Christians apart from the world – they say and do the same things, have the same attitudes and opinions. How do we know how we are supposed to be and what we are supposed to look like?

There is only one way to know. As we immerse ourselves in the Word and are transformed by the renewing of our minds, we begin to think and act like Jesus, who always did the will of the Father. We prove to ourselves that God's will is always good, acceptable and perfect. It is good for you, it is acceptable to Him, and it's perfect before the Father in heaven. There are not three levels of God's will, and there is no such thing as His "permissive" will. You are either in God's will or out of it.

We are transformed by the renewing of our minds. This is how we take what God has put on the inside and bring it to the outside. We can be so conscious of wrong thoughts and actions, of things done in the flesh. But realizing that we are clothed in the robes of righteousness that Jesus has given us causes us to instantly shed that sin every time. We quickly confess our sin to the Father, He forgives us, and we step right back into our place in the Spirit. I don't want to spend a second without my robe of righteousness. It is my protective covering.

Our minds are renewed as we spend time in the

Word. You can never get too much of the Word, because your mind forgets. You might forget tomorrow how blessed you felt today, unless you stir yourself up again in the whole counsel of God's Word. I learn something new every time I study and preach the Word. Our minds have to be continually renewed to the Word of God.

Second Corinthians 3:18 tells us we are **"transformed into the same image from glory to glory, just as by the Spirit of the Lord."** We become increasingly like Jesus by virtue of spending the time in God's Word. The illumination of our righteousness that comes from faith to faith results in us being changed from glory to glory.

You may say, "I wish God would do an instant work in my life and just get me transformed all the way." It can't happen instantly. But we can speed the process along. We have the choice to grow in our understanding – we have the choice to hunger after God's Word and after God's presence.

PUT ON THE NEW MAN – RIGHTEOUS AND HOLY

Ephesians 4:23-24 says:

Be renewed in the spirit of your mind... put on the new man which was created according to God, in true righteousness and holiness.

We have the choice to put on this image of righteousness every single day. As we walk in this understanding of our righteousness, we put on this new creature who is created in Christ Jesus and made absolutely righteous and holy. We are no longer trying to be holy, working hard at obeying a set of rules. Instead we are expressing who we really are inside. We are putting on the new man.

If you don't have the character issues settled and

resolved, you won't be able to keep the faith, prosperity, and healing the Lord showers down on you. Students come to me after our course "Christ-Like Character" and say, "That was the hardest course I ever took in my life because God started cleaning out my closet. It was painful!"

After a few more weeks, they come back and say, "Wow! Now that I am dealing with these issues, the blessings are coming. My faith is really working. I wouldn't trade Christ-like character for anything. The little bit of pain it took to die to myself was worth it." What happened? Jesus became Lord in every area of their life.

We have to give the reins of Lordship to Jesus, die to the old man more and more, and live to the righteousness of God that we have been given. Wow! That's a safe place, that's a holy place. That's where the robes of righteousness start glowing, and we start sensing a tangible anointing on our lives. We begin to rule and reign. God can operate in and through us.

Some may accuse us of being arrogant, but it's not arrogant to understand that God has created us to be righteous and holy – that is what has been imparted to us.

When you walk in righteousness and holiness, people are convicted. Unsaved people may begin to criticize you. You may start receiving persecution for righteousness' sake, because you live a different life than others do. You turn and walk away as soon as a dirty joke is told, so they say, "You know, the problem with you Christians is you think you're holier than everybody else."

The reality is, you *are* holier than everybody else. You've been made holy by the Blood of the Lamb. There's nothing wrong with saying, "I refuse to fellowship with works of unrighteousness and un-holiness." You don't have to. God gives you the power to be able to walk away.

Furthermore, taking a righteous stand doesn't mean that you lose your ability to reach these people. As a matter of fact, it makes them even more curious. I believe it actually increases your ability to reach them. Almost everybody wishes they had the strength to stand up for what they know to be right, but they realize that they cave in to peer pressure all the time. You'd think peer pressure would go away after high school, but it doesn't. It affects some adults all the way through life. They're still comparing themselves to everybody else. They want to "fit in," so they follow the crowd in sinful ways. They disappoint themselves by going against their conscience. When they see someone take a righteous stand, it's like the salmon who is swimming upstream when everybody else is drifting downstream, going with the flow of the world.

They wonder, "How do they do that?" You do it by the power of God. You have put on the image of righteousness. You put on the "new man" created after God, who makes you holy like God. Second Corinthians 5:21 says we are made "the righteousness of God in Him." We receive the fullness of that new nature.

POSITIONED TO LIVE LIKE JESUS

The end result of translation, illumination, and transformation is an ever-increasing awareness or image of righteousness and an ability to receive the fullness of our new nature. We see the heavenly truths change our earthly lives.

We are now positioned to live like Jesus. Romans 6:5-11 tells us:

For if we have been united together in the likeness

of His death, certainly we also shall be in the likeness of His resurrection, knowing this, that our old man was crucified with Him,

You went to the Cross with Jesus two-thousand years ago. God is not bound by space or time. He saw your old man being crucified with Christ.

...that the body of sin might be done away with, that we should no longer be slaves of sin. For he who has died has been freed from sin.

Do you think you will have any more problems with temptation after your funeral? No! Your spirit and soul will go to heaven and await your glorified body. There's nothing earthly or fleshly to be tempted!

Now if we died with Christ, we believe that we shall also live with Him, knowing that Christ, having been raised from the dead, dies no more. Death no longer has dominion over Him.

For the death that He died, He died to sin once for all; but the life that He lives, He lives to God. Likewise you also, reckon yourselves to be dead indeed to sin, but alive to God in Christ Jesus our Lord.

That's what happened. We came alive unto God. We have a direct connection with God. We have His Spirit inside us. We are His kids.

In this passage, Paul is telling believers how we can "check out" of every problem the world may put in our path. His reasoning goes like this: the "old you" (the person who was a sinner) died, and he who is dead is freed from sin. Everyone who is born again is actually dead, so we can't sin anymore. This is some really good news!

Being dead changes everything! For example, when a believer gets offended, you could ask, "Why are you offended?"

They reply, "Don't you know what they did to me?"

"Yeah, but aren't you in Christ?"

"Yeah, so?"

"So then you are dead! You've been crucified with Christ; nevertheless you live, yet not you. It's Christ who lives on the inside of you that's alive."

Dead people don't complain about being taken advantage of, or being left out, or being insulted. In this passage, Paul is telling us the secret of how not to take offense: realize (reckon) that the person who would be offended has died. If you know the date you were born again, you can cite it to the devil! "Hey, that person died. You can't get under my skin. I'm alive unto God!"

Death, hate, fear, sin, offense, self-pity, and mistrust have no more dominion over you. These cannot exercise influence upon or have power over you. You are dead, and a dead man doesn't experience any of these things!

Replacing the old man who died is a whole new person. When the Holy Spirit came into your spirit (the "real you"), a new creation popped into existence. This "you," a person re-created and alive to God, never existed anywhere in space or time before.

2 Corinthians 5:17 says it like this:

Therefore, if anyone is in Christ, he is a new creation; old things have passed away; behold, all things have become new.

Once this is done, it's done. You will never need to

get "born again" again! Remember when Jesus was washing the disciples' feet (John 13:5-11)? Peter said, "Lord, you shall never wash my feet."

Jesus replied, "If I don't wash you, you will have no part with Me."

Peter said, "Then wash all of me."

But Jesus said, "No, Peter, you are already clean." Jesus knew that Peter believed in Him. Jesus knew the end from the beginning. He already knew that Peter was going to make it because of the Word that Jesus had spoken (John 15:3). Jesus said, "A person who has had a bath needs only to wash his feet."

As believers, we get defiled going through the dirt of the day. Stuff tries to get on us, and we need to wash our feet. But we have "had a bath" – we've been made clean by the Blood of the Lamb. Once it's done, it's done. We now walk as a new creation. We walk "in Christ."

Our faith is restored – on an all-new level. We know that **"faith comes by hearing, and hearing by the word of God"** (Romans 10:17). Suddenly you hear and understand the Word of God in a whole new way, and your faith begins to function full force. You are believing for things that used to seem impossible – now you see that God wants to do them for you. You are seeing the miraculous. You enter into a upward spiral of ever-increasing faith! The more you believe, the more you pray, the more you see God move, the more you believe, the more you pray.

When you spiritually hear any part of the Word, the faith is there, and you start receiving it. You start receiving *all* the Covenant promises.

I didn't understand this in my first years of ministry. I was driving back from a ministry trip with some friends and had a head-on collision. The devil tried to kill us – and almost did. A truck came at us, sliding in the rain at forty miles an hour. We were also going forty miles an hour, so the impact was like hitting a brick wall at eighty miles per hour. The angels intervened, and slid the truck off to the side, or it would have taken the top of the car off. As it was, we hit the trailer. I heard this horrible crunch. My face bent the steering wheel flat. We were all injured: we still bear the scars.

Back then I didn't understand Psalm 91. Since that time, I have heard Brother Hagin teach on it, and have dug through it myself. I could teach for weeks on all the nuggets I have found in that psalm! I walked out of that season of meditation saying, "Praise God, He has shown me how to shut the door on the devil. Now that I understand the Covenant promises, I know that is the last time I will be in an accident."

As a Psalm 91 believer, don't get under condemnation and think your faith isn't working if you have a "fender bender." Your car might have been in an accident, but you weren't! No, your faith is working. Satan has a plan to take you out. You are dangerous to his kingdom. If he hasn't been able to take you out, your faith is real, and you can increase it every single day.

POSITIONED TO RECEIVE THE MIRACULOUS

When we become conscious of our position of righteousness with God, we find, right away, that our prayers "avail much." James 5:16b, from the Amplified says, **"The earnest (heartfelt, continuous) prayer of a righteous man makes tremendous power available [dynamic in its working]."** That's good news! Since you've been made the righteousness of God in Christ Jesus, you don't have to try to become righteous to be a person of effectual prayer. You are that righteous man or woman. According to James, if we, the righteous, are diligent and offer up "earnest, heartfelt, continuous prayer," then tremendous power becomes available to us, power that is dynamic in its working. That kind of prayer is going to produce results!

Brother Hagin tells how this verse of Scripture gave him hope: "I decided if I could only become righteous, I could be healed of a deformed heart, incurable blood disease, and almost total paralysis." Then God led him to the realization that he had already been made the righteousness of God in Christ Jesus. He said, "I get it! Now I believe I receive my healing." He received an understanding of righteousness and was healed. He walked in that healing and lived to be eighty-six years old.

We are no longer begging God to do something. As His covenant partners here on earth, we are speaking His infallible Word over situations, praying – both in the Holy Spirit and with our understanding – as He gives us the words. We are declaring the will of God on earth, just as Jesus instructed us to do: "Your kingdom come, Your will be done on earth as it is in heaven." And when we pray according to His Word, He hears us. First John 5:14 and 15 tells us:

Now this is the confidence that we have in Him, that if we ask anything according to His will, He hears us. And if we know that He hears us, whatever we ask, we know that we have the petitions that we have asked of Him.

The Lord is teaching you how to pray prayers that will be answered – because He longs to intervene in the affairs of men, to stop the suffering caused by sin. He wants us to ask Him for things that are impossible with man! In fact, you will begin to see, more and more, how carefully He has worked, generation after generation, through His prophets and finally His own Son to establish His covenant on the earth - so He can answer your prayers!

You realize you have a position with God. You are not a worm, a sinner saved by grace. You were a sinner, now grace has totally transformed you into a son of God, righteous before Him, a partner with Him in His efforts to subdue the earth. God has proven to you that He is faithful, just as He did with Abraham. He has convinced you that He is on your side and wants to answer your prayers.

People who aren't saved don't bother to go to God with their problems. Every now and then, when truly desperate, they may cry out, "God! Help me!" It's their very first prayer - and God answers and actually saves them out of their situation. Usually they make some sort of deal with God: "God, if You get me out of this one, I'll serve You. I'll go to church every Sunday for the rest of my life!" Some people forget their end of the deal once the crisis is over, but others follow through and actually get saved.

POSITIONED FOR DEEP AND ABIDING PEACE

Another benefit of becoming aware of our righteousness is experiencing the peace of God. Isaiah 57:21 says, **"There is no peace," says my God, "for the wicked."** In contrast, Romans 5:1 says, **"Therefore, having been justified by faith, we have peace with God through our Lord Jesus Christ."**

You cannot buy peace with God, and there is no greater possession you can have in this life than the peace with God that comes from receiving this gift of righteousness. It is not a result of your own efforts. An image of sinfulness will cause you to keep trying to earn your way to God. So many people think there is a balance sheet kept in heaven. They will say things like: "I'm just hoping I've done enough good things to outweigh the bad things I did so St. Peter will let me in the pearly gates." This is total ignorance of all that has already been purchased for us.

Peace was something I noticed immediately the day I was born again. The struggle with God in heaven was over. Before Jesus became my Lord, God seemed to be this "cosmic force" that you couldn't really understand. To me, God was kind of like electricity: He could "zap" you at any time if you just tried to touch Him. I pictured Him up there waiting for me to mess up – then He would swat me with a giant heavenly fly swatter.

Then I found out that He wasn't mad at me, that He'd been seeking after me all along, that He loved me, that He sent His own Son for me. One day God told me, "Son, if you were the only person on the planet, I still would have sent My Son for you. I love you with that kind of undying love." I felt like God had picked me up and dipped me in a vat of living love. Now I knew peace – no more struggle trying to earn anything. I found out there was no God to fear.

When you were first born again, you probably experienced the weight of sin being rolled off of your life. Unfortunately, many who have been Christians for awhile have allowed these weights and sins to come back and entangle them once again (Hebrews 12:1). They feel sinful, condemned, and unworthy. They are listening to the lies of Satan, "the accuser of the brethren" (Revelation 12:10).

An image of righteousness helps you see yourself as

God sees you and your peace with God is restored. Romans 8:1 says, **"There is therefore now no condemnation to those who are in Christ Jesus."** You realize that the promises of God are not based on your ability to perfectly obey the rules of God, but on Jesus' perfect life. You now qualify for all the promises for protection and provision. As Psalm 91:10 says, **"No evil shall befall you."** There is no need to worry anymore! You can go to sleep at night and rest assured that you are safe in the hands of God, and that's a wonderful position. Nobody sleeps as well as Christians who know their place in God.

We can have the peace of God which passes understanding (Philippians 4:7). Talk about Holy Ghost stress management! You can start worshiping the Lord in that secret place, abiding under the shadow of the Almighty. You know that He looks at you with absolute love, thinking only love thoughts about you.

God did everything He could to give us a right relationship through Jesus Christ. This is not complicated. It is not a hidden mystery. It can be found by every single believer. It's what God plainly wants each of us to know. It is a very precious thing to have peace with God!

Holiness is simply walking in this righteousness. We've been made righteous. That's how God sees us. All we have to do is walk out what He's made us to be. It's not like a fish out of water: it's like a fish finally back in the water! We spend our whole lives out flopping around on the hard ground and the rocks, when we were designed by God to be swimming in the river. He puts us back in the water, saying, "This is how I created you to be. Just walk in the full awareness of your righteousness."

Some ask, "What do I do with my 'bad habits'?"

Don't just try to get rid of your "bad habits" - replace them with a good "Word habit." Add the Lord and the Word to your life in that area and you will find things dropping off of you. You'll say things like "Wow! I forgot to be addicted to cigarettes today!" You start developing the habits of practicing the presence of God. You introduce an image of righteousness, and the image of sinfulness goes away. I like what faith does in people. It makes them bold! Their stance becomes "God's plan is this. We'll settle for nothing else!"

The world that God created is begging for us to cause it to line up with His plan. It was created to be put under the dominion of faith people. We're just moving into our place, acting like God's kids.

POSITIONED TO RULE AND REIGN

We now have dominion in life. Romans 5:17 says, **"Much more those who receive abundance of grace and of the gift of righteousness will reign in life through the One, Jesus Christ."** We now reign in life by Him. We rule and reign over the circumstances, over the devil, over demon spirits.

People without the revelation of righteousness say, "Be careful now, brother. You don't want to make the devil mad!" No, we don't tiptoe around the devil anymore. Jesus didn't! And He has given us His authority (Matthew 28:18, Mark 16:15-18, Luke 10:17). We don't let demons have their way in our lives. They're not going to run roughshod over us; they're not going to steamroll us in any way. We're going to continue to stand steadfast and have victory over them.

AS HE IS, SO ARE WE –
IDENTIFICATION WITH JESUS

Our identification is now with Jesus. First John 4:17 says, **"Love has been perfected among us in this: that we may have boldness in the day of judgment; because as He is, so are we in this world."**

Jesus is totally victorious today. He has dominion over everything in life; He's the Ruler of the Universe. And as He is today, in His position of authority, so are we in this world. In the sphere of influence that God has given you – the people and things that you are responsible for – you have the same kind of dominion and authority that Jesus has over the entire universe. As He is, so are we in this world.

See yourself exercising faith the way Jesus exercises faith from heaven. Intercede for others the way Jesus ever lives to make intercession for you. It doesn't have anything to do with us: we can't produce it. It has everything to do with Jesus – and we just receive in His name. We say, "Jesus is my Lord. And I receive every single day, more and more understanding of the position that You, Father God, have given me in Christ Jesus."

POSITIONED FOR NEVER-ENDING FELLOWSHIP

When we are aware of our righteousness and of the indwelling Holy Spirit, we are positioned for never-ending fellowship with God and with Jesus. First John 1:1-4 says:

That which was from the beginning, which we have heard, which we have seen with our eyes, which we have looked upon, and our hands have handled, concerning the Word of life – the life was manifested, and we have seen, and bear

**witness, and declare to you that eternal life
which was with the Father and was manifested
to us.**

The life of God was manifested to the Apostles when
Jesus came.

**That which we have seen and heard we declare
to you.**

Aren't you glad that we have their declaration, their
witness? Aren't you glad they wrote these things down, so
we could have them two-thousand years later?

**...that you also may have fellowship with us; and
truly our fellowship is with the Father and with
His Son Jesus Christ.**

When we have fellowship with the Father and the
Son, we're also having fellowship with the early saints.

**And these things we write to you that your joy
may be full.**

The Lord made this scripture come alive to me in an
experience I had while I was a student at Rhema Bible
Training Center. During that time, I went to Healing
School every day and sat under Brother Hagin's ministry.
He only directed Healing School for three years and I had
the opportunity to attend for two of those years. There,
Brother Hagin would demonstrate everything he was
teaching us in our classes. It was awesome. Every single
week, there was a move of the Spirit of God in healing
school. I would sit on the front row and soak it up like a
sponge.

One day Brother Hagin came to the service and said, "I
feel impressed of the Lord that we should just pray today."

So we all turned around and knelt down at our chairs and began to pray. My knees had just touched the floor when suddenly I was in a trance.

A trance is a spiritual vision on a high level where your senses are actually suspended. You're not conscious of your physical body – you're caught up in the realm of the Spirit into another place.

The place in the Spirit I experienced while in this trance was so much more real to me than natural, every-day reality. I was in a place very much like the apartment I lived in while at Rhema. I heard a knock at the door. When I opened the door, there stood Jesus. I saw His robes and His hands and His feet, but I couldn't see His face for the Shekinah glory. His face was radiant with a bright-white light – so bright, I couldn't even look up at it.

As I looked, I saw He had an envelope in His hand. He held the envelope out to me.

I asked, "What is this?"

He said, "It's a love letter from the Father."

I took it and opened it. As I began to read, my heart melted and I began weeping. (Later, after the trance was over, I discovered that the seat of the metal folding chair where I'd been kneeling was completely covered with tears. I had obviously wept through the whole trance.)

This letter from the Father said, "Son, I love you with an undying love; if you had been the only person on the planet, I still would have sent Jesus to die just for you."

As I stood there overwhelmed, all of a sudden the vision repeated itself. There was another knock at the door. I opened the door again, and there stood Jesus. He had an envelope in His hand, and I took it from Him. I opened it up and there was another letter from the Father.

As I continued to read, more words of grace poured out into my heart.

Then, it happened a third time: there was a third knock at the door, I opened it up, and there stood Jesus again.

It was probably fifteen years after I had this trance that it finally dawned on me that when Peter fell into a trance in Acts 10:9-16, his vision was repeated three times as well. I thought, "Peter and I must be really slow learners. It takes a lot of repetition to show us something. But, then again, Peter is good company to be in!"

The third time, Jesus didn't have a letter in His hand. Instead, He said, "Are you ready to go?"

I asked, "To go where?"

He said, "Let's go see the Father."

The next thing I know, we're in the throne room of God. I saw these stone walls with gold shields leaning up against them. (I hadn't seen this in Scripture before that time, but in 1 Kings 10:17, Solomon had three-hundred shields of gold made and placed them in the palace in the forest of Lebanon.)

Then Jesus led me to a table, and I sat down. The table ended just a few feet to the right of me. I didn't even look in the other direction, but I knew it just kept on going into eternity. There was no end to this table.

Have you ever seen that painting of the Marriage Supper of the Lamb with the beautifully-set table that goes on forever? I knew this table looked like that.

Jesus sat Himself across the table from me, and then I looked to the right and, all of a sudden, I saw God the Father's hands on the table. As with Jesus, I couldn't see God's face because of the glow of the Shekinah glory, but I could see both of their hands.

It was then that I noticed for the first time the nail scars in the wrists of Jesus. When we get to heaven, we're all going to have glorified bodies that don't have any marks on them. Jesus will be the only person in heaven who is scarred – He'll always bear in His body those marks that have paid for our eternity.

I was there, overwhelmed at being in the presence of Jesus, My Lord, and God the Father. I was in such unfamiliar territory that it was hard for to me to address God the Father. When I was finally able to speak, I began to express my heart to Him, saying, "Father, it's just such an honor to be here in Your presence with my Lord and Savior, Jesus." I couldn't go on – I was overwhelmed once again, realizing who He was and the price He had paid for me.

Suddenly, I realized that I didn't see the Holy Spirit anywhere. I asked, "Father, I see You, and I see Jesus, but where's the Holy Spirit?"

What He answered changed my life forever.

I saw His finger point right to my belly. He said, "Why, He's right there in you."

Suddenly, I got it.

When you get to heaven you're not going to see the Holy Spirit; He's in you. He's a person, but He dwells on the inside of each believer. Through Him, we have this deep, deep communion with the Father and with the Son. They don't break fellowship – They are always in communion. As long as we stay in fellowship with the Holy Spirit inside us, we are drawn right up to the table, to be seated with the Father and with the Son and share in Their communion.

My life was changed from then on. I walked around with an understanding that I could talk with the Holy Spirit. I prayed to the Father in Jesus' name, I talked to the

Lord Jesus, but I also looked down at my belly and talked with the Holy Spirit.

You may ask, "Are we instructed to talk to the Holy Spirit?"

Well, we know that the Holy Spirit is just as much God as the Father is and Jesus is. Yes, we can talk to the Holy Spirit. And since He dwells in us, He is closer than the other two. I suggest we talk to Him often!

Many people use the word "intimacy" to describe this deep relationship we have with God. I wish we had a better word to describe it that would make people less uncomfortable. As earthly humans, we use the word "intimacy" in a sexual sense, as when a husband and wife are being intimate. But when we talk about being intimate with God, we're talking about God having more knowledge of us and us having more knowledge of God than we do of any other person.

We need the right word to talk to men about being close with God and familiar with Him. "Intimate" is a good word, but sometimes our earthly senses get us off track and we miss the purpose that God's trying to achieve.

"Communion" is the word God uses to describe the place we have with Him - where we know God and we know that we are known by Him; where we have a fellowship with Him that is just so tight that we realize that we're not going to be strangers when we get to heaven.

As you grow in familiarity with God and with the Lord Jesus and with the presence of the Holy Spirit, God is going to reveal so much about His kingdom to you while you're on the earth that you're not going to be a stranger when you get to heaven. You will feel like family. You will feel right at home. You are not going to be blown away by everything.

This "feeling of family" is what Jesus purchased for us. This is the earthward side of this relationship, the earthward side of redemption. When we are free from an image of sinfulness, we can come into God's presence like family. We realize that we have a place at our Father's table. We have the blessing of heaven resting upon our lives. The Lord wants to draw us up into a knowledge of that place because that's the place where our faith works, that's the place where we have total confidence and boldness in this life.

MAKING HEAVENLY TRUTH REAL IN OUR LIVES

There is no denying that these heavenly truths are in the Word of God. Some say that they are not for us today. Some say they were only for the early Church. Others say they are only for heaven. I say, "I'm sorry, but you are too late to convince me that faith does not work. I have experienced too many miracles!"

The world may call this radical faith. But Jesus calls it "getting-the-job-done" faith. If you want to get the job done, you have to walk in this kind of faith, which is produced by an understanding that we have been made the very righteousness of God in Christ Jesus.

CHAPTER TWELVE

WHY CHRISTIANS SUFFER NEEDLESSLY

WHEN STUDYING FAITH, questions often arise, such as "Why do Christians suffer?" and "Can faith overcome suffering?"

It's important for us to understand that there are certain things that we *will* suffer as believers. We are actually told in the Word of God that we are going to suffer for a variety of reasons. We will explore these at the end of this chapter. But first, let's take a look at fifteen reasons why Christians suffer needlessly.

REASON #1: LACK OF KNOWLEDGE

The first reason why Christians suffer needlessly is they have little knowledge of the truth of the Word of God. Hosea 4:6 says, **"My people are destroyed for lack of knowledge."** An old saying says, "Ignorance is bliss," but exactly the opposite is true. Ignorance can be destruction. You can be destroyed through lack of knowledge. The reality is that God has provided so much for us, but when people don't know all that's been provided, they can't take advantage of it.

People don't know the seriousness of the Gospel. It is literally a matter of life and death.

We can see that ignorance brings destruction very clearly in the area of salvation. First Timothy 2:4 says God wants all people to be saved and to come to the knowledge of the truth. Yet because of their ignorance of who Jesus really was and who He really is today, many people will burn in hell for eternity. Because the vast majority of people are not saved, is this an indication that it's not God's will for people to be saved? No! The Bible makes it very plain that God wants everybody saved, yet many never come to a knowledge of the truth. In the same way, it is God's will for everyone to walk in health, provision, safety, and peace. The fact that the vast majority of people are not walking in all that Jesus has provided for them does not change God's provision. Their ignorance keeps them from receiving God's perfect will.

Knowledge of the Father and the Son changes everything. Second Peter 1:2-3 says:

Grace and peace be multiplied to you in the knowledge of God and of Jesus our Lord, as His divine power has given to us all things that pertain to life and godliness, through the knowledge of Him who called us by glory and virtue.

All of these things – grace and peace and all things that pertain to life and godliness – are going to be available to us through knowledge of God's Word. You've heard the phrase, "Knowledge is power." In no place is this more true than in the Christian faith. Knowledge – truly and literally – is power for you.

Knowledge of God's Word helps us wake up and stop

sinning. First Corinthians 15:34 says, **"Awake to right-eousness, and do not sin; for some do not have the knowl-edge of God."** The ability to put sin out of your life comes through knowledge. Great deliverance from the opposi-tion of the devil comes through knowledge of God's Word. Proverbs 11:9 says, **"Through knowledge the righteous will be delivered."**

In fact, if we were to do a "Top Ten List," this is what would go at the top of the list. "Lack of knowledge" is the #1 reason why people suffer needlessly. The world is cer-tainly going to suffer, because of their lack of knowledge, but even born-again Christians severely lack this knowl-edge because, unfortunately, these truths are not taught in many places where Christians gather.

REASON #2: FAILURE TO ACT UPON WHAT THEY DO KNOW

The second reason Christians suffer needlessly is they don't act upon the Word that they do know. You could have some knowledge but not act on it and get the same, negative results as someone who did not know. In Matthew 7:24, Jesus said:

"Whoever hears these sayings of Mine, and does them, I will liken him to a wise man who built his house on the rock: and the rain descended, the floods came, and the winds blew and beat on that house; and it did not fall, for it was founded on the rock."

James 1:21-25 says:

Therefore lay aside all filthiness and overflow of wickedness, and receive with meekness the implanted word, which is able to save your souls.

But be doers of the word, and not hearers only, deceiving yourselves.

For if anyone is a hearer of the word and not a doer, he is like a man observing his natural face in a mirror; for he observes himself, goes away, and immediately forgets what kind of man he was.

But he who looks into the perfect law of liberty and continues in it, and is not a forgetful hearer but a doer of the work, this one will be blessed in what he does.

If you hear the Word, you're responsible for it. If you do it, you'll be blessed. If you don't do it, then you are deceiving your own self. The Greek word for "deceiving" here is *paralogizomai,* which means "to reckon wrong, miscount, to cheat by false reckoning, to deceive by false reasoning." You have taken the Word of God (the *logos*) but miscounted it, figured it wrong, and cheated yourself! James says you will soon forget what you heard. This puts you in the same vulnerable position as those who have never heard - with a house built on the sand.

People have told those of us who teach the Word, "You teachers are going to be held by a higher standard. You are very accountable. The Bible says that not many people should desire to be teachers" (James 3:1).

It is true that a teacher is going to be held more accountable. If you're going to stand up and proclaim these truths and say, "This is how the kingdom of heaven works, and this is how I'm working within the kingdom of heaven," people expect you to live what you preach, to walk the walk after you talk the talk.

But the reality is that *everybody* who hears the

teacher is accountable for what the teacher has taught, because as soon as we teach it, the listeners also have knowledge of that Word. If it is the Truth, we're all accountable for it.

REASON #3: OPPOSITION TO THE TRUTH

The third reason Christians suffer needlessly is opposition or open rebellion to the truth. Second Timothy 2:24-26 KJV says:

And the servant of the Lord must not strive; but be gentle unto all men, apt to teach, patient, in meekness instructing those that oppose themselves; if God peradventure will give them repentance to the acknowledging of the truth and that they may recover themselves out of the snare of the devil, who are taken captive by him at his will.

You've heard the saying, "You are your own worst enemy." People who oppose truth actually oppose themselves. They don't realize what they're doing, but they are destroyed for lack of knowledge. The knowledge was available, but they rejected it.

Uninformed believers are without excuse, even if these truths are not proclaimed in most churches. Such knowledge is available to people in books and on Christian radio and television. Christian satellite networks make it available twenty-four hours a day. Granted, there's a lot of "fluff" and error you have to search through to find solid teaching and preaching, but there's enough out there for people to get the necessary knowledge and apply it to their lives.

This scripture says that it's necessary for God to give some people "repentance to the acknowledging of the truth." Some Christians are always resistant to any new truths they hear.

When you hear a scripture taught in a way you have never heard before, you have a choice. You can immediately reject it as "radical," or you can examine it and meditate on it. You should not automatically accept every doctrine that is new to you. Be like the Bereans, who **"received the word with all readiness, and searched the Scriptures daily to find out whether these things were so"** (Acts 17:11). This is how the Holy Spirit teaches: He compares scripture with scripture, spiritual things with spiritual things (1 Corinthians 2:13).

The end of those who oppose themselves and don't acknowledge the truth is they find themselves in the snare of the devil, they are taken captive by him at his will. They suffer!

REASON #4: REBELLION AGAINST AUTHORITY

The fourth reason Christians suffer needlessly is rebellion against authority. Numbers 16:1-7 and 19-33 tell of the rebellion against Moses and Aaron and the price the rebels paid. The ground split underneath them and the earth swallowed them up. The rebels and their wives and their little children went down alive into the pit, along with everything they owned. Then the earth closed upon them. What a vivid picture! Unfortunately, when someone is in rebellion against authority, it affects their whole family.

You can't rebel against authority. First Timothy 2:1-2 instructs us as believers to first of all pray – with supplication, intercession and giving of thanks – for all those in authority. I believe this is two-part. We pray for those in governmental authority in the natural realm, but also for those in authority over us in the spiritual realm. To me, the spiritual realm is first and foremost.

I pray for the people I consider in authority over my life: my pastor as well as those who have been given apostolic and prophetic authority within the Church. God has specifically given some ministers a broad-based voice to deliver His Word to His Church. We need to pay attention to what they're saying. These ministers have an international platform – often on television. Of course, not everyone on television is preaching the full truth of the Gospel in an accurate way, so use discernment.

We need to pray regularly for those who we know are preaching the Word. I used to pray regularly for Kenneth Hagin. He's gone on to be with the Lord, so he doesn't need my prayers anymore – that's for sure! But I still pray for Kenneth and Gloria Copeland and Joyce Meyer and others who are preaching solid truth. I pray that God would cause their ministries to flourish, that they'll touch more lives, and more people would be established in the things of God because of what they're teaching and preaching.

After we pray for the spiritual leaders in the Church, we pray for the governmental leaders in the natural realm. We absolutely have to be praying for our president; we have to be praying for the governors of the states; for the senators and congressmen; all the way down to anyone with the least bit of authority in our lives. Don't you want to pray for those who teach your kids in the classroom? School teachers need to encourage the children to live uprightly before the Lord. They should demonstrate the things of God. Everybody in a position of authority needs our prayer.

We should pray for and honor our leaders. Open rebellion to any godly leader will produce negative consequences in our lives. (This doesn't mean that we have to agree with - or go along with - secular, ungodly leaders. It means that we pray for their salvation, that God would send spiritual laborers into the harvest to bring them salvation. If they refuse, then our prayer is that they be removed from office and replaced with godly leaders.)

REASON #5: LIVING IN SIN

The fifth reason Christians suffer needlessly is because they are living in sin. Proverbs 13:15 KJV says, **"The way of transgressors is hard."** You can't get a good harvest from a bad seed, and sin is a bad seed.

In Galatians 5:19-21, Paul gives us a long list of the sins of the flesh, such as adultery, fornication, uncleanness, lewdness, idolatry, sorcery, hatred, contentions, jealousies, envy, murders, drunkenness, and revelries. He concludes with the warning, **"those who practice such things will not inherit the kingdom of God."**

There is a difference between going to heaven after you die and inheriting the kingdom of God. People who don't understand the difference have said, "You can't go to heaven if you sin any one of these sins."

But remember, Paul is addressing Christians here. When he lists all of these things that we can easily identify as sins, he's saying, "Obviously, if you're born again, you qualify to go to heaven, but if you do these things, you can't possibly expect to receive your full inheritance. If you neglect to walk uprightly before the Lord, you're not going to inherit all that God has for you to inherit on this earth. You can't expect the blessing of God to come upon you if you are living in sin."

Galatians 6:7-9 tells us that sowing to the flesh is going to result in reaping a harvest of corruption or destruction.

Do not be deceived, God is not mocked; for whatever a man sows, that he will also reap.

For he who sows to his flesh will of the flesh reap corruption, but he who sows to the Spirit will of the Spirit reap everlasting life. And let us not grow weary while doing good, for in due season we shall reap if we do not lose heart.

In James 5:14-15, we have instructions on one of the ways that God heals people – through the laying on of hands, and anointing with oil. James says:

Is anyone among you sick? Let him call for the elders of the church, and let them pray over him, anointing him with oil in the name of the Lord. And the prayer of faith will save the sick, and the Lord will raise him up. And if he has committed sins, he will be forgiven.

As the elders lay hands on believers and anoint them with oil, bodies will be healed and sins forgiven. Of course, not every sickness is a result of sin, but if your sickness is a result of sin, and you've called for prayer, after you get everything right before God, then not only will you be healed, but your sins will be forgiven as well.

REASON #6: NOT DISCERNING THE BODY OF CHRIST

The next reason Christians suffer needlessly is they don't discern the Body of Christ. First Corinthians 11:17-32 is a familiar passage of Scripture which is often read in communion services. If you study it carefully, you'll see that Paul was writing about divisions in the Body of Christ in Corinth. Believers weren't honoring one another and the result was weakness, sickness, and early death:

> **For he who eats and drinks in an unworthy manner eats and drinks judgment to himself, not discerning the Lord's body. For this reason many are weak and sick among you, and many sleep (1 Corinthians 11:29-30).**

Paul said many people actually die early because they're not discerning the Lord's Body – they're eating and drinking unworthily.

I noticed when I was serving as a pastor that some people did not take communion. I'd ask them afterwards, and they'd say, "I don't want to bring damnation on myself, because I'd be eating unworthily." Then they'd start describing some sin in their life. They were afraid that the grape juice and wafer would cause sudden death. That's superstition!

That's not what Paul was talking about in this passage. He was addressing Corinthian church services where some of the wealthy people acted ostentatiously and brought excessive amounts of food for themselves. They were eating gluttonously, and they were drinking and getting drunk. Other believers who didn't have much were ashamed to eat their scant meal next to such an excessive display. Paul says they weren't honoring one another. He asked, "Don't you have homes to eat and drink in? But honor one another and tarry one for another when you come together." In other words, "Look out for one another and share."

When Paul spoke of not discerning the Lord's Body, he was saying that all of us are members of the Body of Christ. It's damning to ourselves to treat members of the Body of Christ poorly and without respect and honor. We must consider all Christians equal and worthy of reverence and be like-minded in blessing them. To do otherwise is a sin against the Church, which is Christ's Body here on the earth.

REASON #7: UNFORGIVENESS

Matthew 18:32-33 tells the parable about the servant who was forgiven a tremendous debt, but would not forgive his fellow servant for a very small debt. The unforgiving servant was called before his master because he wouldn't extend to somebody else what had just been extended to him.

His master was angry and said:

"You wicked servant! I forgave you all that debt because you begged me. Should you not also have had compassion on your fellow servant, just as I had pity on you?"

His master then delivered him to the tormentors, until he should pay all that was due. Jesus concludes His teaching, telling His disciples in verse 35, **"So My heavenly Father also will do to you if each of you, from his heart, does not forgive his brother his trespasses."**

Being delivered to the tormentors sounds like serious suffering!

In Mark 11:25, right after His well-known teaching on faith, Jesus said, **"If you have anything against anyone, forgive him."** Basically, Jesus is saying if you don't forgive, your faith won't work, because faith and forgiveness are tied together. You can't walk in offense and unforgiveness and expect your faith to work. You can't afford to take offense – it ruins your faith.

We've got to be free of all these things or we will suffer needlessly.

REASON #8: ENVY AND STRIFE

James writes in James 3:13-18:

Who is wise and understanding among you? Let him show by good conduct that his works are done in the meekness of wisdom. But if you have bitter envy and self-seeking in your hearts, do not boast and lie against the truth. This wisdom does not descend from above, but is earthly, sensual, demonic.

For where envy and self-seeking exist, confusion and every evil thing are there.

But the wisdom that is from above is first pure, then peaceable, gentle, willing to yield, full of mercy and good fruits, without partiality and without hypocrisy.

Now the fruit of righteousness is sown in peace by those who make peace.

Envy and strife are all earthly, sensual, and demonic wisdom. We've got to be free of those things that produce division in the Body of Christ.

REASON #9: LUSTING AFTER EVIL THINGS

In 1 Corinthians 10, Paul points out mistakes the Israelites made in the wilderness and identifies a number of different traps that can result in needless suffering. In verses 5 and 6 we read:

But with most of them God was not well pleased, for their bodies were scattered in the wilderness. Now these things became our examples, to the intent that we should not lust after evil things as they also lusted.

In addition to the list of the sins of the flesh given under Reason #5, we could add lusting after anything that does not bring glory to God.

REASON #10: IDOLATRY

A number of things not to do are identified in the verses that follow. First Corinthians 10:7 says, **"And do not become idolaters as were some of them. As it is written, 'The people sat down to eat and drink, and rose up to play.'"** This is a quote from Exodus 32:6, in reference to the time when the Israelites created the golden calf and worshiped it while Moses was up on the mountain receiving the Ten Commandments.

Few people in modern times would be tempted to worship a golden calf, but there are still many people with idols in their lives. Today, an idol could be anything you put before the Lord. It could be your career, your possessions, your "fun." If getting out on the golf course on a Sunday morning is more important than going to church, then suddenly, that's an idol; it's a false God. Paul is warning us against these things, because in the end, they will cause suffering.

REASON #11: FORNICATION AND SEX SINS

In 1 Corinthians 10:8, Paul writes, **"Nor let us commit**

sexual immorality, as some of them did, and in one day twenty-three thousand fell." This refers to the story found in Numbers 25:1-8, where the people committed whoredom with the daughters of Moab. They also sacrificed to false gods, and it brought a plague on them, which killed twenty-three thousand people. Fornication is a negative seed and they reaped a negative harvest. Fornication and sexual sins have far-reaching consequences, bringing suffering to families for generations to come. You don't have to look far to find horror stories from sexually transmitted diseases, especially HIV and AIDS. And the high cost of infidelity has destroyed marriages and families.

REASON #12: TEMPTING CHRIST

First Corinthians 10:9 says, "**Nor let us tempt Christ, as some of them also tempted, and were destroyed by serpents.**" Exodus 17 tells of how the Israelites tempted the Lord in the desert, and how Moses struck the rock with his staff and the water poured out. Verse 7 says, "**And he [Moses] called the name of the place Massah and Meribah, because of the contention of the children of Israel, and because they tempted the Lord, saying, "Is the Lord among us or not?"**

In Numbers 21:5-9, the people continued to speak against God and Moses, saying, "**Why have you brought us up out of Egypt to die in the wilderness?**" They were given manna and water supernaturally, yet instead of being grateful, they said, "**Our soul loathes** [abhors and despises] **this worthless** [miserable, contemptible, unsubstantial] **bread.**"

The complainers were bitten by fiery serpents, and many of them died. Remember, Paul said these stories were given to us as examples. He puts these two stories together, saying God's chosen people were bitten by the serpents because they continued to doubt that God was among them, even though He was working miracles on their behalf. If we don't revere what Christ has done for us, if we don't acknowledge those things with gratitude, the Bible calls it "tempting the Lord" and "tempting Christ."

REASON #13: MURMURING AND COMPLAINING

Paul's "Not To Do List" continues in 1 Corinthians 10:10 – **"Nor complain, as some of them also complained, and were destroyed by the destroyer."** The Old Testament is filled with stories of the Israelites murmuring and complaining. Often they complained to Moses, but Moses understood that the complaint was really against God. In Exodus 16:8, Moses told the people, **"The Lord hears your complaints which you make against Him. And what are we? Your complaints are not against us but against the Lord."**

Perhaps the most amazing story of murmuring is found in Numbers 16:41-50. This occurs just after those who led the rebellion against Moses and Aaron were swallowed up by the earth and the 250 men who had supported the rebellion were consumed by fire from the Lord. Verse 41 says, **"On the next day all the congregation of the children of Israel murmured against Moses and Aaron, saying, "You have killed the people of the Lord."**

There is no way Moses and Aaron could have killed these rebels – they were swallowed by the earth and consumed by holy fire. Immediately the glory of the Lord appeared over the Tabernacle. God told Moses and Aaron, **"Get away from among this congregation, that I may consume them in a moment."** (v. 45). A plague came upon the people, but Aaron ran among them with incense, making atonement for them. The plague was stopped, but not before 14,700 people died.

In Numbers 14:27, God said, **"How long shall I bear with this evil congregation who complain against Me? I have heard the complaints which the children of Israel make against Me."** God takes it personally when we complain. Murmuring and complaining keep people out of the blessing of God and in a place of suffering.

REASON #14: PRIDE AND INDEPENDENCE FROM GOD

We must avoid arrogance and pride. In Proverbs 8:13, God says, **"Pride and arrogance and the evil way and the perverse mouth I hate."** Proverbs 16:18 says, **"Pride goes before destruction, and a haughty spirit before a fall."** Pride is a haughty attitude and a fall is total destruction. Pride and arrogance cause destruction in our lives because they promote an attitude of independence from God.

Jeremiah 17:5-8 vividly pictures the contrast between the man who tries to live independently without God, trusting his own abilities, and the man who trusts in the Lord:

> **Thus says the Lord: "Cursed is the man who trusts in man and makes flesh his strength, whose heart departs from the Lord.**
>
> **"For he shall be like a shrub in the desert, and shall not see when good comes, but shall inhabit the parched places in the wilderness, in a salt land which is not inhabited.**
>
> **"Blessed is the man who trusts in the Lord, and whose hope is the Lord.**

"For he shall be like a tree planted by the waters, which spreads out its roots by the river, and will not fear when heat comes; but its leaf will be green, and will not be anxious in the year of drought, nor will cease from yielding fruit."

The man who trusts, relies, and hopes in the Lord is like a tree by the river, abundantly supplied with everything he needs. He isn't affected even when bad times come. In contrast, the proud, independent man who trusts in himself is like a dried up bush in a parched, salty desert. He misses all the good that comes to him. God hates pride because it cuts us off from His blessing.

First Timothy 3:1-7 is a passage that tells the qualifications to be a leader in the church. Paul warns Timothy not to pick a new convert **"...lest being puffed up with pride he fall into the same condemnation as the devil."** The Greek word translated "pride" is *tuphoo* which literally means "to raise a smoke, to wrap in a mist." When we are puffed up with haughtiness or pride we can no longer see clearly, we become blind with pride or conceit, we are "rendered foolish, stupefied, or confused."

The Bible warns us that if we become proud, we fall into the condemnation of the devil.

REASON #15: WORKING YOURSELF NEARLY TO DEATH

There is one more reason why Christians suffer needlessly – they work themselves nearly to death. In Philippians 2:25-30, Paul tells how Epaphroditus worked so hard that he became sick: **"Because for the work of Christ he came close to death, not regarding his life, to supply what was lacking in your service toward me"** (v. 30).

Divine Faith & Miracles

Even in serving God, you have to keep things in balance. That means you must take time to smell the roses. You don't work yourself into the grave and say, "I'm serving the Lord, and if He takes me early, He takes me early."

No, you must take time off working for the Lord to refresh yourself. You have to decide to stop working to spend time with your family. I really enjoy it when I do spend time with my kids. I look forward to the times when I take one of them out for individual time alone with Dad. This lets each child know how special they are to me. It's important: it's vital for their lives, and it's vital for me as well. The time off keeps me from working myself so hard I ruin my health and suffer needlessly for the Lord.

SCRIPTURAL SUFFERINGS FOR CHRISTIANS

We have been examining the question, "Can faith overcome suffering?" We have looked at a long list of different reasons why people suffer needlessly. If you eliminate these fifteen things, you will have removed the handle the devil uses to grab hold of your life and shake it up and down whenever he wants to.

There are, however, times when suffering is scriptural. We are told in the Word of God that there are certain things that we will suffer as believers. Jesus warned His disciples of these things – and told them what to do. Let's take a look at what they suffered.

HOW DID THE DISCIPLES AND APOSTLES SUFFER?

There is no question about it: the apostles and disciples suffered persecution. In Mark 10:29-30 Jesus said:

Assuredly, I say to you, there is no one who has

left house or brothers or sisters or father or mother or wife or children or lands, for My sake and the gospel's, who shall not receive a hundredfold now in this time – houses and brothers and sisters and mothers and children and lands, with persecutions – and in the age to come, eternal life.

As followers of Christ, we will be incredibly blessed, but we will also suffer persecutions.

SUFFERING FOR THE WORD'S SAKE

Mark 4:17 says we will suffer for the Word's sake:

And they have no root in themselves, and so endure only for a time. Afterward, when tribulation or persecution arises for the word's sake, immediately they stumble.

This refers to the process that happens whenever a believer receives a promise by faith. Troubles always come to test whether we will stand our ground and hold fast to our confession or not. Those with no root in themselves – who haven't taken the time to meditate on the Word and receive illumination – "immediately stumble." The Greek word for "stumble" here is *skandalizo* which means "to put a stumbling block or impediment in the way, upon which another may trip and fall; to cause a person to begin to distrust and desert one whom he ought to trust and obey; to cause to fall away." Satan tries to convince the believer that he can't trust God and brings circumstances to make it look like the Word is not going to work this time. Mark 4:6 tells us what happens next: **"But when the sun was up it was scorched, and because it had no root it withered away."**

SUFFERING FOR RIGHTEOUSNESS' SAKE

Another way the disciples and apostles suffered was persecution for righteousness' sake. In His Sermon on the Mount, Jesus said we'd be blessed for hungering after righteousness: **"Blessed are those who hunger and thirst for righteousness, for they shall be filled"** (Matthew 5:6). Four verses later, He pronounced a blessing on those who are persecuted for righteousness' sake:

> **"Blessed are those who are persecuted for righteousness' sake, For theirs is the kingdom of heaven.**
>
> **"Blessed are you when they revile and persecute you, and say all kinds of evil against you falsely for My sake.**
>
> **"Rejoice and be exceedingly glad, for great is your reward in heaven, for so they persecuted the prophets who were before you"** (Matthew 5:10-12).

The Message, a phrase-by-phrase contemporary paraphrase of the Bible, puts that passage like this:

> **"You're blessed when your commitment to God provokes persecution. The persecution drives you even deeper into God's kingdom.**
>
> **"Not only that – count yourselves blessed every time people put you down or throw you out or speak lies about you to discredit me. What it means is that the truth is too close for comfort and they are uncomfortable. You can be glad when that happens – give a cheer, even! – for**

though they don't like it, I do! And all heaven applauds. And know that you are in good company. My prophets and witnesses have always gotten into this kind of trouble."

SUFFERING FOR JESUS' NAME'S SAKE

A third reason the disciples and apostles suffered was for Jesus' name's sake. In Matthew 10:21-22, Jesus gave them a warning and a promise:

"Now brother will deliver up brother to death, and a father his child; and children will rise up against parents and cause them to be put to death. And you will be hated by all for My name's sake. But he who endures to the end will be saved."

After the Resurrection, the apostles began to minister in the name of Jesus and suffered persecution from the religious Jews. Acts 5:17-40 tells how they were thrown in prison for healing the multitudes, but that night, they were released by an angel, who instructed them to go to the Temple the next morning to teach. They did, and were arrested again, beaten and finally released. In Acts 5:41, we are told: **"They departed from the presence of the council, rejoicing that they were counted worthy to suffer shame for His name."** We will see this element of rejoicing again and again in the accounts of scriptural suffering.

SUFFERING FOR HAVING A STRONG CHRISTIAN WITNESS

In Acts 7 we find the account of the stoning of Stephen, the first Christian martyr. He had been called before the High Priest and those who sat on the Jewish

Council and falsely accused of blasphemy. As he stood to defend himself, his face shined like the face of an angel. He preached an amazing sermon, giving a panoramic view of God's dealings with the Jewish people from Abraham on. Then he pointed out that the Jews had always been a stiff-necked people and asked why they always resisted the Holy Spirit.

> **When they heard these things they were cut to the heart, and they gnashed at him with their teeth. But he, being full of the Holy Spirit, gazed into heaven and saw the glory of God, and Jesus standing at the right hand of God, and said, "Look! I see the heavens opened and the Son of Man standing at the right hand of God!" (Acts 7:54-56).**

This was too much for the Jewish leaders. Yelling, hissing and booing, they drowned him out. Then they dragged him out of town and pelted him with rocks.

> **And they stoned Stephen as he was calling on God and saying, "Lord Jesus, receive my spirit."**

> **Then he knelt down and cried out with a loud voice, "Lord, do not charge them with this sin." And when he had said this, he fell asleep (Acts 7:59-60).**

As with the disciples, the grace of God was upon Stephen – he had a glorious vision of Jesus welcoming him to heaven. And just like Jesus, he totally forgave those who tormented him.

In 2 Timothy 3:12, Paul wrote, **"Yes, and all who desire to live godly in Christ Jesus will suffer persecution."** In other words, there's going to be persecution if you have a strong Christian witness in this world. If you walk in the Spirit, you're going to suffer for it. People are going to reject you, because you're anointed and they're convicted of sin, just by being around you.

In John 16:33, Jesus said, **"These things I have spoken to you, that in Me you may have peace. In the world you will have tribulation; but be of good cheer, I have overcome the world."** In all the things that we would suffer because of persecution, Jesus said we could be of good cheer or good comfort. He has overcome the world and so, therefore, we will overcome the world.

The "Faith Hall of Fame," found in Hebrews 11, is a list of men and women of God who – when persecuted – were courageous and did mighty exploits for the Lord. They were victorious over their circumstances. Then in Hebrews 11:35 we read, **"Others were tortured, not accepting deliverance, that they might obtain a better resurrection."** They refused to deny their faith in God, even to the point of dying for their beliefs.

In Philippians 1:21, Paul wrote, **"For to me, to live is Christ, and to die is gain."** There is no downside to the Christian life. Even when you die, you go directly to heaven and see Jesus face to face (Philippians 1:23).

The Apostle Paul was no stranger to suffering persecution. He gave a long list of things he suffered for the sake of preaching the Gospel in 2 Corinthians 11:23-27:

> **In labors more abundant, in stripes above measure, in prisons more frequently, in deaths often. From the Jews five times I received forty stripes minus one.**

305

Three times I was beaten with rods; once I was stoned; three times I was shipwrecked; a night and a day I have been in the deep; in journeys often, in perils of waters, in perils of robbers, in perils of my own countrymen, in perils of the Gentiles, in perils in the city, in perils in the wilderness, in perils in the sea, in perils among false brethren; in weariness and toil, in sleeplessness often, in hunger and thirst, in fastings often, in cold and nakedness.

Earlier in that same epistle, Paul called these sufferings "light afflictions." Can you imagine? In 2 Corinthians 4:17 he wrote:

For our light affliction, which is but for a moment, is working for us a far more exceeding and eternal weight of glory.

Paul compared the two as though on a scale, weighing out what we're going to receive for all eternity against whatever it is we suffer here. He then declared, "Compared to the glory that we're going to receive, you will call these things 'light afflictions.' You'll say, 'I would gladly bear all those things in order to receive the fullness of what I'm going to have in God's glory.'"

Despite the persecution Paul and others faced, they finished their course, accomplishing all God had planned for them to do. In 2 Timothy 4:7-8 Paul wrote:

I have fought the good fight, I have finished the race, I have kept the faith.

Finally, there is laid up for me the crown of righteousness, which the Lord, the righteous Judge, will give to me on that Day, and not to me only

but also to all who have loved His appearing.

In addition to these biblical accounts of the suffering of Stephen and Paul, Church history tells us that of the Lord's remaining eleven disciples, all were killed for preaching the Gospel except John, who survived numerous tortures and exile.

Fortunately, in America we seldom suffer persecution. We may experience a little bit of rejection and little bit of criticism. People may say that we're "politically incorrect" because we say, "Jesus is the only way to heaven" instead of, "All roads lead to Nirvana." But what we suffer here is nothing compared to what many people throughout the world have suffered - and are still suffering - because of their faith.

DOES SICKNESS TEACH US ANYTHING?

We have seen that the disciples and apostles suffered - but it's important to note that their sufferings did not include poverty and sickness.

Yet there are those in the Body of Christ today who claim that Christians suffer from sickness as a way to learn the lessons that God is trying to teach them. We go into this a great deal in our course on Divine Healing, but let's briefly touch on the following question: "Does sickness teach us anything?"

John 14:26 says, **"But the Helper, the Holy Spirit, whom the Father will send in My name, He will teach you all things, and bring to your remembrance all things that I said to you."**

Jesus said the Holy Spirit, the Helper, would be the One to teach us. The Holy Spirit is now here. So, why would God teach us with sickness and disease instead of the Holy Spirit Whom Jesus sent?

Think about it: sickness and disease don't exist in heaven, so God would have to steal some from the devil. To think that God would steal sickness from the devil in order to teach you something is ludicrous!

You've heard people say, "But I learned so much when I was on the bed of affliction." That's because they finally got humble enough to sit down and get serious with the Lord and plugged into the Word. But they could have gotten the same benefit from the Word if they'd plugged in without getting sick.

That's the reality. People get desperate when they are sick, and they finally do what they should have done when they were well. God intends that we learn from the Word and the Spirit, not from the consequences of disobeying the Word. I've been sick before, and here's what I learned from it: it hurts, it feels awful, it's terrible, it's a curse. I don't want to have anything to do with it. That's what I've learned from sickness: avoid it like the plague!

OVERCOMING SUFFERING

We have seen how sin and improper teaching have kept people locked into patterns of suffering. But what about those who have studied the Word and know the Scriptures concerning the promises of God, who are not operating in rebellion, sin, idolatry, or pride. We are to fight the good fight of faith: identify with Christ, reckon it paid for, refuse to suffer again when Jesus already paid the price.

Once during a service, a young Bible School student had a vision that makes the substitutionary sacrifice of Christ so real. In the vision, she was standing with the other women at the foot of the Cross. She wept as she watched Jesus suffer so, knowing it was for her healing that He was beaten and for her sins that He would soon die. Suddenly unseen arms lifted her up toward the top of the cross until she was face to face with Jesus. He looked into her eyes for a long moment.

Then He asked her, "Will you agree with Me that it is finished?"

IT IS FINISHED!

Jesus paid the price! He suffered for us, so we don't have to suffer what He suffered. As Christians, we are to identify with His sufferings and see why we are liberated from the worst parts of life. He bore so much for us.

Romans 8:2 is a great verse to meditate on when you need to identify with Christ's sufferings. It says, **"For the law of the Spirit of life in Christ Jesus has made me free from the law of sin and death."** There is a law of sin and death. But there is also a law of the Spirit of life – which is far more powerful. The law of the Spirit of life in Christ Jesus has set you completely free from the law of sin and death. I identify with Christ, agreeing with Him that "It is finished." I honor all that He did for me. I refuse to let what Jesus purchased for me be taken from me. I refuse lying symptoms that exalt themselves against the knowledge of God (2 Corinthians 10:5).

Then I take the five infallible steps of faith. I begin to meditate on the specific promises in the Word of God that apply to the current condition. I wait for illumination, reminding myself of verses the Lord has illuminated for me in the past, stirring up my faith. I pray the prayer of faith, declaring the eternal Word of God, changing the facts with the truth. Then I stand fast with my confession until possession comes.

RESISTING SIN: THE SUFFERING THAT *DOES* BRING GLORY AND HONOR TO THE NAME OF JESUS

We have seen how, as Christians, we can avoid much of the suffering that people in the world will experience. But there are verses in the Bible that imply that believers *will* suffer. There is a suffering that will guarantee that your faith will not be compromised and you will receive miracles. That suffering comes as we resist sin. We are to strive against sin and self-will.

Sometimes cutting off sin and the habit patterns that came from ignorance is easy, but sometimes it is a struggle. Sometimes we suffer! In this, Jesus is our example. Luke 22:41-44 is the account of the Lord's struggle in the Garden of Gethsemane:

And He was withdrawn from them about a stone's throw, and He knelt down and prayed, saying, "Father, if it is Your will, take this cup away from Me; nevertheless not My will, but Yours, be done."

Then an angel appeared to Him from heaven, strengthening Him. And being in agony, He prayed more earnestly. Then His sweat became like great drops of blood falling down to the ground.

Gethsemane was the Lord's great agony, His place of suffering. His temptation was, "Don't go to the Cross." It would have been a sin for Him to refuse to go to the Cross. This is the greatest example He gave us of struggling against sin and self-will. He knew He needed to go to the Cross so that He could purchase our redemption. John tells us that a few days earlier Jesus had prayed, **"Now My** soul is troubled, and what shall I say? 'Father, save Me from this hour'? But for this purpose I came to this hour" (John 12:27). Jesus successfully overcame the temptation to do His own will.

In His prayer of consecration, Jesus prayed, "Father, if there is any other way We can pay the price to redeem all these people from sin, let's do that. Please deliver Me from being beaten and crucified. Deliver Me from being separated from You. But if there's no other way, let Your will be done, not Mine." Matthew 26:44 tells us Jesus prayed that same prayer three times. After this, the Father immediately sent an angel from heaven to strengthen Him. He was empowered in the Spirit.

Jesus came out of the Garden of Gethsemane totally anointed to face the torture and death that was before Him. He could have stopped the process several times: He could have escaped when the arresting soldiers fell to the ground when He said, "I am He" (John 18:5,6). It was dark and Jesus had "passed through the midst" of angry mobs before (see Luke 4:28-30). Both Pilate and Herod gave Jesus a chance to defend Himself. Pilate did not want to kill Him. But Jesus endured His sufferings with supernatural strength, remaining silent throughout the proceedings. (He walked in such favor with God, perhaps He knew if He said anything He would have been released – and ruined God's carefully-timed redemptive plan!)

He went through the pain and the shame of torture in the power of the Spirit. He literally experienced the worst beating any human being had ever experienced, followed by the cruel torture of crucifixion. Yet by the strength of the Holy Spirit inside, He remained compassionately aware of the needs of those around Him. He encouraged the women of Jerusalem, saying, **"Do not weep for Me, but weep for yourselves and for your children"** (Luke 23:28). He forgave the repentant thief on the cross next to Him. He forgave the soldiers who crucified Him. He spoke to John the Apostle and arranged for him to take care of His mother.

We find another references to Jesus' great suffering in the Garden of Gethsemane in Hebrews 12:3-4:

> **For consider Him who endured such hostility from sinners against Himself, lest you become weary and discouraged in your souls. You have not yet resisted to bloodshed, striving against sin.**

This is a description of what Jesus did: He resisted to bloodshed, striving against sin. The temptation to walk away from His crucifixion was so great that He sweat great drops of blood, agonizing over the idea of being separated from God the Father and from the Holy Spirit.

This scripture says, "You have not yet resisted to bloodshed, striving against sin." Have you ever been tempted and the temptation was so great, and you resisted it so much, that you began to sweat great drops of blood? No. It hasn't happened. Jesus had the greatest temptation of anyone, yet never sinned. He's our example of how we need to strive against sin.

First Peter 4:1-2 says:

> **Therefore, since Christ suffered for us in the flesh, arm yourselves also with the same mind, for he who has suffered in the flesh has ceased from sin, that he no longer should live the rest of his time in the flesh for the lusts of men, but for the will of God.**

In other words, the thing that we are to suffer is ceasing from sin.

If you've ever decided and made a stand against a specific sin in your life, you realize how much your flesh begins to suffer. Your flesh cries out: "No! I want to eat those forty-two donuts," or "No! I want to go after that woman!"

Your spirit-man immediately says, "No! No!" You rein your flesh in and force it to be subject to the Word of God, in agreement with your spirit and your soul. You can do this because of the fellowship you have with the Lord. This ceasing from sin is what God is really calling us to suffer. That's suffering enough.

IT TAKES FAITH TO WALK UPRIGHTLY

The very first application for our faith is to develop Christian character, because only with the help of God can we cease from sin by dying to the flesh. We must use faith to walk uprightly before the Lord, living a holy and righteous life. Once we learn that God will answer our prayers, we pray for deliverance from evil and then exercise our faith. Christ is our example, and we need to follow Him.

People really underestimate the power of morality. Christian character produces morality, and morality - living right before the Lord - is good seed sown. When you walk in upright Christian character, your whole life suddenly becomes a positive seed that you're sowing into your future. It prepares a blessing down the road for you and for others.

As we become aware of negative seeds sown in our lives - things done through ignorance and disobedience that are now causing us to suffer needlessly - we can cut them off. As we purpose to walk uprightly before the Lord, walking in faith will produce a holy and righteous life that is constantly blessed by the Lord. We will have God's favor and prosper in everything we do.

If you have a sense of divine destiny, if you know God's purpose for your life, you will be vision-driven and purpose-driven, rather than driven by the lusts of the flesh. Knowing that many lives will be eternally changed by your obedience helps you see the importance of each and every choice that you make.

As Christians, we hear about keeping on the "straight and narrow way" (Matthew 7:14) and how difficult it is. I heard one minister say that every year, God made the way for him a little bit narrower. Things that he used to wink at or allow in a his life were no longer acceptable. God was asking him to walk a closer and straighter path.

For me, the longer I walk with the Lord, the more it seems like a tightrope; it's so narrow. I've got to be so careful in what I do and how I live, because I realize fulfilling what God's called me to do may make an eternal difference in millions of people's lives.

Some may say, "I'm not called to be an evangelist, so that doesn't apply to me. My obedience won't make a difference in whether millions of people spend eternity in heaven." You never can tell. As you walk uprightly before the Lord, ceasing from sin, and being blessed of the Lord, doing what He's called you to do, you might be the one who wins the next Reinhard Bonnke or the next Billy Graham to the Lord. Or you may win somebody who wins somebody, who wins somebody – *how* it happens doesn't matter. What does matter is that it is essential for you to be obedient to what God has called you to do. It literally could mean millions of souls spending eternity in heaven rather than in hell.

The more you realize your divine purpose, the more

clearly you see how important it is for you to walk uprightly before the Lord. You continue to make quality choices and decisions to follow after God – even when it's hard. You become willing to pay the price it takes to be a vessel of honor, fit for the Master's use.

USE YOUR FAITH WHEN YOU ARE TEMPTED!

Remember when Jesus was tempted by the devil in the wilderness? Jesus resisted Satan with the Word of God. Afterwards, Luke 4:14 tells us **"Jesus returned in the power of the Spirit to Galilee, and news of Him went out through all the surrounding region."** Jesus came away from that trial in the power of the Spirit, totally anointed to go and fulfill His ministry.

When tempted to sin, believe God for a way out. First Corinthians 10:13 promises us:

> **No temptation has overtaken you except such as is common to man; but God is faithful, who will not allow you to be tempted beyond what you are able, but with the temptation will also make the way of escape, that you may be able to bear it.**

Every temptation you face is one that is common to all mankind, and God will always give you a way of escape. By faith, you know there is a way out of every situation. Even before your eyes can see it, you know it's there.

Jesus said in John 16:33:

> **"These things I have spoken to you, that in Me you may have peace. In the world you will have tribulation; but be of good cheer, I have overcome the world."**

Jesus said that trouble will come, even to believers.

But He said you could have peace "in Him." In fact, you can be cheerful, knowing you're going to overcome just as Jesus overcame the world. You will make it. You'll be able to go the distance and fulfill what God has called you to do.

THE RIGHT FOCUS

Let God begin to get your focus just right concerning why He wants you to have faith. He will give you a clear picture of how to get His blessings in your life and how to walk uprightly before Him.

You will discover a whole different perspective on why we desire to go forth in faith. The point is not pursuing faith so that you can have the cars and the money and all the other things – that's the by-product of living a life before the Lord as He uses you to impact other people's lives. It's great to be blessed, drive a nice car, and live in a nice house. I can testify: God has done all those things in my life as I've served Him in the ministry for thirty-five years. But I also can testify of the really lean times and the price I've had to pay to get to where I am today.

I had to be willing to say, "Yes, Lord. I'll do this job. I'll serve in this position. I'll do whatever You ask me to do. I know You have a higher purpose and I want You to form in me everything that needs to be formed. Work out everything that has to be worked out in my life, and make me a vessel fit for the Master's use."

The only way you're going to be able to do this is by faith.

You realize you're not part of those who get criticized as the "name it, claim it, blab it and grab it" bunch. That's not your purpose at all. Your purpose is to glorify God, and you know you have to be built up in faith and lay hold of that which God wants you to have in order to fulfill what God has called you to do.

It's not always going to be easy, even on the road of faith. Obstacles will come to discourage you. You must decide that you are bound and determined to fulfill what God has called you to do, that you'll pay whatever price is necessary.

As you continue on in a life of faith, you will produce fruit that will be a blessing to many and receive a harvest that will be a blessing to you. You will be reigning in life by the power of Jesus Christ.

CHAPTER THIRTEEN

WHY YOU CAN RECEIVE A MIRACLE RIGHT NOW!

JESUS PASSIONATELY WANTS YOU TO RECEIVE miracles in your life. I believe that some of you have already started to receive miracles while you were reading this book. Many others will begin to see miracles come streaming into your lives like a procession of gifts, delivered by the hand of God's immeasurable grace.

WHAT GOD HAS DONE FOR ME, HE'LL DO FOR YOU

I want to tell you why I believe that you can receive a miracle right now, but I would first like to share the rest of the testimony of my miraculous first month as a Christian. You will see why I believe so completely in the miracle-working power of God, and why I believe that you can also receive the miracle you need right now. What God has done for me, He will do for you, because as Acts 10:34 says, **"God shows no partiality."**

You may remember that I was saved after reading most of the four Gospels. When I got to John 16:33, I read the words of Jesus, **"In the world you will have tribulation; but** be of good cheer, I have overcome the world." I immediately heard the Lord call me by name and say, "Doug, I'm alive, and I'm the Lord." Of course, I got out of my bed and on my knees and prayed a prayer to ask Jesus to come into my heart and to take over my life.

"I DON'T HAVE TO GET HIGH ANYMORE!"

The following week, the rock band in which I played drums was on the road in Fort Lauderdale, Florida. One night, I came in from playing at the nightclub and decided to read my Bible and pray. I had only been saved for five days and knew nothing about the Christian life. I had been drinking at the club and smoking pot on the way to the hotel. When I went to read my Bible, I noticed that the pages looked really fuzzy. I couldn't focus on the words. After a period of time, I realized that I was even holding my Bible upside down! Then I had this frightening thought: *Maybe drugs and alcohol don't mix with being a Christian.* My heart sank, because at this time in my life I smoked pot all day, every day, and always drank in the clubs at night.

Even though I began my spiritual search as an alternative to getting high on the hard drugs I had started using, I couldn't imagine not smoking pot and drinking every day! I suddenly felt trapped – so I said a very simple prayer: "Lord, if drugs and alcohol don't mix with being a Christian, You'll just have to take them out of my life, because I am powerless to stop. This is just what I do every day." At the time I prayed that, I had no idea of the power of the prayer of consecration.

The next night was the final night of our contract. We decided to drive all the way across the state after the gig in order to get home as soon as possible. About halfway home, I began to feel really sick. By the time we arrived at the guitar player's apartment, I felt violently ill. I ran into his bathroom, locked the door, and began vomiting. All of a sudden, I felt my throat close up like someone's hand reached right into my esophagus and squeezed it shut. Immediately, I began to lose consciousness. The lights dimmed and everything went black.

Then, just as suddenly as it had closed, my throat opened up. I gasped a great big breath of air. As I began to breathe normally, my vision returned, and I found myself lying on the floor. My body was racked with pain as if I had the flu. Again I began to vomit violently and the whole experience repeated itself.

I must have screamed out, because my band mates started pounding on the door asking what was going on. When I regained consciousness the second time, it hit me: I was dying. I thought to myself, *I must have come down with a terminal illness, but God in His mercy made sure that I received Christ as my Lord the week before so that I would go to heaven instead of hell.* But my next thought was *I don't want to die like a typical rock musician on the floor of a bathroom with my head in a commode, and leave everyone thinking that I died of a drug overdose!*

Suddenly, my sole purpose in life was to get out of that bathroom, get to the hospital, and die with a little bit of dignity in a clean bed. That's all I wanted from the Lord. I thought to myself, I'll get up and unlock the door. My friends can call the ambulance to get me to the hospital, and then I can die.

To my great astonishment, as I began to push up on the toilet seat, the power of God hit me at the top of my head and shot straight through my body. All of a sudden, I was standing up straight - and all the pain and sickness had miraculously left! I felt like my body was stronger and cleaner than it had ever been. I actually thought that I had begun to float up toward the ceiling, so I looked down at my feet to see if they were still on the ground. I was sure that I was at least six inches off the floor.

I hurriedly washed my face and unlocked the door. When I walked into the other room, my eyes were opened as wide as saucers. The guys in the band looked at me with astonishment.

"Man, are you all right?" they asked. "We thought you were dying."

"I thought I was dying too," I replied. "But now I feel better than I've ever felt in my life."

One of them said, "Wow, that's really weird, dude."

"I know," I admitted. "I don't know what happened, but I really have never felt better in my life."

They looked at me, and I looked at them. Finally one of them spoke. "Well, if you feel all right, do you want to get high?"

Then it hit me. That's what this was all about. I didn't need to get high anymore. At that time I didn't understand anything about demonic powers and how they can cause addictions. I sure didn't know that a spirit of drug addiction and alcoholism had oppressed me and that it tried to choke me to death while Jesus was kicking it out of my body. All I knew was that I would never have to get high again.

So I said to the guys, "No thanks! The Lord has made it so that I'll never have to get high again. That's what happened in the bathroom. You guys might have to get high, but I don't."

They said, "Well, we don't have to get high either. We're going to, but we don't *have* to."

DIPPED INTO A VAT OF LIVING LOVE

After being saved one week and delivered from a spirit of drug addiction and alcoholism the second week, I felt like I was ready for anything that God wanted to send my way.

My mother had a small bookcase in her home where she put all her Christian books. I began looking through her little Christian library and found a book by Pat Boone entitled *A New Song*. Now, rock musicians of the early '70s didn't consider Pat Boone the hippest dude in the music business. I had hair almost to my waist; I wore wild stage clothes and multicolored snakeskin shoes with lightning bolts on the sides. When I pictured Pat Boone, with his white buckskin shoes and white belt, crooning old ballads, I wondered if he could hold my attention through a whole book. Boy, was I wrong!

A New Song told of Pat's spiritual journey and baptism in the Holy Spirit. It started when Pat's wife, Shirley, learned about the infilling of the Spirit. She realized that this experience was for her and she wanted it right away. Not having anyone around to pray for her, she simply asked the Lord to fill her with His Holy Spirit all by Himself. She received by faith and immediately began praying in another tongue as the Lord graciously answered her prayer.

When I read her testimony, I immediately thought that I should ask the Lord for the same blessing. In my spiritual naivety I said out loud, "Lord, this sounds really cool to me. Would You baptize me in the Holy Spirit, too?" I had no sooner finished the sentence than a language that sounded to me like a blend of Russian and Chinese came flooding out of my innermost being and then out of my mouth. I felt a rushing wave of the presence of the Lord, which I can only describe one way: I felt like God literally picked me up and dipped me into a vat of living love.

I sensed that everything in my life had drastically and radically changed. I felt so full of the love of God that all I desired was for everyone I knew to be saved and have the same kind of miraculous experiences I was having. I wanted to lay hands on everyone I knew and pray for them.

I was alone at my parent's house at the time of this experience. As I walked downstairs, my mom's dogs came running up to me, so I knelt down and prayed for them. I walked outside and looked up at the trees and the majesty of God's handiwork and was completely amazed. I looked at the detail of the pine trees that made up the forest. I looked at the incredibly blue sky with the amazingly fluffy white clouds. I even thought that I could see the air. Since I wasn't on acid, I knew that this was an encounter with the power of God!

From that time on, I had an insatiable desire to read and understand the Word of God. Over the next week, I began devouring the Bible and every Christian book I possibly could. Then on the fourth week of my new life as a Christian, I had a wild thought which I can only describe it as a true revelation from heaven. I thought to myself, *Maybe I should go to church.*

JUST BETWEEN GOD AND ME

You see, I had experienced all of these miracles – the new birth, deliverance from a spirit of drug addiction and alcoholism, and the baptism in the Holy Spirit – without having darkened the door of any church. This had been simply between God and me alone. Jesus was so real to me that I was ready to abandon everything about my life and follow Him on whatever path He had for me.

No church could be blamed - or credited - for my experience with God. Because I had such a powerful and profound experience with the Lord, and because I didn't have a lot of bad doctrine to unlearn, I seldom have had any problem hearing the voice of the Lord and finding His direction for my life. I have never doubted the miracle-working power of God and have found it fairly easy to get most of my prayers answered. I feel as though my whole life is a miracle, from the day I was saved when Jesus called me by my name, until today.

Don't get me wrong: I still have many unanswered prayers, but most of them have to do with fulfilling the call of God on my life. These are the kind of answers that can only come to pass as you walk out the plan and purpose for which God has commissioned you. It takes a lifetime to see them all come to pass. I also have new personal needs and family needs that continually arise. We will all need a constant stream of miracles flowing from God's throne into our lives.

I marvel that God has called me to be the steward over a ministry that is training several thousand ministers a year all over the world. I frequently tell people that they came way too late to tell me that God doesn't do miracles today. I tell them, "I am a miracle! I could have been dead and burning in hell today, except for the magnificent grace and miracle-working power of God. Instead I am blessed to be bearing fruit for God's Kingdom."

TOTALLY FREE FROM PAIN

When I think back on my first six months as a Christian, I remember how much I witnessed to my band mates. They were really open. One started reading the Bible with me, and I got the other one to attend a church service with me. He was raised Catholic, and his father had attended a Catholic conference where he must have been baptized in the Holy Spirit, because my friend said I sounded just like his dad. The service he attended with me was at a Catholic church, the only place he would agree to go. A Spirit-filled Catholic priest and a Spirit-filled Baptist preacher were holding healing services together. We arrived after the service started, so we sat on the back row. What happened next really blew my friend's mind. The ministers started flowing in the gifts of the Spirit, receiving various words of knowledge concerning ailments that people had, then ministered healing to them. Suddenly, one of the ministers pointed to the back pew and said, "The Spirit of God is resting on someone in the back row. You have a back problem, and Jesus is healing you right now."

As soon as he said those words, I felt the power of God come over me like a warm, electric current. For years I had suffered from lower back pain due to a junior-high-school football injury. I was so used to the pain being there that I was in total shock when the pain suddenly left. I began weeping and jumped to my feet and began praising God at the top of my lungs.

I had brought my friend in hopes of getting him saved – then suddenly, I received a dramatic miracle. I was hoping the whole experience would be enough to inspire him to receive the Lord, but he resisted. I think he simply believed I had lost my mind. Well, crazy or not, I was the one totally free of pain!

Just a few years ago, while I was thinking about my former band mates, I began praying for them and suddenly was prompted to try to contact them. I did an on-line search for their names and found the one who had begun reading the Bible with me. A few years after I left the band, he moved to southern California to play on several albums with another former band mate of his. The recording work was for a Christian artist who led my friend into making a decision for Christ. My friend has since recorded twelve Christian albums and even played the part of Jesus in a Hollywood movie. Isn't that just like God? Isn't Jesus wonderful?

THE MIRACLES DON'T HAVE TO STOP!

My new life in Christ began with miracles. Perhaps you, too, got off to a good start and saw miracles when you were first born again. But now it seems you are bogged down. You are still doing what everyone has told you to do, but you are not seeing miracles anymore. Why did the miracles stop? What went wrong?

I believe it's because we stray from the simplicity of grace and the gift of righteousness. In this book, we have seen how having an inner image of righteousness is so foundational to receiving from God. Recently I have been greatly encouraged by *Destined to Reign*, written by Joseph Prince, Pastor of New Creation Church in Singapore. He has put his finger on the problem: we are mixing "law" and "grace."

The term "law" for today's modern Christian is not just referring to the Law of Moses. It also refers to all of the Christian legalism that has been added to the Christian faith throughout the Church age. This Christian law, or legalism, is the product of well-meaning but ignorant Christian preachers and teachers. When they try to mix law with grace, they neutralize grace. I know that these ministers are trying to help believers live a holy life, but often they have a misguided idea of what a holy life should look like. It is not an external, legalistic holiness, obtained by keeping rules. No, true holiness is an inner working of the Spirit, revealed from the inside out.

In our course "Christ-Like Character," I stress the issue with our students that we obtain Christ-like character the same way we obtain healing or provision: by faith. We simply meditate on all of the true virtues of Christ and His character, and we begin to be conformed into the image of His character by faith. When you engage faith and prayer with your meditation, you are accessing the abundance of grace and the gift of righteousness.

With God, it does not matter who you were when you were first saved. With God, it doesn't even matter who you were yesterday. If today you are repentant for any wrong thing done yesterday, and you are now endeavoring to walk in your righteousness, you can be that person with a heart that does not condemn you. You can be that person John describes in 1 John 3:21-22:

> **Beloved, if our heart does not condemn us, we have confidence toward God. And whatever we ask we receive from Him, because we keep His commandments and do those things that are pleasing in His sight.**

The power of God's grace should not be underestimated. It is through this power alone that we obtain the supernatural strength to live a righteous, holy life and can therefore exercise great faith in God's Word.

Grace is not a license to sin; rather it is the power *not* to sin. Our image of righteousness does not come because we are keeping the rules. We can't keep all of them all the time in our own strength. And that's the point. We need Jesus. We must receive the abundance of grace.

THERE IS NOTHING WRONG WITH YOU!

Sometimes we blame ourselves or our faith when things don't work out as we think they should. We reason: *There is nothing wrong with God or His Word, so it must be my fault. There must be something wrong with me.*

True, there is nothing wrong with God; there is nothing wrong with Jesus; there is nothing wrong in heaven; there is nothing wrong with God's Word. His Word is forever true, and *it* says that because of the Blood of Jesus and the grace of God, there is nothing wrong with you!

CONVICTED OF RIGHTEOUSNESS, NOT SINFULNESS

In John 16:7, Jesus told His disciples that it would work out to their advantage for Him to go away, because He would send the Holy Spirit. Jesus then described the ministry of the Holy Spirit, which He intended to bring great encouragement to the Church. Sadly, most Christians have misunderstood and seen the ministry of the Holy Spirit as a ministry of condemnation.

You see, the Holy Spirit has a ministry of conviction to all the inhabitants of the earth: to unbelievers, to believers, and to Satan's forces of darkness. In John 16:8-11, Jesus describes three different types of conviction that the Holy Spirit will deliver to these three different groups.

First, the Holy Spirit convicts the unbeliever of sin. He constantly impresses on their consciousness, "You must receive Christ in order to have your sin removed."

Second, the Holy Spirit convicts Satan and his losers of judgment. He continually says to them, "You have been found guilty of high treason and your judgment is imminent."

Third, the Holy Spirit says something quite different to His purchased possession, the apple of His eye, those who have run to God and made Jesus both Savior and Lord. What does the Holy Spirit convict this group of – those who are now known as the Body of Christ, and who will eternally be the Bride of Christ? He says to each and every one of them, "You are a righteous child of God, the beloved of heaven. You have been made righteous by the Blood of the Lamb, clothed in His robes of righteousness, and forever seated at the table of the blessing of the Lord."

When the Bible says the Holy Spirit "convicts" you of righteousness, that means He tells you every good thing that you have ever heard from heaven concerning how much God loves you and how He thinks only love thoughts toward you.

You couldn't be more loved by God. You couldn't be more accepted, for you are in the Beloved. You are in Christ. All the work done by the Blood of Jesus – shed for you on the Cross – was to make you righteous and holy and acceptable to God. No work on your part need be added to make you more righteous. By God's great grace, this free gift of perfect cleansing, holiness, and righteousness was purchased for you and hand-delivered to you by none other than Jesus Himself.

If you listen carefully, you will be able to discern that this is all you will hear from heaven and from the Holy Spirit of the Living God. You will not hear condemnation – no, not from heaven! You *might* hear condemnation coming from your own soul, prompted by the accuser of the brethren, the devil. But never will condemnation proceed from the lips of the Father, or from Jesus, or from the Holy Spirit.

You might ask, "Then how does God correct us?" By now, you have probably figured out that I will always say,

"He corrects you through His Word, as a loving Heavenly Father who encourages you and never condemns you." God will say, "You can do better, because I have recreated you to *be* better. I'll show you all of the mysteries of My kingdom whereby I have given you power to do your best, even power to do exploits in the name of My Son Jesus."

LEGALISM REARMS THE ENEMY

Here's a final thought from Pastor Prince: Anytime we add legalism, it neutralizes our faith. Satan, the accuser of the brethren, is always watching for us to mess up so he can tell us all about it. If we add legalism to the simplicity of the gospel, it actually rearms the enemy of our soul.

A STEADY STREAM OF MIRACLES

When Pastor Prince began to teach this "radical" grace, members of his congregation began to receive miraculous healings, supernatural debt cancellation, healed marriages, and great deliverances from addictions. Following the miracles came explosive church growth. You see, when people receive a steady stream of miracles, the word will get out. Believers are drawn to answered prayer. Believers are drawn to believing churches.

THE BOTTOM LINE: MIRACLES ARE OUR DAILY BREAD

I want to get straight to the bottom line: You can receive a miracle right now because miracles are the children's bread and you are a child of God. John 1:12 tell us, **"But as many as received Him, to them He gave the right to become the children of God."**

Jesus called miracles "the children's bread" in the amazing story of a woman who surprised Jesus with her great faith. A Canaanite woman, a non-Jew, chased Jesus down when He was trying to get away from the crowds. She desired deliverance for her daughter who was terribly demon possessed. Because Jesus had been sent to fulfill the covenant with Israel first, He tried to send the woman away. He even called her a dog, the name the Jews used to refer to non-Jews. Jesus said in Mark 7:27, **"Let the children be filled first, for it is not good to take the children's bread and throw it to the little dogs."**

Unmoved by His rejection, she answered in verse 27, **"Yes, Lord, yet even the little dogs under the table eat from the children's crumbs."**

In Matthew's account of this same story, Jesus answered her, **"O woman, great is your faith! Let it be to you as you desire"** (Matthew 15:28). Notice Jesus couldn't call her "daughter," for she was not a Jew, He called her only "woman." Yet this woman had such great faith that it caught Jesus' attention!

In Mark 7:29, Jesus said to her, **"For this saying go your way; the demon has gone out of your daughter."** Jesus said the demon went out of her daughter when she answered Him with the saying, "Yes, Lord, yet even the little dogs under the table eat from the children's crumbs." In other words, at the moment she proclaimed her faith in Jesus, she received the miracle for her daughter.

This woman wasn't a covenant child of God. She did not keep the Law of Moses. Yet she received a miracle. How much easier it is for us to receive miracles! We are the children of God!

When Jesus called miracles "the children's bread," I believe He was saying that miracles are as basic to the spiritual lives of the children of God as bread is basic to their bodies. Miracles should not take us by surprise! They should be our daily bread. God wants us to continually walk in the realm of the miraculous, asking in faith and receiving answers to our prayers.

Jesus, the giver of all miracles, identified Himself as the "true bread from heaven" (John 6:32). In verse 33, He called Himself "the bread of God." He is called the "bread of life" in verses 35 and 48, and the "living bread which came down from heaven" in verse 51. Miracles can't be separated from the giver of miracles. Jesus is the bread of life, and He brings miracles – which He calls "the children's bread" – to the Father's children. When you received Jesus, you came into the presence of the One who can give you every miracle you will ever need. These miracles can all be accessed with that divine gift given you when you receive His Word: the divine gift of faith.

YOU CAN'T EARN A MIRACLE BY KEEPING THE RULES

What God did for me, even when I was a brand-new believer and knew so little, He will do for you. I didn't keep any rules. *I didn't even know any rules!* It took me four weeks to figure out I should go to church! You can't "earn" a miracle by keeping the rules. Miracles are a gift the Father wants to give you. Have faith in God's great grace, not in your own ability to keep any religious rules!

There is nothing wrong with you. You are made to be the righteousness of God in Christ. Don't let the devil tell you that it's not working because you are not good enough, obedient enough, haven't prayed enough, etc. Don't rearm the enemy of your soul!

RECEIVE YOUR MIRACLE RIGHT NOW!

Take the five infallible steps of faith. Hear what God

is saying to you through meditation and illumination. When you engage faith and prayer with your meditation, you are accessing the abundance of grace and the gift of righteousness. Pray the prayer of faith and continue to confess and hold fast to what God has told you. You don't have to do it perfectly! You don't have to have the perfect prayer or the perfect confession. When you mess up, just hang out with Jesus some more. Let the Holy Spirit convict you some more of how much God loves you, how He sings and rejoices over you.

Receive the abundance of grace and the gift of righteousness. Hold fast: it's just a matter of time until you have possession of what God has promised!

Simply believe God, and through your divine faith, receive your miracle today!